PROCEDURES AND DECISIONS OF THE SCOTTISH SOLICITORS' DISCIPLINE TRIBUNAL

PROCEDURES AND DECISIONS
OF THE
SCOTTISH SOLICITORS' DISCIPLINE TRIBUNAL

IAN S. SMITH
BSc, BL, Solicitor

JOHN M. BARTON
MA, LLB, WS

With a Foreword by
Kenneth A. Ross, LLB
President of
The Law Society of Scotland

PUBLISHED ON BEHALF OF
THE LAW SOCIETY OF SCOTLAND
by
T & T CLARK
EDINBURGH
1995

T&T CLARK LTD
59 GEORGE STREET
EDINBURGH EH2 2LQ
SCOTLAND

ISBN 0 567 29288 6

British Library Cataloguing-in-Publication Data
A catalogue record for this book is available from the British Library

Typeset by Fakenham Photosetting Ltd, Fakenham, Norfolk
Printed and bound by Bell and Bain Ltd., Glasgow

CONTENTS

CONTENTS

CONTENTS

CONTENTS

PREFACE

This volume consists of an analysis of the constitution, workings and decisions of The Scottish Solicitors' Discipline Tribunal (formerly known as the Scottish Solicitors' Discipline Committee). It does not contain the views of the authors, both of whom are closely associated with the Tribunal. Until the coming into force of the provisions of the Law Reform (Miscellaneous Provisions) (Scotland) Act 1990, it was in many cases the practice of the Tribunal to order that there should be no publicity of its decisions; this meant that these decisions were not readily available to the profession at large. Since the coming into force of the 1990 Act virtually all decisions of the Tribunal now receive publicity. However, it is believed that it will be useful for the profession to have access to the principles upon which the decisions which have been made by the Tribunal over the years, as well as the decisions of the Court following on appeals taken against decisions of the Tribunal.

It should be stressed that although the authors have endeavoured to paraphrase the provisions of the Solicitors (Scotland) Act 1980 with regard to the constitution and procedures of the Tribunal, in a particular case this volume should not be regarded as a substitute for the precise provisions of the 1980 Act and The Scottish Solicitors' Discipline Tribunal Procedure Rules 1989 which are readily available in the *Parliament House Book*. It is hoped, however, that the analysis will prove helpful to persons who are not familiar with the detailed workings of the Tribunal.

It should be borne in mind when considering the terms of the decisions of the Tribunal as precedents that some aspects of professional standards have developed over the years. Penalties imposed by the Tribunal have not been quoted, first, because the maximum penalties have considerably increased over the years and penalties imposed some years ago in many cases bear no relation to what would be imposed by the Tribunal today in similar circumstances and, secondly, because penalties imposed take into account the particular circumstances of individual cases, they cannot be relied on as guidance as to what penalty the Tribunal would impose in another case which may *ex facie* appear similar.

When the Clerk to the Tribunal receives a Complaint, an Appeal or other Application this is marked in a Register and given a unique reference number which consists of a chronological number representing the order in which the case is presented (irrespective of the year in question) together with a further number representing the year in which the case is presented. For example,

PREFACE

'Case 333/83' represents Case No 333 received by the Tribunal and was presented in the year 1983, and it is this identification number which is used in this volume to identify cases from which extracts have been quoted. Although the reference numbers will help to put the case in context as regards date, it should be remembered that the year quoted is the year when the case first was presented to the Tribunal and the circumstances giving rise to the case may have arisen in some cases considerably before that year and of course the case may not have been finally disposed of in the year in which it was first presented.

In this volume the following expressions are used:

'the 1980 Act'	The Solicitors (Scotland) Act 1980 as amended.
'Section – –'	Where a section is referred to without reference to a particular statute, the section is contained in the 1980 Act.
'Schedule 4'	Schedule 4 to the 1980 Act.
'the Tribunal'	The Scottish Solicitors' Discipline Tribunal.
'the Discipline Committee'	The Solicitors' Discipline (Scotland) Committee (now The Scottish Solicitors' Discipline Tribunal).
'the Council' 'the Society' 'the Law Society' 'the Council of the Law Society'	These expressions all refer to the Council of the Law Society of Scotland.
'the Court'	The Court of Session.
'the Procedure Rules' 'the 1989 Rules'	The Scottish Solicitors' Discipline Tribunal Procedure Rules 1989.
'the Code of Conduct'	The Code of Conduct for Scottish Solicitors promulgated by the Law Society of Scotland (October 1989) now incorporated in the Code of Conduct (Scotland) Rules 1992.

The Decisions reviewed are those issued by the Tribunal prior to 28th February 1995.

Ian S. Smith
Inverness
John M. Barton
Edinburgh
3rd April 1995

FOREWORD

The Discipline Tribunal is a forum which, fortunately, few solicitors ever visit. Yet, although the Law Society may act as a filter for complaints about professional conduct, it is the Tribunal which is the real arbiter of what is right and wrong in professional terms. Of course an appeal lies to the Court of Session but in *Sharp* the Court made it very clear that where a solicitor strays across the boundary into professional misconduct is really a matter for the profession to determine. This test is set at what the competent and reputable solicitor would regard as serious and reprehensible. So all of us in practice have a part in setting the standards which the Tribunal enforces.

Like most areas of law the rules of professional conduct are not static. The pressures of modern practice have brought new difficulties in areas such as conflict of interest, taking instructions from an intermediary, keeping the client fully informed, replying to correspondence, recording deeds timeously and controlling workload. These are everyday problems for solicitors and it is not surprising that all of them are the subject of Discipline Tribunal decisions. This book by Ian Smith and John Barton sets out, for the first time, the procedures of the Tribunal, the principles which it applies and the practical effect of these in cases before it. Much of the material has not been easily available before. For those who advise their colleagues on professional conduct matters and appear before the Tribunal it will be invaluable.

The authors bring a special authority to their work. John Barton has acted as Clerk to the Discipline Tribunal for many years and has a unique knowledge of its working. Ian Smith was a member of the Law Society Council where he had great experience of professional practice matters and now sits as a Vice-Chairman of the Discipline Tribunal.

But this book is not just for those who sit on and appear before the Tribunal. It is for all of us in practice who encounter daily delicate decisions about how to deal with clients and, on their behalf, with other solicitors. For younger members of the profession it provides a thorough overview of the standards of conduct which are expected and for more senior members a useful reminder of how important these standards are.

I am delighted that the Council of the Society has agreed to issue the book widely and I am confident that those who read and use the book will greatly benefit.

Kenneth A. Ross
President
The Law Society of Scotland

TABLE OF CASES

TABLE OF DISCIPLINE TRIBUNAL DECISIONS

TABLE OF DISCIPLINE TRIBUNAL DECISIONS

TABLE OF REFERENCES TO CODE OF CONDUCT FOR SCOTTISH SOLICITORS

TABLE OF STATUTES

TABLE OF STATUTES

TABLE OF RULES

TABLE OF RULES

1

CONSTITUTION OF THE DISCIPLINE TRIBUNAL

1.01 ORIGINS OF THE TRIBUNAL

The Scottish Solicitors' Discipline Tribunal was originally established by section 24 of the Solicitors (Scotland) Act 1933 as the Solicitors' Discipline (Scotland) Committee. This name gave rise to the misconception that it was a committee of the Law Society; and it was principally to overcome this confusion that the name changed in 1976.

Originally the conduct of solicitors was a matter for the Court of Session, and when the Discipline Committee was set up, the Court of Session retained the exclusive right to suspend a solicitor from practice or to strike a solicitor off the Roll. In such cases the Discipline Committee heard the particular Complaint and presented a formal report to the Court; and it was only in connection with lesser offences that the Discipline Committee had the power to impose the penalty of a fine of an amount not exceeding £100.

The Solicitors (Scotland) Act 1949 which established the Law Society of Scotland, provided that the objects of the Law Society should 'include the promotion of the interests of the profession of solicitors in Scotland and the interests of the public in relation to that profession'; and to reinforce these principles, the Council of the Society was specifically empowered to present Complaints to the Discipline Committee. The Law Society has fulfilled its duty under this provision and the Society has presented most of the Complaints which have come before the Discipline Committee and the Discipline Tribunal.

1.02 OPERATIVE STATUTE

The constitution, procedure and powers of the Tribunal are now set out in Part IV of and Schedule 4 to the 1980 Act. The Tribunal has no powers outwith this statute apart from those given to the Tribunal under section 31 of the Legal Aid (Scotland) Act 1986.

1.03 PROCEDURE RULES

Section 52(2) of the 1980 Act empowers the Tribunal to make Rules for regulating the making, hearing and determining of Complaints and Appeals to the Tribunal and the 1989 Rules are made under the provisions of this section. Persons having any business in relation to the Tribunal are strongly advised to consult and familiarise themselves with the Procedure Rules which contain various important provisions regarding the forms to be used by parties to proceedings, time-limits, lodging of productions, and generally the rules and procedures to be followed in matters relating to the Tribunal.

In terms of rule 39 it is provided:

> The Tribunal may from time to time dispense with any requirements of these rules respecting notices, affidavits, documents, service or time, where it appears to the Tribunal to be just to do so.

In terms of rule 40 it is provided:

> The Tribunal may extend, and with consent of parties may at their discretion reduce, the time for doing anything under these rules.

Parties should not however rely on the Tribunal relaxing any of the requirements of the Procedure Rules and if the Tribunal does make any relaxation this may carry with it a direction regarding expenses.

1.04 AREAS OF JURISDICTION OF THE TRIBUNAL
These are:
1.   Complaints of Professional Misconduct (section 53).
2.   Complaints of Inadequate Professional Services (section 53(A)).
3.   Appeals against determinations or directions made by the Council in relation to Inadequate Professional Services (section 42A(7)).
4.   Proceedings for enforcement of directions made by the Council relating to Inadequate Professional Services (section 53(C)).
5.   Applications for restoration to the Roll of Solicitors by a person who has been struck off the Roll by the Tribunal (section 10).
6.   Appeals against decisions by the Council to suspend or withdraw or impose restrictions relating to Investment Business Certificates (section 53D).

1.05 WHO MAY MAKE A COMPLAINT TO THE TRIBUNAL
A.   The Council of the Law Society. The Society may (and normally does) appoint a solicitor to act as Fiscal (section 51(1)). In terms of the Procedure Rules such Complaint requires to be in a stipulated form.

B.   Any other body or any member of the public. Such Complaint also requires to be in the stipulated form and to be accompanied by a sworn Affidavit.

Whether or not such Complaint is in the required form, the Tribunal may remit the Complaint to the Council (Schedule 4, para 8A).

Thereafter any further procedure is in the discretion of the Law Society, and if the matter were to proceed, it is to be expected that the Council would proceed under head A and instruct a Fiscal to prosecute a fresh Complaint in its own name. However if the Council decides to take no further action, there is no obligation to report the matter back to the Tribunal. The Tribunal has declared that it has no power to recall such remit (Case 870/93).

C.   Any of the undernoted persons can make a complaint in the form of a report:

The Lord Advocate.
Any Judge.
The Dean of the Faculty of Advocates.
The Auditor of the Court of Session.
The Auditor of any Sheriff Court.
The Scottish Legal Aid Board.
The Scottish Legal Services Ombudsman.

The Tribunal can appoint a solicitor to prosecute any complaint (report) made by these persons and the expenses of that solicitor so far as not recoverable from the solicitor complained against are paid out of the funds of the Tribunal. The Tribunal otherwise has the usual powers to award expenses in relation to such complaints (see Case 802/90 at para 5.08).

1.06 POWERS OF THE TRIBUNAL

A.   *Where*

(*a*) Professional Misconduct is established against a solicitor; *or*

(*b*) a solicitor (whether before or after enrolment) has been convicted by any court of an act involving dishonesty or has been sentenced to a term of imprisonment of not less than two years; *or*

(*c*) an incorporated practice has been convicted by any Court of an offence which conviction the Tribunal is satisfied renders it unsuitable to continue to be recognised by the Council under Section 34(1A); *or*

(*d*) the Tribunal is satisfied that an incorporated practice has failed to comply with any provision of the 1980 Act or Rules made under the Act;

the Tribunal may

(*a*)   order that the name of the solicitor be struck off the Roll; *or*

(*b*)   order that the solicitor be suspended from practice as a solicitor for such time as it may determine; *or*

(*ba*) order that any right of audience held by the solicitor by virtue of section 25A be suspended or revoked (section 25A relates to rights of audience before the Court of Session, etc);

(*c*)   impose on the solicitor or, as the case may be, the incorporated practice a fine not exceeding £10,000 (but not if dealing with a case where the solicitor has been convicted of an act involving dishonesty or has been sentenced to a term of imprisonment of not less than two years); *or*

(*d*)   censure the solicitor or, as the case may be, the incorporated practice; *or*

(*e*)   impose such fine *and* censure; *or*

3

(*f*) order that the recognition under section 34(1A) of the incorporated practice be revoked; *or*

(*g*) order that an investment business certificate issued to a solicitor, a firm of solicitors or an incorporated practice be—

    (i) suspended for such time as it may determine; or

    (ii) subject to such terms and conditions as it may direct; or

    (iii) revoked.

In relation to the foregoing it should be noted that

1. The Tribunal may impose a fine and/or censure a former solicitor, notwithstanding that his name has been struck off the Roll or he has since the misconduct, conviction or sentence, as the case may be, ceased to practise or been suspended from practice. There are similar provisions dealing with incorporated practices which have ceased to be recognised (section 53(3A)).

2. The power to suspend or revoke any right of audience under section 25A can be exercised independently or in conjunction with any other power.

3. Where the Tribunal censures and/or fines a solicitor it may order that the solicitor's Practising Certificate be subject to restriction.

4. It is not competent for the Tribunal to impose a fine if it decides to strike a solicitor off the Roll or suspend a solicitor nor if it is dealing with a case following on a solicitor being convicted of an act involving dishonesty or sentenced to imprisonment for not less than two years.

5. When ordering that a solicitor be struck off the Roll or suspended, or when a right of audience under section 25A is suspended or revoked, the Tribunal may make the order take effect on the date on which the written Findings are intimated to the Respondent. Otherwise such Decision does not take effect until the expiry of the days of appeal or at the conclusion of any appeal (see Case 679/ 86 referred to at para 17.01). Section 53(6A) makes a special provision for the taking effect of an order revoking recognition of an incorporated practice.

6. An order revoking, suspending or making conditional an Investment Business Certificate may be made to take effect on intimation of the order (section 53(6B)).

7. The Secretary of State has power to increase the maximum fine of £10,000.

8. Any fine imposed is forfeit to the Crown. This is in contrast to an award of compensation to a client in respect of Inadequate Professional Services under section 53A(2) (*d*).

9. The Tribunal has no power to modify a period of suspension or a specified period for which a solicitor's Practising Certificate is restricted (See Case 820/ 91 at para 5.04).

The Tribunal was advised by Senior Counsel in an Opinion dated 30th November 1981 that in a case where the contraventions of the Solicitors (Scotland) Accounts Rules which were libelled against a solicitor were committed prior to 22nd December 1980, when section 24 of the Law Reform (Miscellaneous Provisions) (Scotland) Act 1980 came into force (section 24 raised the maximum fine which the Tribunal could impose from £250 to £2,500), it was the powers in force at the date of the hearing which governed the fine which the Tribunal was entitled to impose and not the maximum fine available when the offences were committed.

NB The foregoing Opinion may have to be reconsidered in the light of article 7(1) of the European Convention of Human Rights and the Decision of the European Court of Human Rights in the case of Peter Frederick Welch issued on 9th February 1995.

All the foregoing provisions relate to an individual solicitor or incorporated practice, and it is not competent for such a Complaint to be taken against an unincorporated firm. Accordingly, where two or more solicitors in a firm are implicated in a particular matter, it is the practice for such Complaint to be against each named solicitor. The Tribunal has said:

> The Respondent's Answers contained a plea to the competency of this Complaint and in response to a call contained in the Answers, the Complainers produced an Extract from the Minute of Meeting of their Complaints Committee 'B' held on [. . . . .] which narrated as follows:—
>
> *COMPLAINT BY* ['A, B & Co'] *AGAINST* ['C, D & E']
>
> It was reported that Messrs [C, D & E] had failed to answer the Society's various letters and in particular a letter dated 27th January which informed them that unless a reply was received in seven days the matter would be put before the Complaints Committee.
>
> Resolved to recommend to the Council that a Case be brought before the Discipline Tribunal against [C, D & E] for professional misconduct in respect of their failure to reply to the Society's correspondence and in respect of any other matters which the Fiscal considered to be appropriate.
>
> This Minute was approved without comment at a meeting of the Council of the Law Society of Scotland held on [. . . .].
>
> Counsel for the Respondent submitted that the Complaint was incompetent in that the Council of the Law Society had at no time authorised the making of a Complaint against the Respondent personally, and he referred to the above mentioned Minutes and the Correspondence from the Law Society which was addressed to the Respondent's firm throughout. Counsel referred to the provisions of Section 51 and 53 of the Solicitors (Scotland) Act 1980 in which the proceedings of this Tribunal are wholly directed against individual Solicitors and he submitted that the Complaints Committee and the Council of the Law Society had fundamentally erred in deciding to make a Complaint against a firm of Solicitors, namely Messrs [C, D & E]. In addition, Counsel pointed out that prior to September 1978, the correspondence referred to in the Complaint had been with Messrs [F & C] and that two of the more recent letters had in fact been addressed to an associated firm, Messrs [G, D & E].
>
> The averment of professional misconduct contained in the Complaint contained two specific charges against the Respondent, namely:—
>
> (a) that he showed gross discourtesy to other professional advisers in that he failed to respond or even acknowledge timeously twenty-eight letters sent by [A, B & Co.] to him seeking information in regard to the Trust and

(*b*) that he showed discourtesy to the Complainers by failure timeously to reply to letters from them enquiring in regard to progress thereof.

Counsel for the Respondent made a further submission seeking to have the charge under (a) dismissed because it had not been authorised under the said Minutes of the Complaints Committee and the Council of the Law Society of Scotland; and he argued that it was incompetent for the Council to delegate to the Fiscal the power to extend the prosecution to include:

Any other matters which the Fiscal considered to be appropriate.

The Fiscal acknowledged that the powers of the Tribunal are limited to dealing with individual Solicitors but he explained that when a Complaint against a firm of Solicitors is received by the Law Society of Scotland, there is frequently no means of knowing which person in the firm is responsible for the matter, particularly when the Complaint relates to a failure to reply to correspondence. It was therefore understood that any resolution of the Law Society Council to proceed to this Tribunal with a Complaint against a firm of Solicitors implied that the Complaint should proceed against the partners or any of them.

Section 51(1) of the Solicitors (Scotland) Act 1980 provides that '... for the purpose of investigating and prosecuting Complaints, the Council (of the Law Society) may appoint a Solicitor to act as Fiscal'. It was not disputed that the powers of the Tribunal are limited to dealing with individual Solicitors and the Tribunal accepts the Fiscal's argument that a resolution to proceed with a complaint against the firm of Messrs [C, D & E] in fact gives authority to the Fiscal to proceed with a Complaint against the individual partners or any of them. In the Fiscal's investigation made in terms of the last mentioned section of the 1980 Act, it was found that the partner at fault was the Respondent and in the view of the Tribunal the Fiscal correctly framed his Complaint against him.

Having accepted the principle that the Respondent is the individual against whom the Complaint should have been made, it is to be considered whether it was right that the Complaint should relate to circumstances covering a period or periods when the Respondent might have been practising on his own or as a partner in another firm. The Tribunal takes the view that it was competent for the Fiscal to refer in the Complaint to actings of the Respondent prior to the establishment of his present firm . . . .

The present Complaint bears to be at the instance of the Council of the Law Society of Scotland, and it is the opinion of the Tribunal that it is not competent for the Tribunal to question the authority of the Fiscal or the extent of his instructions in the presentation and conduct of a Complaint (Case 519/81).

In a Complaint against two solicitors (the Respondents), who were latterly in partnership but where formerly the first Respondent had employed the second Respondent, the Tribunal said:

This Complaint is directed to the Respondents' conduct in the defence of an action of Reparation.

At the beginning of the Hearing, Mr [X], who was representing the Respondents, submitted pleas to the effect that the proceedings were incompetent, and that the Statement of Facts was irrelevant and insufficient to support the Complaint.

Mr [X] referred to the Rules of the Committee which provide for any Complaint to be against 'a Solicitor' and he argued that it was incompetent to make a Complaint against more than one Solicitor, particularly when the Complaint did not distinguish the extent of the liability of each individual Solicitor. In referring to the circumstances of this particular Complaint, he pointed out that all the relative correspondence had been addressed to the Respondents' firm and that it had been their Clerk, [Z], who had written and signed all the letters on behalf of the firm. Mr [X] accepted the civil liability of a firm for the negligence of its employee in such circumstances but he questioned whether the actings of a Clerk could ever impute dishonourable conduct on the part of the members of a firm unless in circumstances such as where the Respondents had themselves written the letters or if the letters had been written on their instructions.

Mr [X] conceded that there could be a competent Complaint against the whole members of a firm in circumstances where there was joint responsibility as with a breach of the Accounts Rules, but this was in contrast to a Complaint of professional misconduct arising from dishonourable conduct such as embezzlement which could only be on the part of an individual Solicitor. Mr [X] also criticised the wording of the Statement of Facts which accompanied the Complaint in respect that it failed to distinguish the personal actings of each individual Respondent, and the Respondents' firm, which was not and could not in itself be the subject of a Complaint.

The Committee carefully considered Mr [X's] submissions and the observations made by [the solicitor for the Complainers] in reply and they are satisfied that the form of the Complaint was in accordance with the Rules and that the individual Respondents were not prejudiced in respect that the matter had been brought before the Committee in a single Complaint. They are also satisfied that the Statement of Facts contains a case relevant to support the Complaint . . . (Case 297/69).

B. *Where a charge of Inadequate Professional Services is established*
In terms of section 53A(1) the Tribunal may take such of the following steps as are set out in section 53A(2) as it sees fit, namely:

(*a*) to determine that the amount of the fees and outlays to which the solicitor shall be entitled for the services shall be—

(i) nil; or

(ii) such amount as the Tribunal may specify in the determination, and by order direct the solicitor to comply, or secure compliance, with such of the requirements set out in subsection (3) as appear to it to be necessary to give effect to the determination;

(*b*) to direct the solicitor to secure the rectification at his own expense of any such error, omission or other deficiency arising in connection with the services as the Tribunal may specify;

(*ba*) to order that any right of audience held by the solicitor by virtue of section 25A be suspended or revoked (section 25A relates to rights of audience before the Court of Session, etc);

(*c*) to direct the solicitor to take, at his own expense, such other action in the interests of the client as the Tribunal may specify;

(*d*) to direct the solicitor to pay to the client by way of compensation such sum, not exceeding £1,000, as the Tribunal may specify.

The requirements set out in subsection (3) are:

(*a*) to refund, whether wholly or to any specified extent, any amount already paid by or on behalf of the client in respect of the fees and outlays of the solicitor in connection with the services;

(*b*) to waive, whether wholly or to any specified extent, the right to recover those fees and outlays.

In relation to the foregoing it should be noted that

1. Before making a determination the Tribunal may submit the solicitor's account for the fees and outlays to the Auditor of the Court of Session for taxation.

2. Where a solicitor in respect of whom a complaint of Inadequate Professional Services is made was, at the time when the services were provided, an employee of another solicitor, a direction under section 53A shall specify and apply to that other solicitor as well as the solicitor in respect of whom the complaint is made.

3. A direction of the Tribunal under section 53A shall be enforceable like an extract registered decree arbitral in favour of the Council bearing a warrant for execution issued by the sheriff court of any sheriffdom in Scotland.

4. The Secretary of State has powers to increase the maximum sum of £1,000 that may be awarded by way of compensation.

5. Section 56A(1) and (2) provides that any Decision of the Tribunal in relation to Inadequate Professional Services shall not be founded on in subsequent court proceedings in a claim for negligence except that any monetary award may be taken into consideration by the court upon making an award of damages.

6. A payment which may be ordered by the Tribunal in terms of section 53(A)(2) (*d*) is by way of compensation to a client and is not a fine forfeit to the Crown, as are payments made under section 53(2) (*c*).

7. The powers of the Tribunal in relation to headings A and B are entirely separate and accordingly a finding of Professional Misconduct will not entitle the Tribunal to make an order in relation to Inadequate Professional Services unless the latter is separately averred and established.

C. *Appeals under section 42A(7)*

In Appeals under section 42A(7) against determinations or directions by the Council relating to Inadequate Professional Services, the Tribunal may in terms of section 53B

> quash, confirm or vary the determination or direction being appealed against.

Section 42A(8) defines 'solicitor' in relation to such cases as including a firm of solicitors or an incorporated practice.

The specialities of appeals under section 42A(7) are considered at para 2.06.

D. *Exclusion from giving legal aid advice and assistance*

Under section 31 of the Legal Aid (Scotland) Act 1986, the Tribunal may make an order to exclude a solicitor (for a specified period or without limit of time) either from being selected to advise or act for any person to whom legal aid and or advice and assistance is made available or from giving advice and assistance to or from acting for a person to whom legal aid is made available on the ground that there is good reason for excluding him arising out of

(*a*) his conduct when acting or selected to act for persons to whom legal aid or advice and assistance is made available;

(*b*) his professional conduct generally;

(*c*) in the case of a member of a firm of solicitors or a director of an incorporated practice, such conduct on the part of any person who is for the time being a member of the firm or a director of the practice.

The Legal Aid Board must be informed of any such order.

E. *Applications for restoration to the Roll*

A solicitor whose name has been struck off the Roll (other than by order of the Court of Session) shall only be entitled to have his name restored upon application to the Tribunal (section 10) and the Procedure Rules contain detailed procedure and styles for such Application. The Tribunal insists that the accompanying Affidavit be sworn before a Justice of the Peace and that the supporting letters are from solicitors who are in practice as principals.

The Tribunal intimates such Application to the Law Society and it is accepted that the Council of the Society has an interest to answer the Application and to be represented at the hearing. (The corresponding position in England was considered by *R* v *Master of the Rolls*, ex parte *McKinnell* [1933] All ER 193.)

It is open to the Applicant to request that the hearing of his Application is in public. There have been no recent decisions of the Court of Session in relation to applications for restoration but it has been observed in England by Lord Donaldson MR that a solicitor who had been guilty of a serious offence should only be restored to the Roll in exceptional circumstances.

F. *Other Applications*

There are occasions where the Tribunal has ordered that a restriction on a solicitor's Practising Certificate made under section 53(5) shall continue until the solicitor satisfies the Tribunal that he is fit to hold a full certificate, and at the appropriate stage it is open to the solicitor to make application to the Tribunal to have such restriction withdrawn. The Procedure Rules do not contain any specific provisions for this procedure, but it is usual for the solicitor to lodge a formal Application which the Tribunal intimates to the Law Society, and thereafter the Application is set down for hearing.

1.07 MEMBERSHIP OF THE TRIBUNAL (Schedule 4, Part I)

The Tribunal consists of:

(*a*) ten solicitor members who are solicitors recommended by the Council, appointed by the Lord President. The 1980 Act allows for the appointment of a further four solicitor members;

1.07 MEMBERSHIP OF THE TRIBUNAL

(*b*) eight lay members who are neither solicitors nor advocates, appointed by the Lord President after consultation with the Secretary of State.

1.08 CHAIRMAN
The Tribunal appoints a Chairman and also Vice-Chairmen who preside at its meetings.

1.09 QUORUM
The Tribunal is deemed to be properly constituted if:
(*a*) at least three solicitor members are present, *and*
(*b*) at least one lay member is present, *and*
(*c*) the number of solicitor members present exceeds the number of lay members present, *and*
(*d*) there are present not more than three solicitor members for every lay member.

Four solicitor members and two lay members are usually called to each meeting.

As a matter of practice the first item on the agenda for meetings of the Tribunal is the verification that there is a quorum present.

1.10 CLERK
The Tribunal appoints its own Clerk (who must not be a member of the Tribunal).

1.11 PAYMENT OF MEMBERS
Lay members of the Tribunal are paid by the Secretary of State a fee for their attendance together with subsistence and travelling expenses. Solicitor members are not paid any fee for their attendance but are paid subsistence and travelling expenses.

1.12 PERIOD OF TENURE OF MEMBERS
Members are appointed for not more than five years but may be reappointed in the same manner as new members are appointed. It is not the practice for solicitor members to continue after they have retired from practice or have attained the age of 65. The Lord President may from time to time terminate the appointment of any member and he may fill any vacancy in the same manner as new members are appointed.

1.13 PRIVILEGE
It is understood that the Tribunal and its members have absolute privilege. The making of a Complaint (or an Appeal under section 42A(7) or section 53D(1) of the 1980 Act) to the Tribunal or the giving of any information in connection with a Complaint (or such an Appeal) confers qualified privilege (Schedule 4, para 7, and Schedule 4, para 23).

2

INITIAL PROCEEDINGS

2.01 THE CHARGE

Rule 2 of the Procedure Rules makes provision for the form of Complaints. In an Appeal to the Court of Session by the Council of the Law Society against a Decision of the Solicitors' Discipline (Scotland) Committee to dismiss a Complaint the Lord President stated *inter alia* in his Opinion:

> In the course of the hearing before us the relevancy and specification of head 1 of the complaint against Mr [A] and head 2 of the complaint against Mr [B] were criticised. The criticism was derived mainly from the circumstance that having set out on averment what they offered to prove against these solicitors the complainers in Stats 16 and 17 of the complaint purported to define the misconduct alleged against each of them under three separate heads This we are told is the practice of the Law Society in framing complaints and it is an entirely laudable one. In this case, however, head 1 of the complaint against Mr [A] and head 2 of the complaint against Mr [B] do not by themselves sufficiently disclose any act of professional misconduct. Head 1 of the complaint against Mr [A], for example, merely alleges misrepresentation that he acted for a client for whom he then did not act. If the misrepresentation was innocent it would not plainly be professional misconduct to make it. The vital ingredient which is absent from head 1 is that of Mr [A's] knowledge and is only to be discovered here by reading head 1 together with the whole averments which preceded Stats 16 and 17. We have only to say that this is undesirable and that when the Council of the Law Society proceeds to define the precise act of professional misconduct alleged against a solicitor that definition should, like a Summary Complaint or a charge in an Indictment, contain within itself all the ingredients necessary to disclose the offence. (*Council of the Law Society of Scotland* v *M and W*, Court of Session, unreported, 16.1.75).

2.02 PRIOR CIRCUMSTANCES NOT FOUNDED ON

In considering matters in the Complaint which are the subject of averments of Professional Misconduct, the Tribunal may have regard to earlier events for the purpose of considering whether subsequent events constitute Professional Misconduct and thereafter in assessing the gravity of the conduct and determining the appropriate decision for the Tribunal to make (as in Case 815/91). Accordingly, it is frequently the practice of the Law Society to narrate circumstances in a Complaint, which of themselves might have amounted to Professional Misconduct or Inadequate Professional Services and where the Respondent had been advised/warned as to his conduct by the Law Society, as background and to indicate that the subsequent actings of the Respondent were at a time when he was aware of the earlier advice/warning of the Law

2.02 PRIOR CIRCUMSTANCES NOT FOUNDED ON

Society. In such circumstances, the Law Society states that it is not seeking a finding of Professional Misconduct or Inadequate Professional Services in respect of such earlier events. The Tribunal has said:

> The events arising on 7th June 1983 were in themselves serious in that they demonstrated the Respondent's disregard of elementary requirements of the Accounts Rules and in particular his duty to ensure that all transactions should be recorded in his books of account. Taking into account the prior circumstances occurring since December 1978 and in particular his previous failure to maintain his cash books and make satisfactory entries for all transactions nothwithstanding previous warnings which had been given [by] the Law Society, the Tribunal are satisfied that the particular breaches of the Accounts Rules which became apparent on 7th June 1983 were reprehensible and that they amount to professional misconduct on the part of the Respondent.

> The original Answers as lodged on behalf of the Respondent had contained a plea of competency on the basis that the circumstances arising in paragraphs 2 and 6 were *res judicata*, and Counsel for the Respondent did indirectly refer to the fact that these events had been the subject of a prior finding of the Tribunal. In considering whether the matters arising on 7th June 1983 amounted to professional misconduct, the Tribunal disregarded such knowledge that they had of any previous finding against the Respondent, but the Tribunal are of the opinion that notwithstanding that a prior conviction may have related to the events occurring between 13th December 1978 and 4th August 1982, they were nevertheless entitled to take earlier circumstances into account in considering whether the recent failures which had subsequently occurred in themselves amounted to professional misconduct (Case 580/83).

In finding the solicitor guilty of Professional Misconduct in respect of a breach of rule 8 of the Solicitors (Scotland) Accounts Rules 1981 as at 7th June 1983, the Tribunal said:

> Section 35(3) of the Solicitors (Scotland) Act 1980, which re-enacted section 20(3) of the Solicitors (Scotland) Act 1949 provides that if any Solicitor fails to comply with Accounts Rules made under that Section, 'that failure may be treated as professional misconduct . . .'. In considering that provision, it was observed by the Lord President in an appeal from this Tribunal decided on 20th October 1982:

>> Whether such a failure should be treated as professional misconduct must depend upon the gravity of the failure and a consideration of the whole circumstances in which the failure occurred including the part played by the individual Solicitor in question [*Sharp* v *Council of the Law Society in Scotland* 1984 SC 129 at 134].

> It was submitted by Counsel for the Respondent with reference to the foregoing *dicta* that the circumstances occurring between 13th December 1978 and 4th August 1982 were irrelevant for the purposes of determining whether the subsequent events as narrated in paragraphs 7 and 8 amounted to professional misconduct. Counsel argued that in interpreting the words 'gravity of the failure' and 'a consideration of the whole circumstances' it was the duty of the Tribunal to look only at the gravity of the failure as disclosed in paragraphs 7 and 8 and only to consider the whole circumstances as contained in these paragraphs; and Counsel used the analogy of a Road Traffic charge to point out the irrelevancy of previous

12

events in determining whether a particular course of events amounted to careless driving.

Since the decision of the Court on 20th October 1982, it has been the practice of Fiscals for the Law Society to set down previous contraventions of the Accounts Rules in order to demonstrate the seriousness of the conduct which is the subject of the Charge set out in a Complaint and this was the first occasion on which it had been argued that such prior circumstances might be irrelevant.

Upon a careful consideration of the matter, the Tribunal is of the opinion that the analogy of a Road Traffic Offence is not appropriate in that the background information is not being made available to assist in deciding whether the particular events were in breach of the relevant regulations but whether the events constituting the breach were of such gravity as might appropriately be stigmatised with a finding of professional misconduct. In the opinion of this Tribunal it is appropriate for the Tribunal in considering the gravity of the conduct to examine the Solicitor's previous record of compliance with the Accounts Rules, particularly in relation to any warnings or other advice which he may have had (Case 580/83).

See also Case 746/89 at para 16.10 and Case 861/93 at para 19.08.

2.03 DISMISSAL OF COMPLAINT/APPEAL WITHOUT SERVICE

Subject to Part IV of the 1980 Act, the Tribunal may dismiss a Complaint against a solicitor or an incorporated practice

(a) without requiring the solicitor or the incorporated practice to answer the allegations made against him or, as the case may be, it or without holding any inquiry if—

(i) it is of the opinion that the Complaint discloses no *prima facie* case of Professional Misconduct on the part of the solicitor, or of failure on the part of the incorporated practice to comply with any provision of the 1980 Act or of rules made under the 1980 Act or, as the case may be, of provision of Inadequate Professional Services; or

(ii) the Complainer fails to comply with any of the Tribunal's Rules of Procedure (made under section 52 of the 1980 Act). (Schedule 4, para 9.)

Subject to Part IV of the 1980 Act the Tribunal may dismiss an Appeal under section 42A(7) or section 53D(1) of the 1980 Act without holding an inquiry if

(a) it is of the opinion that the Appeal is manifestly ill founded; or

(b) the Appellant fails to comply with any of the Tribunal's Rules of Procedure (made under section 52 of the 1980 Act). (Schedule 4, para 24.)

In practice where the Tribunal receives a Complaint from the Council (or an Appeal from a Solicitor) it is considered by the Chairman and Vice-Chairmen and thereafter if they consider that a *prima facie* case is made out in the Complaint (or the Appeal, as the case may be) they authorise service of the Complaint (or the Appeal, as the case may be) on the Respondent solicitor (the Law Society in the case of an Appeal by a solicitor). Otherwise the Complaint/Appeal is considered at the earliest meeting of the Tribunal.

2.04 SERVICE OF COMPLAINT/APPEAL
This is effected by the Clerk in accordance with the Procedure Rules. In the case of an Appeal by a solicitor under section 42A(7) of the 1980 Act (against a finding of Inadequate Professional Services by the Council), the Tribunal is also required to give notice of the Appeal to the person who made the original complaint to the Council.

2.05 FURTHER CONSIDERATION
In the event of a solicitor lodging answers to a Complaint or the Council lodging answers in an Appeal by a solicitor against a determination of Inadequate Professional Services or regarding an Investment Business Certificate by the Council, or in the event of the expiry of the period for lodging answers without answers being lodged, the Chairman and Vice-Chairmen will again consider whether or not the case should proceed to a hearing and if they are of the opinion that a hearing is not appropriate, they will report the matter to the next meeting of the Tribunal and at that stage it is again open to the Tribunal to dismiss the Complaint or the Appeal without a hearing.

In an Appeal to the Court against a Decision of the Tribunal to dismiss a complaint by a lay complainer after having received a Complaint and Affidavit from the Complainer and Answers from the solicitor, together with adjustments from each party, it was argued that the Decision was *ultra vires* of the Tribunal on the basis of the provisions of rules 4 and 5 of the Tribunal's Procedure Rules 1978 which correspond to rules 5 and 6 of the current Procedure Rules (the 1989 Rules). The Court said:

> This submission rested upon the provisions of Rules 4 and 5 of the Tribunal's Rules of Procedure which, so far as relevant for present purposes, are in these terms:
>
> 4. On receiving a complaint made, in the opinion of the Tribunal, in accordance with Rule 2, the Tribunal shall take the same into consideration, and they may from time to time and either before or after fixing a day for the hearing require the complainer to supply such further information and documents in support of the complaint as they think just. In any case where, in the opinion of the Tribunal, no *prima facie* case against the solicitor is disclosed the Tribunal may, without further procedure and whether or not an opportunity to supply further information and documents may have been given to the complainer as aforesaid, make an order in writing dismissing the complaint.
> 5. If, in the opinion of the Tribunal, any complaint as originally lodged with the Clerk to the Tribunal or as supplemented in accordance with the procedure in Rule 4 discloses a *prima facie* case against the solicitor, the Tribunal shall serve on the solicitor a full copy of the complaint and affidavit as lodged . . . and . . . as supplemented, and shall allow answers to be lodged within such time as the Tribunal may appoint. If answers are lodged, a full copy thereof shall be sent by the solicitor to the complainer, and a certificate that this has been done shall be sent by the solicitor to the Clerk of the Tribunal. On the expiry of the date appointed for lodging answers and whether answers have been lodged or not, the Tribunal may, if on considering the documents lodged they are of opinion that no further action by them is called for, make an order dismissing the

complaint; but otherwise the Tribunal shall fix a day for hearing the complaint and shall serve a notice thereof on the complainer and on the solicitor complained against . . . . .

Under reference to these Rules it was, it was said, quite clear that a decision as to the relevancy of a Complaint falls to be taken once and for all when the Tribunal has to consider whether to order service upon the respondent. At that stage, on an examination of the averments in the Affidavit of the Complainer, supplemented by any further information or documents which the Tribunal may have required the Complainer to supply, the Tribunal may dismiss the Complaint without further procedure if, in their opinion, no *prima facie* case against the solicitor [is] disclosed. The argument was that Rule 4 so provides because, as the Tribunal observe in the Note appended to their decision dated 4th September 1979, proceedings against a solicitor are quasi criminal and charges must be specific and detailed and be established beyond reasonable doubt. If, on the other hand, the Tribunal is of opinion that a *prima facie* case is disclosed it is required under Rule 5 to serve the Complaint upon the solicitor and to proceed thereafter in terms of that Rule. A *prima facie* case is a case supported by averments relevant and sufficiently specific to instruct professional misconduct if they are proved. A decision to order service is a decision that the test of relevancy has been passed and it is not open to the Tribunal thereafter to dismiss the Complaint on the ground of relevancy. Reading Rules 4 and 5 of the Rules together the power to dismiss conferred by Rule 5 is not concerned with either relevancy or specification, and is designed to be exercised where, for other reasons, the Tribunal decides that no further action by them is called for. In the events which happened in this case, accordingly, the Tribunal has no power to dismiss the Complaint for the reasons which they gave.

It would we think be unfortunate if the language of Rules 4 and 5 compelled us to accept this attractively simple argument. A Complaint against a solicitor is not a criminal charge. Consideration of the Rules of Procedure as a whole strongly suggests that it is not intended that the proceedings of the Tribunal should be conducted with the formality of a criminal process. Indeed the function of the Tribunal is such that if the Rules permit it to do so, it should, before rejecting any complaint from a member of the public, give the Complainer a reasonable opportunity to specify crucial facts in dispute which he will require to prove if his Complaint is to go to inquiry. A flexible approach by the Tribunal in our opinion must, we think, be in the public interest. We are accordingly happy to find that Rules 4 and 5 cannot and should not be construed in the rigid and narrow way for which the petitioner contends in this case. A *prima facie* case within the meaning of these Rules is merely a case which is sufficient to call for an answer. When a Complaint from a member of the public comes before a Tribunal it is accompanied only by an Affidavit of the complainer himself. Such an Affidavit may and often, of necessity, will, contain inferential averments—Averments of the Complainer's belief of the existence of certain alleged facts not within his own knowledge. Confronted by such an Affidavit a Tribunal is entitled to ask itself how much more information it should ask for before calling for an answer. It is also entitled to decide to order service where the Complaint rests on inferential averments which, if well founded, would support a charge of professional misconduct, so that they may see to what extent these averments are in dispute before demanding further specification. It is in the public interest that the Tribunal should be able to proceed in this flexible way and to delay demanding from complaining members of the public further specification of the facts necessary in proof of inferential averments in their Affidavits until such specification is seen to be necessary. As Rule 4 shows that the Tribunal is entitled to call for further information from time to time throughout any proceedings and as we read the power to dismiss contained in Rule 5 the language used is wide enough to permit dismissal on grounds of relevancy and specification after answers have been lodged, and after an opportunity has been given to the Complainer to set out the facts which he offers to prove in support of crucial inferential averments which have been denied by the respondent. In the result therefore we hold, upon a proper construction of Rules 4 and 5, that the Tribunal were entitled upon a consideration of the Complaint and Affidavit, as adjusted to meet the Answers, to dismiss the Complaint as irrelevant by exercising the power conferred upon them by Rule 5 . . . . (*S* v *B*, Court of Session, unreported, 25.2.81).

2.06 APPEALS RE INADEQUATE PROFESSIONAL SERVICES

In terms of section 42A of the 1980 Act, where the Council of the Law Society receives, from any person having an interest, a complaint that professional services provided by a solicitor in connection with any matter in which he has been instructed by a client were inadequate and the Council, after inquiry and after giving the solicitor an opportunity to make representations, upholds the complaint and makes a determination or direction under this section, the solicitor may within 21 days of the date upon which the determination or direction is intimated to him appeal to the Tribunal against the determination or direction.

The section (section 42A) does not set out any basis on which the Tribunal requires to proceed with the Appeal but para 23 of Schedule 4 to the 1980 Act directs that in relation to any such Appeal to the Tribunal the provisions of para 11 of Schedule 4 should be varied to read as follows:

> For the purpose of inquiring into the appeal the Tribunal may administer oaths and received affirmations, and the appellant and respondent shall each be entitled—
> (*a*) to require the evidence of parties, witnesses and others interested, and
> (*b*) to call for and recover such evidence and documents and examine such witnesses as they think proper . . . .

Also para 25 of Schedule 4 provides that

> The Tribunal shall give notice of the appeal . . . and shall enquire into the matter, giving the appellant and the complainer [the person by whom the original complaint was made] reasonable opportunity to make representations to the Tribunal.

Section 53B of the 1980 Act provides that on an Appeal under section 42A(7) the Tribunal 'may quash, confirm or vary the determination or direction being appealed against'. It should be noted that there is no provision for any such decision being remitted back to the Law Society.

There are therefore a number of ways in which the Tribunal might approach such an Appeal and the Tribunal has thus far only had to consider a limited number of such Appeals.

In an Appeal where the respective solicitors representing the Appellant and the Council of the Law Society informed the Tribunal that various productions lodged on behalf of the Council of the Law Society and the Appellant were admitted and no witness was called by either the Appellant or the Law Society to give evidence and the original complainer did not appear, the Tribunal were referred to Sheriff I. D. Macphail's book, *Sheriff Court Practice*, para 18–110, where he stated:

> The appellate court may also intervene where, although the judge has not erred in law, misapprehended or misused the facts, considered any irrelevant matter, or left out of account any relevant matter, the court is satisfied that his conclusion is vitiated by an error in weighing the relevant considerations, by giving too little or too much weight to one or more of them. The weighing of the relevant considerations has been called 'the balancing exercise'. If the court is satisfied that there has been an error in the balancing exercise or that the judge's conclusion is so plainly wrong that there must have been such an error, the court may interfere.

The Tribunal took the view that the 'balancing exercise' as set out by Sheriff Macphail properly represented a process which may be exercised by the Tribunal in considering an Appeal against a finding of Inadequate Professional Services and they then proceeded to deal with the Appeal on that basis (Case 839/93).

In another Appeal to the Tribunal by a firm of solicitors against a finding of Inadequate Professional Services by the Law Society, the agent for the Appellants appealed on four separate grounds.

The first ground was that the Law Society had not given the Appellants an opportunity to make representations as required by section 42A(1) (*b*) of the Solicitors (Scotland) Act 1980. The agent referred to the specific terms of section 42A(1) which provides that where 'the Council [of the Law Society], after inquiry and after giving the solicitor an opportunity to make representations, uphold the complaint, they [may] take such of the steps mentioned in subsection (2) as they think fit'. With reference to the foregoing, the agent emphasised the word 'and'. He submitted that the functions of 'inquiry' and the 'opportunity to make representations' were successive and that the Law Society's correspondence with the Appellants, commencing with a letter of 20th May 1992 and continuing to a letter of 24th September 1992, was all part of the information-gathering exercise. He pointed to the papers being passed to the Committee member acting as reporter who then presented his findings to the Committee. The agent submitted that this was the stage when the Appellants should have been given the opportunity to make representations. He particularly observed that the Appellants had not been given the opportunity to comment on any matters which the reporter may have misunderstood, or to make a plea in mitigation.

The Appellants' second ground of appeal was to the effect that, in any event, it was inappropriate and unreasonable for the Law Society to proceed without giving the Appellants an opportunity to appear personally to explain their position and make representations, in view of the complexity of this particular case. The agent submitted that it was unreasonable not to have allowed either the Appellants or the complainer the opportunity to comment on the Report, but did not insist that the Appellants should have been given the right to an oral hearing.

The Law Society Fiscal disputed the Appellants' agent's interpretation of section 42A(1) (b). He explained that when the provisions relating to Inadequate Professional Services originally came into effect, the Law Society had adopted the practice of giving the solicitor the opportunity to make submissions either orally or in writing before issuing its final determination but it had been found from experience that this procedure resulted in unacceptable delays for both the complainer and the solicitor. In its opinion, the critical word 'and' was not consecutive but simultaneous and upon adopting the present procedure, the Law Society had endeavoured to achieve a fair balance. In support of the present procedure, the Fiscal contrasted the position with that of a planning appeal where the reporter is statutorily obliged to issue a proposed finding and seek representations. The Fiscal also specifically referred to the paragraph in the initial letter from the Law Society to the effect that 'your written responses and any further correspondence which follows thereon shall be considered as fulfilling the terms of section 42A(1) (b) of the Solicitors (Scotland) Act 1980 as amended' and he submitted that either by contract or acquiescence the Appellants, by their letter of 24th September 1992, had permitted the Law Society to proceed. The Fiscal also illustrated the reasonableness of the procedure by taking the analogy of an arbitration in that the Law Society refers the matter to a reporter in order to reach a decision, that even then the matter is still not final as the solicitor has the right of appeal to the Discipline Tribunal and that there is a further safeguard in that this Tribunal has the right to hear witnesses, in contrast to an appeal to a Sheriff Principal.

The Fiscal also relied on the suitability of the new Law Society procedure in responding to the second ground of appeal. The Tribunal in its Decision stated:

> The Tribunal appreciated the very full submissions made by each party. The practice recently adopted by the Law Society may have been seen as fair and reasonable having regard to the desirability of reaching an early conclusion in such a complaint. Nevertheless a finding of inadequate professional services, possibly involving as in this case, the denial of significant fees and the prevention of any recovery of outlays can be a serious matter for the solicitor. The powers conferred upon the Law Society are specifically set out in section 42A of the Solicitors (Scotland) Act 1980 and whilst it is desirable to find a course of action which is both expedient and fair to all parties nevertheless the Tribunal must have paramount consideration to the terms of the statute and any course of action, however reasonable, which does not fulfil these requirements must be invalid.

> Turning to the words of the statute, it is significant that section 42A(1) (b) contains two distinct phrases 'after inquiry' and 'after giving the solicitor an opportunity to make representations'. Each phrase is introduced by the word 'after' and it is reasonable to conclude from this that the Law Society is required to carry out two distinct and separate functions, and that a party challenging the operation of this Section is entitled to be satisfied that each function is separately carried out. [The

agent for the Appellants] went further and suggested that the use of the word 'and' implied that the operations should be carried out consecutively. The Tribunal does not accept this aspect of [the agent for the Appellants] case although in practical terms, it may be difficult to demonstrate that a solicitor is being given a fair opportunity to make representations if the separate inquiries are still proceeding. Turning to the particular case, inquiries undoubtedly commenced with the Law Society's letter of 20th May 1992 and the indications are that they continued until the Appellants' letter to the Law Society of 24th September 1992. It was implied by [the Fiscal] that the terms of the Law Society's letter of 20th May also commenced the consultative stage whereby the solicitor was able to make representations particularly in view of the specific reference to section 42A(1) (b) in that letter. However it cannot be accepted that the requirements of a particular statutory provision are necessarily fulfilled merely by stating to another party that a particular course of action is deemed to satisfy that provision. The Law Society must be able to point out that a separate and distinct opportunity was given to the Appellants to [make] representations and that such opportunity was given at an appropriate stage in the whole proceedings. Nor can it be implied from the terms of [the Appellants'] letter of 24th September 1992 that he had waived his right to make representations. It remained the obligation of the Law Society to give the solicitor that opportunity and if he intended to waive his entitlement to make representations, such intention would require to be specifically declared by the solicitor[s].

Looking at the particular circumstances, it is the Tribunal's opinion that the correspondence up to and including 24th September was solely associated with the Law Society's operation of making inquiries. The appropriate Committee of the Law Society then passed the whole papers to one of their members to prepare a Report. This is a practical arrangement and in the absence of a prior fact-finding inquiry, the provision of such Report is a reasonable means of establishing the facts upon which a decision was to be made. Until shortly prior to the consideration of this particular Complaint, it had then been the Law Society's practice to give the solicitor the option of an oral hearing or the alternative of making written submissions and undoubtedly that procedure satisfied the requirements of section 42A(1) (b). An oral hearing is potentially the fullest method of inquiry as it allows an adjudicating body to ask supplementary questions and gives the party attending the hearing the opportunity of making further submissions based on any point which might arise at such a hearing; but significantly, [the agent for the Appellants] did not insist on the option for an oral hearing. In the opinion of the Tribunal, the words 'after giving the solicitor an opportunity to make representations' does not necessarily imply that there should be an oral hearing and such hearing could not reasonably be insisted upon by any party. Nevertheless these words in the statute require the Law Society to confer with the solicitor in regard to the disposal of the Complaint and this requires a positive approach to the solicitor which is separate from the fact-finding exercise of an inquiry.

In this case, the reporter appears to have perused the Appellants' files and prepared a lengthy Report covering each of the separate heads of complaint and this Report and his recommendation were subsequently placed before the appropriate Committee of the Law Society. This practice crystallises a given set of facts and provided detailed material on which the Committee can reach a decision for recommendation to the Council. The Council of the Society, through its Committee, came to a decision accepting the factual content of the Report and determining the penalty to be imposed on the Appellants—without any further communication with the Appellants. The Statute does not specify the nature or subject matter of the representations which may be made by the solicitor, but as the direction follows the reference to an inquiry, it is reasonable to presume that the solicitor should have the opportunity to comment on the outcome of the inquiry and natural justice requires that the solicitor should also have the opportunity to make submissions in relation to the possible disposal of the matter, particularly in view of the significant powers available to the Law Society. The previous practice of the Law Society had been to issue their Schedule containing findings in fact and opinion together with the intended disposal in a proposed form—giving the parties or at least the solicitor a limited time in which to make comment thereon, and such procedure undoubtedly satisfied section 42A(1) (b). However it is the opinion of the Tribunal , that in this case the Appellants were not given the opportunity to make representations to the extent to which they were entitled under section 42A(1), and accordingly it is appropriate that the Tribunal should uphold the Appeal and quash the determination and direction made under section 42A(2) (Case 848/93).

In yet another appeal by a solicitor against a decision of the Law Society making a determination of Inadequate Professional Services the question arose as to whether the Tribunal should hear evidence. The Tribunal, in the Note to its Decision said:

It had been made known to the Tribunal that [the original complainer] intended to give evidence and to lead the evidence of her husband; and in anticipation of this, [the agent] for the Appellant submitted that it was not appropriate for the Tribunal to hear evidence in this Appeal. He referred to the normal appeal procedure and in particular to the statement of Sheriff Macphail in his volume on *Sheriff Court Practice* at para 18–109:

The underlying rationale of the appellate court's restrictive approach to the review of discretionary decisions is that it is of the essence of a judicial discretion that on the same material different minds may reach widely different decisions any one of which may reasonably be thought to be the best, and any one of which, therefore, a judge may make without being held to be wrong.

An appeal court ordinarily proceeds on the basis of the facts which are established before the lower court, and if an appeal court were to hear evidence, it would in effect amount to a rehearing. [The agent for the Appellant] acknowledged the provisions of paragraphs 11 and 23 of the Fourth Schedule of the 1980 Act, noting that paragraph 11 which empowers the Tribunal to administer oaths and receive affirmations, with each party being entitled to require evidence, had existed prior to the legislation relating to inadequate professional services but that paragraph 23 had been introduced by the Solicitors (Scotland) Act 1988 under which the present appeal procedure was introduced. However [the agent for the Appellant] observed that the hearing of evidence in an appeal was most unusual and he submitted that it should only be permitted in certain restricted circumstances. It was significant that the operative section of the 1980 Act regarding appeals, namely section 53B, did not empower the Tribunal to remit the subject matter of an appeal back to the Council of the Society. Occasionally a new matter will arise which was not available at the earlier stage in proceedings. Whereas a Sheriff Principal has the power to remit the subject matter back, this Tribunal does not have that power and in these circumstances it would be open to the Tribunal to hear evidence. [The agent for the Appellant] added that there was no indication that any evidence which might have been led before the Tribunal could not have been available at the time of the enquiries carried out by the Council and in such circumstances it was therefore inappropriate to hear evidence in this Appeal.

[The agent for the Council of the Law Society], pointed out with reference to the Appellant's productions that credibility was an issue and that if it were to be the Appellant's intention to challenge the Report which had been before the Law Society's Committee, it was appropriate for the Tribunal to hear evidence to resolve the issue.

[The original complainer] adopted [the agent for the Council's] submissions.

In considering this matter, it was noted that the particular Law Society Committee had not heard oral evidence before coming to its decision. However the Committee had extensive powers to call for relevant documentation and there was no reason to believe that all material information was not available when the Committee Member prepared his Report. The Report and the subsequent Disposal Schedule had been produced to the Tribunal and the Appellant had lodged certain material documents, but the Tribunal did not have access to the whole files which were before the Law Society Committee. There was no suggestion that there was any new information which was not available at the time of the Law Society enquiries; and in the opinion of the Tribunal it would now be inappropriate to open up the factual findings of the Committee on the basis of the limited documentary evidence which was presently before the Tribunal. It is significant that section 42A(1) (*b*) makes provision for 'the Council, after *inquiry* and after giving the solicitor an opportunity to make representations' whereas the operative provision in the section 53B directs that 'on *an appeal* to the Tribunal under section 42A(7), the Tribunal may quash, confirm or vary the determination or direction being appealed against'. The introductory provision of this last mentioned section is the reference to 'an appeal'. There is no provision for a rehearing and although the Tribunal has in the Fourth Schedule been given power to hear evidence, it is apparent that this is a supportive provision in relation to the whole appeal process. The standard procedure in an appeal is to proceed on the basis of the facts as established by the inferior *forum* and the Tribunal is not persuaded that in this case it should go behind the facts as established by the relevant Committee of the Law Society as reflected in the Disposal Schedule (Case 860/93).

3

INCIDENTAL PROCEDURE

3.01 AMENDMENT OF COMPLAINT/ANSWERS

The Procedure Rules of the Tribunal do not contain any provision for the adjustment or amendment of pleadings but in practice an amendment of the Complaint by the Complainer, or the Answers by the Respondent may be made at any time with leave of the Tribunal. However, the Tribunal will not permit such an amendment if it feels that there would be prejudice to the other party to the proceedings; any such possible prejudice may in certain circumstances be overcome by the opposing party agreeing to the amendment or by adjourning the proceedings. In the event of a Complainer becoming aware of circumstances which might constitute an aggravation of the Complaint or justify additional charges, it is usual for such matters to be included in a further Complaint so that the Respondent may have reasonable opportunity to answer the same.

3.02 WARRANT TO CITE WITNESSES, ETC

Schedule 4, para 12, provides:

> On a petition by the complainer or the respondent to the court, or to the sheriff having jurisdiction in any place in which the respondent carries on business, the court or, as the case may be, the sheriff, on production of copies (certified by the clerk of the Tribunal) of the complaint and answers, if lodged, together with a statement signed by the clerk specifying the place and date of the hearing of the complaint and certifying that notice to that effect has been given to the complainer and to the respondent, and on being satisfied that it would be proper to compel the giving of evidence by any witness or the production of documents by any haver, may—
>
> > (a) grant warrant for the citation of witnesses and havers to give evidence or to produce documents before the Tribunal, and for the issue of letters of second diligence against any witness or haver failing to appear after due citation;
> > (b) grant warrant for the recovery of documents; and
> > (c) appoint commissioners to take the evidence of witnesses, to examine havers, and to receive exhibits and productions.

NB. In terms of Schedule 4, para 23, these procedures are applied to Appeals to the Tribunal under section 42A (7) or section 53D (1) of the 1980 Act.

3.03 BANKERS' BOOKS

The Bankers' Books Evidence Act 1879, section 7, provides that

> On the application of any party to a legal proceeding a court or judge may order

that such party be at liberty to inspect and take copies of any entries in a banker's book for any of the purposes of such proceedings ...

and in terms of the (English) Solicitors Act 1974, section 86, the definition of legal proceeding is extended to

the [English] Solicitors Disciplinary Tribunal or any body exercising functions in relation to solicitors in Scotland ... corresponding to the functions of that Tribunal.

3.04 PLEAS IN BAR OF PROCEEDINGS

The Tribunal has on a number of occasions had to consider cases where the question was whether the proceedings before the Tribunal might be barred by other considerations. These have included the following cases in each of which it was held by the Tribunal that it was not barred from proceeding with the case before it.

A. *Plea of* res judicata

In a case where a solicitor had been acquitted of charges of embezzlement in the High Court and a Complaint was subsequently taken by the Law Society against the solicitor averring Professional Misconduct on virtually the same set of facts as had been used in the High Court case except that the Law Society did not aver embezzlement, the Tribunal held that *res judicata* did not apply.

Reference was made in the Tribunal's Decision to the case of the *Procurators of Glasgow* v *Colquhoun* 1900 2F 1192, which related to a solicitor, David Colquhoun. David Colquhoun and his brother James Colquhoun who had carried on practice as solicitors in partnership were charged with embezzlement. James Colquhoun pleaded guilty, but after a trial David Colquhoun was acquitted. Nevertheless David Colquhoun was expelled from the Faculty of Procurators and was then the subject of a complaint to the Court of Session. The Court repelled a plea of *res judicata* in these proceedings.

The Tribunal thereafter went on to consider the requisites of a plea in law of *res judicata* and said:

It has been broadly stated that the requisites of a plea of *res judicata* are

(a) a proper previous determination of the subject in question,
(b) the parties to the second cause must be identical with, or representative of the parties to the first cause, or have the same interests,
(c) the subject matters of the two actions must be the same, and
(d) there must be identity of *media concludendi* or grounds of action in law or in fact.

The verdict of the jury in the High Court of Justiciary was undoubtedly a 'proper previous determination', and the Fiscal for the Complainers did not challenge Counsel's statement that the subject matter of the two actions was the same. Strictly the identity of the respective complainers differed but the Lord Advocate and the Council of the Law Society of Scotland have a common interest on behalf of the public in relation to the respective proceedings and it is significant that the Fiscal did not seek to challenge the plea on this aspect.

23

There remains the identity of the *media concludendi*. Before the High Court the charges were in effect 'embezzlement' and this is a crime at common law entitling a jury to make a finding of guilty and for the Court to impose the appropriate sentence. The Complaint before this Tribunal contains seven charges but it is charges 1 and 3 which particularly run close to the previous Indictment. The Fiscal emphasised that the consideration by the Tribunal is whether the solicitor has been guilty of 'professional misconduct', but this is merely a generic term which sets a standard below which the solicitor renders himself liable to the punitive measures which are set down in detail in Section 53 of the Solicitors (Scotland) Act 1980. Indeed it is significant to note that where a solicitor has been convicted by a Court of a crime involving dishonesty or is sentenced to a term of imprisonment of not less than two years, most of the punitive measures are open to the Tribunal without professional misconduct having to be established. It is not sufficient for a complainer to aver that a solicitor has been guilty of professional misconduct any more than it is competent for a prosecutor in a criminal court to allege that a person has been guilty of 'a crime'. An accused person is entitled to notice of the particular offence of which he is charged and it is then up to the prosecuting authority to lead evidence sufficient to establish that the accused is in fact guilty of the crime as charged; and similarly in proceedings before this Tribunal the Complaint should contain within itself all the ingredients necessary to disclose the particular offence.

The Solicitors' Discipline Tribunal is a domestic tribunal which has special regard for the interests of the profession of solicitors and the interests of the public in relation to that profession. The powers of the Discipline Tribunal are wholly statutory and although the same standard of proof applies in relation to proceedings before this Tribunal and criminal courts, the considerations entirely relate to the conduct of the solicitor in that capacity, and it is therefore appropriate that an acquittal before a criminal court should not in itself preclude a competent Complaint to this Tribunal . . . .

However, as the Fiscal acknowledged, if a solicitor is charged with murder and is acquitted after a trial in the High Court, it would not be competent for this Tribunal to entertain a Complaint and hear evidence that the offence of murder had indeed been committed by the solicitor; and the critical question is whether any of the charges contained in the present Complaint in effect allege the same criminal conduct of which the Respondent has already been acquitted.

The essential words in each charge in the Indictment were that the Respondent 'did . . . embezzle sums of money'. That phrase, and that phrase alone, contains the alleged criminal conduct which the Crown failed to establish to the satisfaction of the Jury. If the Complaint had only contained a charge which repeated the same words, it would clearly not have been competent for this Tribunal to proceed further (Case 797/90).

See also Case 580/83, reported in para 2.02, and Case 367.75(a), reported in para 3.04 E, in which *res judicata* is referred to.

B. *Plea where solicitor found guilty of Professional Misconduct in respect of breach of Accounts Rules and thereafter appearing again before the Tribunal following a conviction in the Court for embezzlement*

In a case in which a solicitor appeared before the Tribunal and was convicted of Professional Misconduct and sentenced in relation to certain matters regarding the Accounts Rules, but where no allegation of dishonesty was made, and where later the solicitor was found guilty by the Court of embezzlement and sentenced to over two years in prison in relation to various charges, some of which involved the same events as had given rise to the solicitor's initial appearance and conviction by the Tribunal, the Tribunal nevertheless dealt with the solicitor once again when the Law Society, under section 53(1) (*b*) of the 1980 Act, reported the Court conviction for embezzlement to the Tribunal.

The Tribunal noted various submissions by the solicitor on the background of the Court case such as, that he had been found guilty only by a majority of the jury and that an appeal had eventually been abandoned without the solicitor's authority, but the Tribunal refused to look behind the conviction and stated that standing the terms of the statute, the Tribunal was obliged to accept the conviction as it stood (Case 816/91).

C.   *Plea of personal bar against the Law Society bringing proceedings following on the issue of a reprimand and warning*
In a situation where a solicitor was charged with various items of Professional Misconduct, including one which consisted of unconscionable delay in completing an Executry where the Law Society had made previous inquiries into the matter and had issued a letter to the solicitor containing a reprimand and warning as to his future conduct, the Tribunal took the view (in proceedings raised less than two years after the letter was written) that the procedure adopted by the Law Society was extra-statutory and did not affect the Tribunal's duty to consider the matter separately (Case 784/90, also Case 632/85).

D.   *Consideration of Complaint averring Professional Misconduct in circumstances where criminal charges are pending or are warranted*
The Tribunal will proceed to a hearing and a decision in a Complaint against a solicitor averring Professional Misconduct notwithstanding that the averments in the Complaint appear to warrant a prosecution in a Criminal Court even although such a prosecution in the appropriate Criminal Court has not been completed, or even in a case where the expected prosecution has not been instituted. Of course it may in certain circumstances be preferable to await the outcome of any criminal proceedings before proceeding with a Complaint to the Tribunal; but where a Complaint is made to the Tribunal, the Tribunal is obliged to proceed to a hearing and a decision in accordance with its Rules (Opinion of Senior Counsel, 19.7.74).

In Case 851/93 the Tribunal said:

> The Tribunal was also informed that the prior application to the Court* had contained a submission that the hearing of the Complaint by the Tribunal might prejudice any future criminal trial, and that the Vacation Judge had not accepted this contention as a basis for postponing the Tribunal Hearing. Counsel for the Respondent renewed this submission but the Tribunal maintained the view which it has previously expressed on such occasions, namely that it has a duty in terms of its Procedure Rules to proceed with the hearing of any Complaint notwithstanding that there are criminal proceedings pending which may relate to the subject matter of the Complaint.

* The prior application to the Court referred to was an application to the Court of Session by the Respondent for interdict in relation to the intended hearing before the Tribunal.

E. *Consideration of Complaint averring Professional Misconduct following a finding by the Legal Aid (Scotland) Complaints Committee that the Respondent's name should be removed from the legal aid list*
In a Decision issued in 1976, the Tribunal said:

> The Respondent, Mr [A], acted for [X] who was indicted on a charge of attempted murder before the High Court at Glasgow in [...] 1972. [X] was convicted and subsequently lodged an application for leave to appeal. Leave to appeal was granted and on [..] December, 1972 the appeal was sustained and the conviction quashed.

> On [....] 1973, a letter of complaint relating to Mr [A] was sent on behalf of the Lord Justice General to the Supreme Court Legal Aid Committee. In terms of paragraph 20(1) of the Legal Aid (Scotland) Scheme 1958 the Supreme Court Legal Aid Committee reported the complaint to the Law Society of Scotland and in accordance with the provisions of sub-paragraph 2 of the said paragraph, the Law Society referred the complaint to the Legal Aid (Scotland) Complaints Committee (hereinafter referred to as the 'Complaints Committee'). The Complaints Committee were required in terms of their rules to investigate the complaint. The Complaints Committee having decided that the complaint disclosed a *prima facie* case of breach of duty, appointed a Prosecutor who prepared a formal Complaint which was served upon Mr [A]. Answers to this Complaint were lodged and a Hearing took place on [....] 1975. The Complaints Committee found that there had been a breach of duty on the part of the Respondent in respect of all but one of the seven charges set out in the Complaint and the Findings of the Complaints Committee were fully set forth in a Report dated [....] 1975 to the Council of the Law Society. The Report contained a recommendation that Mr [A's] name should be removed from the list of Solicitors undertaking to act for assisted persons under the Legal Aid (Scotland) (Criminal Proceedings) Regulations 1964 and that for a period of three years and this recommendation was accepted by the Council of the Law Society.

> The Complaint presently before this Tribunal adopts the Findings of the Complaints Committee as contained in the said Report dated [..] 1975 and avers that Mr [A] by his failure 'in relation to the charge of attempted murder brought against his client, Mr [X], to precognosce witnesses [B, C, D, E and F] to arrange a consultation with Counsel prior to Mr [X's] trial, to represent Mr [X] at the Pleading Diet and timeously lodge a Special Defence, to cite the necessary witnesses for the defence, properly to instruct Counsel with the necessary papers to enable him to conduct the trial, and at any time to attend Mr [X's] trial or arrange for another Solicitor to attend on his behalf', was guilty of the most serious failure in his duties to his client with the consequence that Mr [X] was convicted of the charge libelled, and that these failures or omissions constitute professional misconduct within the meaning of section 5 of the Solicitors (Scotland) Act 1958.

> The Respondent took pleas to the competency and relevancy of this Complaint. In support of his plea to the competency of the proceedings, [Counsel for the Respondent] contended that this complaint was a contravention of a basic principle (or perhaps more strictly two basic principles) of natural justice which he maintained were part of the Law of Scotland, viz. *Nemo debet bis puniri pro uno delicto* and

Nemo debet bis vexarii . . . pro una et eadem causa. He submitted that the complainer in the present case was the same party as in the proceedings before the Complaints Committee, viz. The Law Society of Scotland; and that the facts alleged were identical; and that while the *nomen juris* was different, viz. in the earlier proceedings, breach of duty was averred whereas in the present process it was professional misconduct, there was no material difference between them and that both required to be established in the manner of a criminal charge. [Counsel for the Respondent] contended that unless there existed clear statutory indication that there should be double punishment, the law of natural justice should prevail. He referred the tribunal to a number of English authorities and to the formulation of the plea of *res judicata* in criminal proceedings by Lord Wheatley in the case of *Cairns* 1967 JC 37 at p 45.

[Counsel for the Respondent] answered the argument that dismissal of this Complaint could lead to inadequate punishment and submitted that if the Complaints Committee had considered that the circumstances as presented to them called for a penalty beyond suspension from the Criminal Legal Aid list it was open to them to recommend to the Council that Mr [A] should be prosecuted before the Discipline Tribunal.

In reply to a question from the Chairman, [Counsel for the Respondent] stated that in his view section 5 of the Solicitors (Scotland) Act 1958 supported his contention. He submitted that this section represented an exception to an erosion of the common law principle which must be construed strictly.

[Counsel for the Respondent] further submitted that if the foregoing were not accepted, the Tribunal should exercise its undoubted right to stop proceedings if these appeared to it to be oppressive or unfair or an abuse of process.

In reply [Counsel for the Complainers] submitted that the sequence of events which had taken place was a necessary progress under statute, and he outlined the procedure whereby any relevant complaint to a Legal Aid Committee had to proceed to the Complaints Committee and be reported to the Council of the Law Society. In his submission, he argued that the present case was closely in line with the case of the *Procurators of Glasgow* v *Colquhoun* 1900 2F 1192, in which the Faculty of Procurators having already expelled from their own body the respondent (who in the Criminal Court had been found guilty of embezzlement) prosecuted a Complaint before the Court of Session and it was held that the Faculty were 'well entitled, as a body of professional men practising in a particular locality to bring under the notice of the Court conduct on the part of their fellow practitioner which they consider to be fitted to endanger the interests of clients and to bring discredit upon an honourable profession'.

The Tribunal found this plea of competency by no means free from difficulty, not least because the original source of the complaint had been a letter to the Law Society from the Lord Justice-General. It was indeed possible (as [Counsel for the Respondent] had argued) to draw the inference that because the Lord Justice General had, in the first instance, addressed his Report to the Law Society and not to the Discipline Tribunal, he regarded Mr [A's] offence as falling short of professional misconduct. The Tribunal, however, felt that such an inference would be a hazardous one: the Lord Justice-General's assessment could, they felt, only be a matter of surmise. The more likely explanation seems to be that because the proceedings in question were under Legal Aid, the Lord Justice-General considered it appropriate to employ the procedure laid down under section 20 of the 1958 Scheme, but the Tribunal are satisfied that the reasoning behind the Lord Justice-General's course of action was not relevant and that the question turned solely on whether the principle of natural justice debarred the Tribunal from hearing and deciding on this present Complaint.

The principle of *Nemo debet bis puniri pro uno delicto* and *Nemo debet bis vexari . . . pro una et eadem causa* was strongly supported by [Counsel for the Respondent] in an extensive series of authorities and there is no doubt that this principle has a place in the Law of Scotland. However the *crux* is the conflict of this principle with the express authority conferred by statute on the Discipline Tribunal. In enjoying this authority, the Discipline Tribunal is a statutory successor of the Court of Session as the *forum* of first instance in dealing with complaints against Solicitors and its powers are clearly set down in the Solicitors (Scotland) Acts 1933 to 1976.

That this principle is subject to qualifications there is no doubt. It is well established that a conviction (or an acquittal) in a criminal court is not a bar to hearing a complaint of professional misconduct based on the same facts. Authority for this is found in Spencer Bower & Turner on *Res Judicata*, 2nd edition at p. 279, 'neither a conviction nor an acquittal before a criminal court on a criminal charge will bar the use of the same conduct before such a tribunal on an application to suspend or expel; for the purpose of the proceeding is not to punish the practitioner for the commission of an offence as such, but to exercise disciplinary power over the members of a profession so as to ensure that their conduct conforms to the standards of the profession'. The New Zealand case of *In re a Medical Practitioner* is an apt example.

This qualification, however, is not closely applicable to the present case: in this case proceedings before both the Legal Aid Complaints Committee and the Discipline Tribunal are *quasi-criminal* and within the same context, viz. professional misconduct. But it is considered that there is a further relevant qualification, viz. where the standing of and the remedies available to the respective Tribunals are different. In the present case the statutory authority of the Discipline Tribunal (as successor of the Court of Session) and the Legal Aid Complaints Committee are different and indeed mutually exclusive—the power of the Complaints Committee to terminate a solicitor's entitlement to remain on the Legal Aid List being a penalty not available to this Tribunal.

On a consideration of the authorities, it appeared to the Tribunal that the principle of *Colquhoun* was applicable to the present case.

The Tribunal felt unable to accept the argument advanced by [Counsel for the Respondent] based on section 5 of the Solicitors (Scotland) Act 1958. In their opinion, the special provisions contained in this section in relation to convictions involving dishonesty or where the sentence is for not less than two years imprisonment, have been included merely in order to relieve the Tribunal of the burden of hearing the facts for a second time and not because the matters would not otherwise be open for consideration by the Discipline Tribunal.

On the foregoing grounds, the Tribunal rejected [Counsel for the Respondent's] plea to the competency.

Turning to relevancy, [Counsel for the Respondent] made two points, first the minor point that the different grounds for complaint were not individually articulated as professional misconduct and he referred to the unquoted decision of the *Law Society* v *M & W* dated [16.1] 75 where the form of a Complaint was criticised as the content of a particular charge could only be ascertained by reference to the accompanying statement of facts. However in this complaint, the individual charges are clearly set out. [Counsel for the Respondent's] second point was that Mr [A's] alleged conduct did not in any event amount to professional misconduct.

[Counsel for the Respondent] relied solely on the observations of Lord Anderson in *X Insurance Company* v *A & B* 1936 SC 225 at p 244, 'a charge of professional misconduct involves an accusation of dishonour and may import an act of crime', and Lord Morrison in the same case at p 250 'the cases show that some dishonourable act or improper motive is essential in an act of professional misconduct'.

[Counsel for the Complainers], however, in replying adduced two later cases where *dicta* such as these have been expressly disavowed e.g. by Lord Denning MR in *Re a Solicitor* [1972] 2 All ER 811 at 815:

> Counsel has quoted cases to show that professional misconduct should only be found where the solicitor has been guilty of conduct which is disgraceful or dishonourable and is such as to be condemned by his colleagues in the profession. I do not think that definition is exhaustive. In my opinion negligence in a solicitor may amount to professional misconduct, if it is inexcusable and is such as to be regarded as deplorable by his fellows in the profession;

and Lord President Cooper in *E* v *T* 1949 SLT 411:

> But there is negligence and negligence; and I am certainly not prepared to affirm the proposition that according to Scots Law and practice professional negligence cannot amount to professional misconduct. . . .

The Tribunal were in agreement with [Counsel for the Complainers'] submission that in this particular case Mr [A] was charged with a breach of practically the whole of the duties incumbent upon any solicitor representing an accused person. The conduct imputed to him appeared to them without question to fall within the descriptions above quoted from Lord Denning and Lord President Cooper.

[Counsel for the Complainers] also cited the decision in *Writers to the Signet* v *Mackersy* 1924 SC 776. In that case the solicitor was found guilty of professional misconduct 'in respect of his reckless disregard of the duty which was incumbent upon him to take ordinary and recognised measures in order to satisfy himself that a claim for damages which he was instrumental in presenting to the Court of trial was . . . genuine', In this particular case, Mr [A] had certain duties to his client and consequently to the court. The charges against Mr [A] allege that he failed to carry out these duties; and the Tribunal are satisfied that if the averments set out in the Complaint are proved, the failure to fulfil the particular duties could amount to professional misconduct. In expressing this opinion, the Tribunal have not attempted to assess the charges individually, for a solicitor's duties in any litigation are undoubtedly interrelated and it may be that whilst a failure to take any particular step might not amount to professional misconduct, the compound of various failures could be so regarded. Accordingly, the plea to the relevancy likewise failed (Case 367/75(*a*)).

F. *Plea that Complaint ought first to have been heard by Legal Aid Complaints Committee before being taken to Tribunal*

Two solicitors who were in partnership were charged with Professional Misconduct in relation to fees charged by them for Criminal Legal Aid. Each Complaint averred that on specific dates the Respondents claimed fees from the Legal Aid authorities for the attendance of the same solicitor for the same period of the day in respect of two separate clients and in making these claims contrary to the specific declaration in each claim form, the Respondents were guilty of Professional Misconduct.

3.04 PLEAS IN BAR OF PROCEEDINGS

Counsel for the Respondent submitted a plea to the competency of the Complaints. He pointed out that the charge of professional misconduct was qualified with the words 'in the whole context of the Criminal Legal Aid Scheme' and he submitted that the matter ought first to have been placed before the Legal Aid Complaints Committee. In support of this submission, he argued that the statutory procedure had not been followed and that prior to the service of these Complaints, his clients had not received any prior notice of the relevant charges.

In reply, the Fiscal for the Complainers pointed out that the various statutory provisions did not specify any particular sequence between the Legal Aid Complaints Committee and this Tribunal and he further argued that it would be absurd if the Legal Aid Regulations were to interfere with the Tribunal's deliberation on any matter of exceptional gravity merely because the particular client was in receipt of Legal Aid. Paragraph 20 of the Legal Aid (Scotland) Scheme 1958 sets down the precise procedure for dealing with a Complaint against a Solicitor 'with respect to his services' and the Fiscal further questioned whether the charge contained in these Complaints related to the 'services' provided by the respective Respondents.

This Tribunal is established under the provisions of sections 50 to 54 of the Solicitors (Scotland) Act 1980 and this Act does not contain any qualification which might restrain the Tribunal from considering a Complaint containing a charge of professional misconduct. The Tribunal is accordingly of the opinion that the provisions of the Legal Aid Regulations do not preclude the Tribunal from considering any Complaint in advance of any other proceedings which may be open to the Complainers or other party and it is accordingly competent for the Tribunal to proceed with the hearing of this Complaint.

Counsel also submitted a plea to the relevancy of the Complaint in that the Complaints did not appear to specify in what way the Respondents had acted as might give rise to a finding of professional misconduct. He questioned whether the Complainers were charging the Respondents with deliberate fraud, or negligence which might be regarded as culpable and he argued that it was the duty of the Complainers to set out precisely what was being claimed as professional misconduct. In reply, the Fiscal for the Complainers confirmed that the Respondents were not being charged with fraud and that he was relying on the inaccuracy of the Respondents' declarations.

In the opinion of the Tribunal, the averment of a number of inaccurate claims in itself founded a relevant Complaint (Case 533/82).

NB. This case is also considered at para 18.03.

3.05 WITHDRAWAL OF COMPLAINTS/APPEALS

Complaints made to the Tribunal in respect of Professional Misconduct and/or Inadequate Professional Services and Appeals made to the Tribunal under section 42A(7) or section 53D(1) of the 1980 Act may not be withdrawn except with the leave of the Tribunal and subject to such conditions with respect to expenses or otherwise as the Tribunal sees fit (Schedule 4, paras 8 and 23).

In practice the Tribunal will usually accept any agreement entered into between the Fiscal for the Law Society and the Respondent solicitor (or between the parties to an Appeal under section 42A(7)) but exceptionally the Tribunal will withhold consent in a matter of public interest.

In Case 871/93 the Tribunal refused an application from the Council (as Complainers) for a Complaint to be withdrawn and said:

In the letter from the Respondent's solicitors in response to the Complaint, it was stated that the allegations in the Complaint were admitted and that taken together, the circumstances amounted to professional misconduct. In respect that the Respondent had expressed his willingness to grant an undertaking not to practise as a principal, the Complainers invited the Tribunal in terms of rule 13 of the Procedure Rules of the Tribunal to grant leave for the Complaint to be withdrawn.

However section 53 of the Solicitors (Scotland) Act 1980 empowers the Tribunal to take certain action in the event of the Tribunal being satisfied that the Solicitor has been guilty of professional misconduct. Whether a particular course of action amounts to professional misconduct is a matter for the Tribunal to determine 'after holding an inquiry', and the Tribunal has a duty to other members of the profession and to the puublic to exercise these powers where the circumstances warrant the same. Having regard to the extent of the Respondent's admissions, there was a strong likelihood that the Tribunal might make such a finding and in the opinion of the Tribunal, it would have been failing in its duty to have allowed the Complaint to be withdrawn without any formal determination.

4

HEARINGS

4.01 PRELIMINARY HEARINGS

Exceptionally the Tribunal may hold a separate hearing to consider some preliminary point such as, for example:

1. Whether an Appeal was lodged timeously and should be allowed to proceed (as in Case 839/92).

2. A plea to the competency e.g. a plea of *res judicata* (as in Case 797/90).

In most cases preliminary pleas are dealt with at the hearing set down to consider the evidence.

4.02 PROCEDURE AT TRIBUNAL HEARINGS

The Tribunal may hear all proceedings in public or private as it thinks fit (Procedure Rules, rule 35). In practice it usually holds its proceedings in private. However, in an application for restoration to the Roll, the Tribunal will give the applicant the opportunity to have the hearing in public.

The Tribunal hears evidence on oath, or by way of affirmation, and the evidence is normally recorded by a shorthand writer.

The Complainer and the Respondent are entitled

(*a*) to require the evidence of parties, witnesses and others interested, and

(*b*) to call for and recover such evidence and documents, and examine such witnesses, as they think proper, but no person shall be compelled to produce any document which he could not be compelled to produce in an action.

The procedure at a hearing of the Tribunal follows very much the procedure in a court hearing but as has been said by the Court (*vide S* v *B*, Court of Session, unreported, 25.2.81), a complaint against a solicitor is not a criminal charge and the proceedings are not conducted with the formality of a criminal process; and although the Tribunal requires a structured approach to the proceedings (and expects its Procedure Rules to be adhered to) it does endeavour to be reasonably flexible in its procedure where it considers that such an approach is in the interests of justice.

4.03 HEARINGS IN ABSENCE OF PARTY

The Procedure Rules provide that each party shall be in attendance at the hearing. However, the Tribunal has no power to compel a party to attend and from time to time hearings proceed in the absence of a Respondent. Sometimes where the Respondent is absent he will be represented by a solicitor or counsel, but if neither the Respondent nor a representative appears for the Respondent, then the Clerk to the Tribunal will give evidence on oath to the Tribunal as to the service of the Complaint on the Respondent, as to whether or not the Respondent has lodged Answers and the service on the Respondent of notice of the time and place of the hearing and thereafter the Tribunal may proceed to deal with the Complaint by the hearing of evidence on behalf of the Complainers taking account of any Answers which the Respondent has lodged (Procedure Rules, rule 9).

The Tribunal has said:

> At the commencement of the hearing, Counsel for the Respondent invited the Tribunal to desert the Diet and dismiss the Complaint in respect of the absence of the Complainers from the hearing. In support of this motion, Counsel submitted that it was a well established principle in criminal proceedings that the Prosecutor must be personally present and he referred to Hume on Crimes, Volume 2, at page 265, Alison's Criminal Law, Volume 2, at page 345 and *Walker* v *Emslie* 1899 3 Adam 102, and he also referred to Rule 8 of the Rules of this Tribunal which requires that each party should be in attendance at the hearing. In reply Mr Balfour pointed to the special provision contained in Hume op. cit. 268 and Alison op. cit. 347 whereby the Prosecutor might be represented by a specially appointed Factor or Attorney. The Tribunal carefully considered this point. It was noted with significance that section 51 of the Solicitors (Scotland) Act 1980 specifically provides for the Council of the Law Society to appoint a Fiscal and that reading strictly, this particular Complaint ran in the name of the Fiscal as follows:
>
>> I, Ian Leslie Shaw Balfour, Solicitor in the Supreme Court, 58 Frederick Street, Edinburgh, having been appointed Fiscal by the Council of the Law Society of Scotland for the purpose of bringing this Complaint on behalf of the Council, hereby request that . . .
>
> In the circumstances, it was the opinion of the Tribunal that Mr Balfour was the duly appointed Fiscal and Attorney for the Council of the Law Society and that it was in order for the hearing to proceed without the need for the attendance of any or all of the members of the Council (Case 534/82).

4.04 FORMAL MATTERS NOT IN DISPUTE

The Tribunal has observed:

> In disciplinary proceedings, the onus of proof always lies on the Complainers, and whilst the Respondent's solicitor has no obligation to assist the Complainers in the prosecution of their Complaint, it must be recognised that this is basically a domestic tribunal frequently involving procedures which are familiar to the parties and to the members of the Tribunal and ordinarily the Tribunal expects that parties or their representatives shall whenever possible seek to confer and agree such formal matters as are not in dispute. It was particularly disappointing that those representing the respective parties did not have the opportunity of meeting prior to the first day of the hearing and because of the detailed nature of the case, it was by then apparently too late for any meaningful agreement to be adjusted. As a result, the Tribunal was required to hear the unchallenged evidence of many witnesses, particularly from the Banking and Building Society sector on matters which could easily have been the subject of agreement (Case 797/90).

4.05 STANDARD OF PROOF

Although the Tribunal is a domestic tribunal the standard of proof before the Tribunal in relation to Professional Misconduct is the same standard of proof as applies in the criminal courts i.e. beyond reasonable doubt (Case 797/90).

4.06 IDENTIFICATION OF RESPONDENT

The Tribunal has said:

> Counsel for the Respondent also challenged that there had been no identification of the Respondent. It is accepted that identification is a standard requirement in a criminal prosecution and that in general the standard of proof before this Tribunal is the same as that required in criminal proceedings. However it is not accepted that this extends to identification. This Tribunal is the disciplinary authority for a profession whose members' names are all recorded in an up-to-date register. The Respondent was present at the hearing and introduced to the Tribunal and in these circumstances there was no requirement of the Complainers to identify positively the Respondent in the course of the evidence (Case 534/82).

4.07 THE CIVIL EVIDENCE (SCOTLAND) ACT 1988

The interpretation section of this Act, section 9, by subsection (c), brings the provisions of the Act to bear on proceedings before the Tribunal.

In an Opinion obtained from Senior Counsel in June 1989 the Tribunal was advised:

First, on the question as to whether the Act had any effect on the standard of proof which should be required by the Tribunal:

> [T]he important distinction to bear in mind is that the Civil Evidence (Scotland) Act 1988 is dealing with rules of evidence and not with standard of proof which is a wholly separate question. What both section 1 and section 2 of the Act are concerned with are essentially questions of sufficiency and competency in determining whether or not a fact is to be taken as proved and therefore allowed to be weighed in the balance which balance is struck by the overall standard of proof determined from another source. By way of example, from time to time the Courts have had to consider whether or not in a civil proceeding what was effectively an allegation of a crime required to be established by a standard of proof which was greater than that normally demanded in civil proceedings. There is a useful discussion of this topic in the Opinion of Lord Allanbridge in *Sloan* v *Triplett* 1985 SLT 294 at 296. Whatever may be the resolution of that issue, it is important to bear in mind that it was not concerned with sufficiency or competency of evidence going to the point, but simply whether or not the point was proof on the balance of probabilities or on a higher scale. It follows that the standard of proof required before the Tribunal is not altered by the provisions of the 1988 Act.

Secondly, in answer to the question 'To what extent does the 1988 Act affect the sufficiency of the evidence which was to be expected by the Tribunal?' Counsel answered:

> It is in this area that the most material changes have occurred, but it is important to understand the purpose behind the new statutory provisions with particular reference to sections 1 and 2 dealing respectively with the removal of the requirement for corroboration and the admissibility of hearsay evidence. Historically both these

matters operated as barriers to, in the one case, competency of a conviction on sufficient evidence, and on the other to the admissibility of competent evidence. The Act simply removes these barriers, but does not in itself do any more than allow the relevant Tribunal both to proceed upon uncorroborated facts if it so desires or admit and take on board hearsay evidence if it equally so desires. I consider that both provisions should be treated with considerable care having regard to the standard of proof demanded before the Tribunal. It is significant to note that consequent upon the limited relaxation of the corroboration rules in personal injury cases in 1968, the Court thereafter proceeded to lay down a number of principles which severely limited the circumstances in which a Court could be 'satisfied' that a relevant fact had been proved in the absence of corroboration. (See particularly *Morrison* v *J. Kelly & Sons Limited* 1970 SC 65 and *McGowan* v *Lord Advocate* 1972 SC 68.) The ultimate result of these judicial interpretations was that it was only where the pursuer could not provide corroboration that the Court was prepared to proceed upon the basis of an uncorroborated fact. In these circumstances with regard to section 1 of the 1988 Act, the Tribunal may competently accept uncorroborated evidence and at least in theory proceed to convict upon it, but I suggest it should be very careful so to do having regard to the standard of proof required and certainly should not so proceed if the fact, upon the evidence before it, could be corroborated and simply was not; *a fortiori* where an uncorroborated fact is opposed by other evidence. The hearsay provision is rather less stringent in as much that it simply admits the evidence for consideration by the Tribunal in as much that by using the word 'solely' it removes the barrier to which I have already made reference. Again however to proceed solely upon hearsay evidence, unless there was no direct evidence available, i.e. because of death or disappearance of witnesses, would in my view be a highly dangerous step for the Tribunal to take bearing in mind the standard of proof. However it is competent now for it so to do and that in my view is the limit that the provisions of the 1988 Act seek to achieve.

4.08 AFFIDAVIT EVIDENCE

The Procedure Rules provide that with the consent in writing of all the parties, the Tribunal may, either as to the whole case or as to any particular fact or facts, proceed and act upon evidence given by Affidavit. Occasionally this procedure is invoked to take the formal evidence of a witness but the practice was the subject of judicial criticism by Lord Cameron in an unreported decision (*Petition S*, 27th October 1981), where the Law Society had founded on the Affidavit evidence of their President.

[T]he part played by the President [. . . .] in this transaction was of critical importance. It is therefore all the more unfortunate, to put it no higher than the Tribunal did not have his evidence before it other than in the wholly unsatisfactory form of an affidavit. It is somewhat extraordinary that in these circumstances the prosecutor, being presumably aware of the importance of the President's evidence, should have issued an invitation to the appellant to agree to accept such evidence without even indicating to what matters that affidavit was to be or likely to be directed: It is even more extraordinary that the appellant agreed to the proposal, knowing as he did the nature and unspecific form of the charge against him—for the President would surely rank among the 'officers' of the Society—unless—and this is a fact which may be relevant to the issue of intention to deceive—the appellant was confident that a presidential affidavit would at least not be harmful to his defence. In view of the admission of the affidavit by agreement no challenge was made of the competence of the procedure and I specifically wish to reserve my opinion as to the competence of such a procedure. The Tribunal obviously found themselves in difficulty in dealing with what was presented to them and in resolving an apparent conflict of evidence. I say 'apparent' because no one can be sure if and to what extent any such apparent conflict would have been resolved if the normal and I venture to think only proper procedure had been followed. The device which the Tribunal adopted was no doubt the best they could devise, but it was plainly unsatisfactory and inadequate in a matter in which not only credibility of witnesses but the accuracy and reliability of their evidence was of major importance in the determination of the questions of fact which the Tribunal was called upon to decide. However, as the appellant agreed to that course—unwisely in my opinion—and no point was taken on his behalf as to the competency of the procedure, I express no opinion on a point which may in any event never require to be decided. What I will say, however, is that the prosecutor having chosen and himself proposed this course must abide by the consequences, and one of these is that in a case where the credibility of the appellant is in issue—although the Tribunal at no stage make an express finding on the matter—he can take little comfort from what the President records in his affidavit, the terms of which are in any event partially disregarded by the Tribunal.

In a more recent case, where the Affidavit had been sworn before the Respondent personally, the Tribunal deprecated the practice of swearing an Affidavit before a party to the proceedings (Case 626/85).

4.09 EXPERT WITNESSES

The Tribunal ordinarily discourages the practice of leading the evidence of individual practitioners as to the acceptability of a particular course of conduct. In one case the Tribunal said:

In the course of the Hearing, Counsel for the Respondent led the evidence of [X], WS, as an expert witness on the ethical considerations arising in this particular Complaint. [X] is a senior partner in the firm of [AB] and a former President of the Law Society of Scotland. He has had a wide experience in the profession and is called upon to provide his opinion on matters of practice. However without in any way diminishing [X's] standing or experience, it should be pointed out that the Scottish Solicitors' Discipline Tribunal is in effect a domestic Tribunal whose membership comprises experienced solicitors and a minority of lay members. The present lay members are themselves members of other distinguished professions with their distinct and separate codes of ethics. The subject matter of this Complaint was in effect the formation of a joint venture which operated as a limited company [for] the provision of finance and the acquisition and improvement of heritable property. These are all matters which are familiar to a solicitor in practice and the individual members of the Tribunal have the depth of experience necessary to adjudicate on the propriety of any course of action within the ordinary sphere of a solicitor's practice. In *E v T* 1949 SLT 411 Lord President Cooper observed:

I shall not attempt to define professional misconduct. But if the statutory tribunal, composed as it always is of professional men of the highest repute and competence, stigmatise a course of professional conduct as misconduct, it seems to me that only strong grounds would justify this Court in condoning as innocent that which the Committee have condemned as guilty.

The duty is clearly on the members of this Tribunal to formulate their opinion on the standards of conduct within the profession. The Tribunal therefore ordinarily discourage parties to lead the evidence of individual practitioners, however experienced they may be, to express their personal opinion regarding the acceptability of a particular course of conduct (Case 761/89).

4.10 FACTS ADMITTED

Very often the facts as averred by the Complainer are admitted or sometimes the Complainer is prepared to amend or delete averments so that those averments which remain are admitted, and the Respondent may then argue before the Tribunal that those facts which are admitted do not in the circumstances merit a finding of Professional Misconduct or Inadequate Professional Services as the case may be.

4.11 TRIBUNAL MUST BE 'SATISFIED'

Notwithstanding the extent of any admission which a Respondent may make in regard to charges contained in a Complaint made against the Respondent, the Tribunal must nevertheless be 'satisfied' in terms of section 53(1) of the 1980 Act that there has been Professional Misconduct on the part of the Respondent before it makes a finding against him (as in Case 807/90). Accordingly, in the absence of any admissions, the Complainer must lead evidence to establish the Complaint, even where the Respondent fails to attend the hearing. Such proof can materially increase the expenses which may require to be met by the Respondent.

5

DECISIONS AND APPEALS

5.01 DECISIONS OF THE TRIBUNAL

At the conclusion of a hearing it is usual for the Chairman of the meeting to announce the decision orally to the parties at that time and thereafter the Tribunal issues (*a*) a written Interlocutor and (*b*) formal Findings, which in the case of a Complaint (Appeal) state the facts proved and, in the case of a conviction, particulars of the conviction and sentence, and in every case the Tribunal adds a Note stating the grounds on which the decision has been arrived at. The Interlocutor and the Findings and Note are signed by the Chairman of the meeting.

The Court has said that in making a finding of Professional Misconduct the Tribunal should specify briefly the character of the misconduct and not merely make a general finding of misconduct without specification (*X Insurance Co* v *A & B* 1936 SC 225 at 237).

The Court has observed in an Appeal against a Decision of the Tribunal:

> [T]he decision of this domestic tribunal ... cannot reasonably be expected to be expressed with the clarity and precision expected of a decision of a professional judiciary. Such strength as the submission for the petitioner possessed was derived from a critical analysis of one or two sentences in a Note which could have been more clearly expressed, but in our judgment the approach of the Tribunal, and the view which they formed, is only to be discovered upon a consideration of the decision as a whole (*MacColl* v *Council of the Law Society of Scotland* 1987 SLT 524).

A copy of every Decision by the Tribunal certified by the Clerk is sent forthwith by the Clerk to the parties, intimating their right of appeal against the Decision. The 'Decision' (for the purposes of determining the days of appeal) is the Findings and Note.

5.02 *IN CUMULO* FINDINGS

Where there are a number of charges in a Complaint which all relate to the same Practice Rule or are otherwise *eiusdem generis* and the Complaint contains an alternative averment of Professional Misconduct *in cumulo*, the Tribunal may make a determination on the basis of the alternative charge if the pattern of behaviour discloses conduct which might be regarded as reprehensible even although the individual failures of the solicitor may not of themselves have amounted to Professional Misconduct when considered in isolation. In one such case the Tribunal said:

None of the items which have been established were of particular gravity, but it is regrettable that the Respondent gravely neglected the affairs of five separate clients during a relatively short period. Taking the whole matter in context, the Tribunal is of the opinion that the Respondent's overall delays were inexcusable and it is with this background that an *in cumulo* Finding of professional misconduct has been pronounced (Case 753/89).

In a case where a solicitor delayed in replying to correspondence from various parties, implementing a Letter of Obligation and recording a Standard Security (Case 811/90), and in another case where there were various breaches of the Accounts Rules (Case 759/89), the respective failures were regarded as *eiusdem generis*.

5.03 PROFESSIONAL MISCONDUCT/INADEQUATE PROFESSIONAL SERVICES

The Tribunal has rejected a submission that it was not open to it to make a finding of Professional Misconduct and Inadequate Professional Services in relation to the same matter in that this would result in double jeopardy. The Tribunal took the view that the provisions for dealing with Professional Misconduct and Inadequate Professional Services are contained in separate sections of the Solicitors (Scotland) Act 1980, as amended, and there is no suggestion within the statute that a finding of Professional Misconduct in relation to any matter relieves the Tribunal of their duty to look at the matter separately under the heading of Inadequate Professional Services. An examination of sections 53 and 53A demonstrates wholly differing purposes. It is significant that in the event of Professional Misconduct being established the remedies open to the Tribunal under section 53 are either punitive towards the solicitor or protective. Such directions are wholly in the public interest and confer no benefit upon the individual client or aggrieved party. In contrast, section 53A is solely concerned with the item of business being dealt with by the solicitor and the effect of the solicitor's conduct in relation to that business and the affairs of the client. The essential feature of the provisions of section 53A is to enable the Tribunal to make orders for the benefit of that client without requiring the client to take a civil action in Court and the whole purpose of section 53A would be defeated if it were to be maintained that the Tribunal was unable to exercise these powers if Professional Misconduct were to be established (Case 831/92).

5.04 NO POWER TO VARY DECISIONS

A solicitor made an Application to the Tribunal requesting the Tribunal to vary the terms of an Order made in terms of section 53(5) of the 1980 Act pronounced by the Tribunal some five years and some months earlier in terms of which the Tribunal directed that any Practising Certificate issued or to be issued to the solicitor should be subject to such restriction as would limit the solicitor to acting in employment with an employer to be approved by the Council of the Law Society of Scotland and that such restriction should subsist for a period of at least five years and thereafter until such time as the solicitor might satisfy the Tribunal that the solicitor was fit to hold a full Practising Certificate. The Tribunal determined that it did not have power to vary an Order which had already been made under the section and accordingly dismissed the Application. The Tribunal added that if the Application had been for the removal of the restriction on any Practising Certificate which might be held by the Applicant, the Tribunal would have been disinclined to grant the same at that time because in pronouncing the original Order the Tribunal expected that the Solicitor would have obtained a limited Practising Certificate within the restrictions imposed by that Order and applied to the Council of the Society for its approval of particular employment within the profession. This would have given him valuable experience of working under supervision and, in due course, the Tribunal would have had the benefit of a report from the Applicant's then employer expressing his opinion as to the suitability of the Applicant towards having an unrestricted Practising Certificate. However, since the original Order had been pronounced, the Applicant had not held any form of Practising Certificate nor had he otherwise been employed within the profession and for these reasons the Tribunal would have regarded it as premature should the Applicant at this stage have applied for the removal of the restriction on any Practising Certificate to be held by him (Case 820/91).

5.05 REFERENCES TO STATUTORY PROVISIONS

In a case where the Tribunal had ordered that a solicitor be suspended from practice for a period of five years, the relative interlocutor of the Tribunal had directed 'in terms of section 53(6) of the Solicitors (Scotland) Act 1958' [*sic*] that the Order was to take effect on the date on which it was intimated to the solicitor. The correct reference should have been to section 53(6) of the Solicitors (Scotland) Act 1980. After the interlocutor had been served upon the solicitor, the Tribunal Chairman made a manuscript alteration substituting '80' for '58' in the principal interlocutor and the corrected interlocutor was thereafter intimated to the solicitor. The solicitor brought an action for reduction of the Tribunal's Decision claiming that it was inept and of no legal effect. He argued that the Order was inept as the 1958 Act had been repealed by the 1980 Act and *esto* the Order was effectual, the unauthorised alteration made by the Chairman had the effect of vitiating the whole Decision. The Court held:

(i) that in making the order it had not been essential that reference was made to the statutory provisions which conferred the powers of suspension;

(ii) that only that part of the interlocutor which related to the power to make a direction under section 53(6) of the 1980 Act had been vitiated by the unauthorised alteration; and the action was dismissed (*Paterson v Scottish Solicitors' Discipline Tribunal* 1984 SLT 3).

5.06 PUBLICITY

Until 3rd June 1991 (when the provisions affecting the Tribunal made in terms of the Law Reform (Miscellaneous Provisions) (Scotland) Act 1990 came into effect) the question of whether or not a Decision of the Tribunal should be made public (with or without naming the solicitor) was a matter much canvassed before the Tribunal; but since the above date the position is that every Decision of the Tribunal must be published in full, except that the Tribunal may refrain from publishing any names, places or other facts the publication of which would, in its opinion, damage, or be likely to damage, the interests of persons other than

    (*a*) the solicitor against whom the complaint was made; or

    (*b*) his partners; or

    (*c*) his or their families,

but where it so refrains it must publish its reasons for so doing.

In practice therefore since the coming into force of the 1990 Act submissions on the question of publicity are now very seldom made to the Tribunal and publicity is given to virtually every Decision, but it does remain possible in a suitable case for publicity to be withheld or restricted (Schedule 4, para 14A).

The Tribunal in certain cases makes its Decision public at the conclusion of the hearing in terms of rule 35 of its Rules and this procedure has been followed in cases where the Respondent's actions have already been the subject of considerable publicity in the national press (as in Case 756/89). Otherwise it is the practice of the Tribunal to publish a Decision at the conclusion of the days of appeal, whether or not a petition of appeal is presented to the Court.

5.07 COUNCIL TO MAKE COPIES OF DECISIONS AVAILABLE

The Council require to ensure that a copy of every Decision published by the Tribunal is open for inspection at the office of the Society during office hours by any person without payment of any fee (Schedule 4, para 18A). In addition, Schedule 4, para 18, requires:

> The file of orders under this Act striking solicitors off the roll, suspending solicitors from practice, or restoring persons to the roll shall be open for inspection at the office of the Society at any reasonable hour by any person without payment of any fee.

5.08 AWARDS OF EXPENSES

Subject to the provisions of Part IV of the 1980 Act, the Tribunal may make in relation to any Complaint against a solicitor (or in any Appeal in relation to Inadequate Professional Services or in relation to an Investment Business Certificate) such order as it thinks fit as to the payment by the Complainer (Appellant) or by the Respondent of the expenses incurred by the other party and by the Tribunal or a reasonable contribution towards those expenses (Schedule 4, para 19).

5.08 AWARDS OF EXPENSES

The Tribunal usually applies the general rule that expenses follow success but in a significant number of cases that rule is modified or not followed. For example:

1. In a case where there was a Joint Minute substantially admitting the various charges but resulting in a change of emphasis in the Complaint,—the Tribunal, looking at the Complaint as a whole, and taking account of substantial concessions made by the Complainers, awarded expenses against the Respondent but granted a 25% relief against the Complainers' account (Case 842/93).

2. In a case (which was heard in 1991 prior to the introduction of the charge of Inadequate Professional Services) when all charges of Professional Misconduct brought against a solicitor were found to be not established but the Tribunal found that the services that the solicitor rendered to his client fell considerably below the standard to be expected of a reasonable and competent solicitor, no award of expenses was made to either party. However, the Tribunal took the view that it was the solicitor's lack of professional diligence which gave rise to his client's anxiety and she and her new solicitor were justified in reporting the matter to the Law Society, thereby prompting the Complaint and accordingly the Tribunal found the solicitor liable in the expenses incurred by the Tribunal in relation to the Complaint (Case 812/91).

3. In a Complaint brought by a Complainer other than the Law Society, where after hearing only the evidence of the Complainer and the Complainer's witness and an apology was made by the solicitor to the Complainer with an acknowledgment that the solicitor's conduct had been open to criticism and the Complainer sought to withdraw the Complaint, the Tribunal allowed the Complaint to be withdrawn on condition that the Complainer bore his share of the expenses of the Tribunal and indemnified the Tribunal in respect of the expenses of the solicitor whom the Tribunal had appointed to represent the Complainer. The Tribunal in making this order observed:

> [B]ut it remains that it is the Complainer who was seeking leave to withdraw the Complaint at a comparatively early stage in the proceedings, when the Tribunal was not in a position to form a view whether it was reasonable for the Complainer to have taken the Complaint. If this had been a Complaint at the instance of the Council of the Law Society, albeit on a matter raised by the present Complainer, the Law Society would have had the opportunity of conferring with their Fiscal at each stage, and in such circumstances it would be reasonable that the Law Society would be obliged to accept the financial circumstances of abandoning a Complaint before this Tribunal. However in the present matter, the Law Society has not had this discretion and accordingly it seems inappropriate that they should now be required to bear a substantial proportion of the cost of the present proceedings (Case 802/90).

4. In a case where the Tribunal did not find Professional Misconduct established but strongly disapproved of the solicitor's conduct and took the view that the Law Society had been fully justified in taking the Complaint to the

Tribunal, the Tribunal found the solicitor liable in the whole expenses of both the Tribunal and the Complainers (Case 754/89).

See also Case 755/89, at para 8.02, and Case 493/81, at para 6.09.

5.09 EXPENSES OF TRIBUNAL

So far as not otherwise recovered from parties the expenses of the Tribunal are paid by the Law Society as part of the expenses of the Society (Schedule 4, para 22).

5.10 RECOVERY OF EXPENSES INCURRED

Schedule 4 of the 1980 Act provides:

20. On the application of the person in whose favour an order for expenses under paragraph 19 is made and on production of a certificate by the clerk of the Tribunal that the days of appeal against the order have expired without an appeal being lodged or, where such an appeal has been lodged, that the appeal has been dismissed or withdrawn, the court may grant warrant authorising that person to recover those expenses from the person against whom the order was made.

21. Such warrant shall have effect for execution and for all other purposes as if it were an extracted decree of court awarded against the person against whom the order of the Tribunal was made.

This procedure is effected by an informal letter to the Principal Clerk of Session with the taxed Account of Expenses, and the Interlocutor of the Court is endorsed on the Findings of the Tribunal.

5.11 COUNCIL TO GIVE EFFECT TO ORDERS

Schedule 4 of the 1980 Act provides:

16. In the case of a decision by the Tribunal—
    (*a*) ordering a solicitor to be struck off the roll; or
    (*b*) ordering a solicitor to be suspended from practice; or
    (*c*) censuring a solicitor or an incorporated practice; or
    (*d*) fining a solicitor or an incorporated practice; or,
    (*e*) ordering that the recognition under section 34(1A) of an incorporated practice be revoked; or
    (*f*) containing a direction under section 53A or an order under section 53C(2); or
    (*g*) confirming or varying a determination or direction of the Council on an appeal under section 42A(7); or
    (*h*) ordering that an investment business certificate issued to a solicitor, a firm of solicitors or an incorporated practice be—
        (i)   suspended; or
        (ii) subject to such terms and conditions as they may direct; or
        (iii) revoked,

    on the expiration of the days of appeal if any without an appeal being lodged or, where an appeal has been lodged, if and as soon as the appeal is withdrawn or a decision by the court is given in terms of subparagraphs (*a*) to (*h*) or in the case of a decision of the Tribunal under section 53(6) or (6B) which has not been varied or quashed by the court or under section 53(6A) which has not been varied by the court, the clerk of the Tribunal shall immediately send to the Council a copy of the decision of the Tribunal certified by him and a copy of the decision by the court in any appeal, and the Council shall forthwith give effect to any order as to striking the solicitor off the roll or as to revoking the recognition under section 34(1A) of an incorporated practice and to any terms and conditions directed by the Tribunal under section 53(5); and in any other case shall cause a note of the effect of the decision to be entered against the name of the solicitor in the roll.

17. The Council shall forthwith intimate any order striking a solicitor off the roll or suspending a solicitor from practice to each sheriff clerk and also to the Principal Clerk of Session, and shall without prejudice to paragraph 14, cause a notice of the operative part of the order to be published in the Edinburgh Gazette.

5.12 CONTEMPT OF THE TRIBUNAL

Senior Counsel advised the Tribunal in March 1982 that in his opinion the Tribunal was not a 'Court' within the meaning of section 19 of the Contempt of Court Act 1981 which would allow contempt proceedings in a matter relative to the proceedings of the Tribunal (Opinion of Senior Counsel, 10.3.82). This Opinion would not necessarily preclude proceedings of Professional Misconduct being taken against a solicitor in respect of the solicitor's actings before the Tribunal.

5.13 MISREPRESENTING A DECISION OF THE TRIBUNAL

In a case where a solicitor had been found guilty by the Tribunal of Professional Misconduct involving various offences including breaches of the Accounts Rules, resulting in a fine with publicity being ordered, the solicitor was later charged with Professional Misconduct in that he had misrepresented the original Decision of the Tribunal. The Respondent had used the word 'unfair' in relation to the earlier Decision and it was submitted by the Complainers that the use of this word was a distortion of the previous Decision. The Tribunal observed that the Respondent had only himself to blame for the previous proceedings before the Tribunal and it was not accepted that the Decision was in any way unfair. However, the Tribunal decided that the Decisions of the Discipline Tribunal, like the decision of any Court, are open to reasonable comment and the particular observation in question by the Respondent fell into that category.

In the second Complaint it was also averred by the Law Society that a letter of the Respondent and his comments to a newspaper were a direct attempt by the Respondent to minimise the situation which the Tribunal had ordered to be published and that the Respondent's misrepresentation of the original Decision constituted contempt. The Tribunal in its Decision said:

> The Fiscal did not seek to suggest that the Scottish Solicitors' Discipline Tribunal is a Court and that the Respondent was guilty of what would ordinarily be regarded as Contempt of Court, but he pointed to the ordinary meaning of the word

'contempt' as being 'scorn' and submitted that the letters contained material which was 'contemptuous' towards the Tribunal. He referred to Lund's 'The Professional Conduct and Etiquette of Solicitors' at page 57 where it is stated in relation to English solicitors that a solicitor's duties towards the Court are also owed to the (English) Disciplinary Committee. Various examples are given in the text; but they all relate to the actual proceedings.

Counsel for the Respondent submitted that 'contempt' proceedings were not appropriate in relation to this Tribunal and he referred to

Attorney-General v BBC [1981] AC 303
Ambard v Attorney-General for Trinidad and Tobago [1936] AC 322
Dunn v Bevan [1922] 1 Ch 276 and
Milburn 1946 SC 301

and asked the question whether there had been an attempt to interfere with the administration of justice. Counsel distinguished the case of *In the matter of a solicitor*, ex parte *the Law Society* 1911 TLR 535, where the solicitor was permitted to visit his client who was in prison under sentence of death 'and in abuse of the privilege thus extended to him he aided and abetted the editor of a newspaper to disseminate in his journal false information in the form of a letter purporting to emanate from and to be written by the convict, although as the (solicitor) knew, no such letter in fact existed'. Counsel also observed that in each of the examples referred to in Lund there had been an attempt to influence or distort the outcome of the proceedings before the English Disciplinary Committee.

The Tribunal in this case also said that:

It is significant that although the present Complaint is concerned with the Respondent's actings in relation [to] a part of this Tribunal's Order, the conduct complained of did not relate to the actual proceedings before the Tribunal and it is on this basis that no separate finding of professional misconduct has been made in relation to the second part of the Complaint.

The Tribunal did however find that statements in a letter which the Respondent wrote to clients of his firm, and a press interview which he gave, were grossly misleading and in finding the Respondent guilty of Professional Misconduct in this respect the Tribunal said:

The original matter before the Tribunal had been particularly serious and although the present Complaint followed directly on the previous subject matter it was an entirely separate issue. The observations contained in the Respondent's letters of '. . . . .' [the letters to the clients] which were adopted by his local newspaper, had the effect of creating a misleading impression. It was the Respondent's decision at that time to write the letters of '. . . . .' [the letters to the clients] and he had a duty to ensure that any comments fairly reflected the decision and the opinions of the Tribunal. The Respondent was less than frank with his comments: they went beyond what might be regarded as reasonable criticism and indeed certain passages in the letters were recklessly misleading. Overall, the letters demonstrate a dishonourable intention to minimise the gravity of the Respondent's previous conduct, and having regard to the importance of the subject matter to him and to the recipients of the letter, the Tribunal is obliged to take a serious view of the Respondent's actings (Case 781/89).

5.14 APPEALS FROM THE TRIBUNAL

Any person aggrieved by a Decision of the Tribunal relating to discipline under the Act may within 21 days of intimation of the Decision to that person appeal to the Court of Session. The procedure for such Appeal is set out in rule 41.19 *et seq* of the Rules of the Court of Session. The form of the Appeal is by way of Petition to the Inner House and the Petition requires to be signed and the whole Process lodged within the 21-day period.

An Appeal against a decision to exclude a solicitor from giving legal aid under section 31(3) and (4) of the Legal Aid (Scotland) Act 1986 should follow the same procedure.

It should be noted:

1. The Decisions of the Tribunal which may be appealed against include not only Decisions under section 53 which relate broadly to cases of Professional Misconduct but also to Decisions of the Tribunal under section 53A relating to Inadequate Professional Services (where the Tribunal considers the case in the first instance) and section 53B where the Tribunal acts as an appellate Tribunal in regard to decisions relating to Inadequate Professional Services made by the Council, and Decisions under section 53D where the Tribunal acts as an appellate Tribunal in regard to decisions made by the Council in relation to Investment Business Certificates.

2. Where the Tribunal has exercised its power under section 53(6) to direct that a Decision ordering a solicitor to be 'struck off' or suspended or a right of audience under section 25A be suspended or revoked, should take effect on intimation of the Decision to the solicitor, section 54(2) (*a*) provides that the solicitor concerned may within 21 days of the intimation apply to the Court for an order varying or quashing the direction insofar as it relates to the date of the order taking effect; and section 54(2) (*b*) makes like provisions with regard to appeals against the dates from which orders against incorporated practices shall take effect. It is the normal practice for such application to be incorporated in the Petition of Appeal.

On hearing an Appeal section 55 of the 1980 Act provides:

> (1) In the case of professional misconduct by any solicitor the court may—
> (*a*) cause the name of that solicitor to be struck off the roll; or
> (*b*) suspend the solicitor from practice as a solicitor for such period as the court may determine; or
> (*ba*) suspend the solicitor from exercising any right of audience held by him by virtue of section 25A for such period as the court may determine [section 25A relates to rights of audience before the Court of Session, etc]; or
> (*bb*) revoke any right of audience so acquired by him; or
> (*c*) fine the solicitor; or
> (*d*) censure him; and in any of those events,
> (*e*) find him liable in any expenses which may be involved in the proceedings before the court.
> (2) Subject to subsection (3), a decision of the court under this section shall be final.
> (3) A solicitor whose name has been struck off the roll in pursuance of an order

made by the court under subsection (1), may apply to the court for an order directing his name to be restored to the roll and the court may make such order.

(3A) A solicitor whose rights of audience under section 25A have been revoked in pursuance of an order made by the court under subsection (1) may apply to the court for an order restoring those rights, and the court may make such order.

(4) An application under subsection (3) shall be by way of petition and intimation of any such petition shall be made to the Tribunal who shall be entitled to appear and to be heard in respect of the application.

The Court have held that an Appeal against a Decision of the Tribunal shall also lie at the instance of any Complainer so long as he is a person aggrieved by the relevant Decision of the Tribunal and that the Council of the Law Society is such a party, being the guardian of the public interest so far as concerns the maintenance of the standards of the profession of solicitors. That guardianship 'is not confined to securing that breaches of the rules are established, but that a proper punishment is awarded where these rules have been breached'. Thus it is open to the Council of the Law Society to appeal a Decision of the Tribunal *inter alia* against the penalty imposed (*Council of the Law Society of Scotland* v *Docherty* 1968 SLT 133; *Council of the Law Society of Scotland* v *M and Another*, Court of session, unreported, 14.12.72).

The Court hears Appeals in chambers.

5.15 DAYS OF APPEAL

Paragraph 13 of Schedule 4 provides that the Tribunal shall add to every Decision a Note stating the grounds on which the Decision has been arrived at. The days of appeal against a Decision of the Tribunal run from the date on which the written Decision of the Tribunal together with the Note of reasons is intimated to the parties. In a case in which the Tribunal issued an interlocutor followed at a later date by a formal Decision with Note of reasons, the Court held that days of appeal should run from the date when the Note was intimated (*Council of the Law Society of Scotland* v *M and Another, supra*).

5.16 APPEAL AGAINST SENTENCE

In an Appeal to the Court against sentence by a solicitor who had been found guilty of Professional Misconduct in that he had acted in the preparation, signature and recording of a standard security in circumstances where he was unable to give impartial advice to the granter because of his own separate interests in the transaction and the Tribunal had suspended the solicitor from practice for a period of ten years, the Court in allowing the Appeal said:

> There is no doubt that the Tribunal were in the best position to assess the gravity of the petitioner's misconduct and it is not for us to substitute our own views on that matter. The Tribunal's decision that a suspension was an appropriate penalty in this case is not one with which we can interfere. To accept the argument that a fine was appropriate would be to ignore the fact that the Tribunal took a very serious view of the petitioner's conduct and that it was only with considerable hesitation that they decided not to order that his name should be struck off the roll.

But we are in no doubt that the period of the suspension which was ordered in this case was excessive in the circumstances. In our opinion the Tribunal gave insufficient weight to the fact that the misconduct of which the petitioner was found guilty was confined to a single transaction involving only one client of his practice, and that although it was persisted in when he ran into difficulty no other criticism had been made of his conduct as a solicitor. Furthermore, any period of suspension must represent a very severe punishment for a solicitor, as was pointed [out] in *Sharp* v *Council of the Law Society of Scotland* 1984 SLT 313 at 319. The named publicity which must be given to the order will itself have an adverse effect on his professional life in the future, irrespective of the length of the suspension. In our opinion the grave and reprehensible nature of the petitioner's conduct would be sufficiently recognised by a suspension from practice as a solicitor for a period of four years. We shall, accordingly, recall that part of the Tribunal's interlocutor and substitute a finding to that effect (*A* v *The Council of the Law Society of Scotland*, Court of Session, unreported, 21.12.90).

In a case where a solicitor appealed to the Court against a suspension from practice for a period of 10 years where the solicitor had been found guilty of various matters giving rise to findings of Professional Misconduct, the Court when refusing the petition, said:

Counsel's principal argument, however, was that the Tribunal had misdirected themselves as to what was necessary to protect the interests of the public in this case. It was pointed out that on 14 February 1989 the petitioner had voluntarily surrendered his practising certificate. He was said to have done so because of his mental health, although this was not strictly necessary because the degree of mental illness required for section 18(1) (*a*) of the Solicitors (Scotland) Act 1980 to apply had not been reached. That step in itself had achieved all that was needed to protect the public in this case because the Council had a discretion in terms of section 15(1) (*a*) as to whether or not to grant the application if and when the petitioner sought to have his practising certificate restored to him. It was said that this would enable the Council to have proper regard to his mental health at the time and by this means to ensure that he did not return to practice as a solicitor until he was fit to do so. Accordingly, if the protection of the public was the aim, an order for the suspension of the petitioner from practice was unnecessary. It was submitted also that this was a harsher sentence than that of striking his name off the Roll, which the Tribunal had expressly decided not to do. This was because in terms of section 10 the petitioner could apply to have his name restored to the Roll at any time, whereas he could only obtain a restoration of his certificate in terms of section 15(2) (*f*) after the period of suspension had come to an end. In the result the Tribunal had, without apparently intending to do so, subjected him to a severe punishment which was not necessary to achieve their declared aim of protecting the interests of the public in this case.

We do not construe the Tribunal's findings in this way. Their task, on being satisfied that the petitioner had been guilty of professional misconduct, was to decide which of the powers available under section 53(2) they should exercise. These are disciplinary powers, to be exercised by way of punishment according to their assessment of the gravity of the offence. The Tribunal's duty to protect the interests of the public is a factor to be taken into account, since this is one of the principal objects of the Act. But it is a factor bearing on the question what is the appropriate punishment, not an end or purpose in itself. And it has an obvious bearing on the question of sentence in this case, not only because of the petitioner's state of health but also because of the deplorable nature of his conduct. As we read this passage, therefore, the Tribunal's concern was to mark the gravity of the conduct, in the general public interest, by a period of suspension of a sufficient length.

On this view the Tribunal did not misdirect themselves as to what was appropriate by way of sentence in this case. The petitioner's state of health was taken into account by their refraining from striking him off the Roll on the one hand, and by their recognition on the other that at the conclusion of the period of suspension section 15(2) (f) would come into play and it would then be a matter for the Council to consider whether the petitioner was fit to hold a practising certificate at that time. But the Tribunal decided also that it was in the general public interest that solicitors who were guilty of such serious acts of misconduct should be suspended from practice for a substantial period. In our opinion this was a decision which the Tribunal were entitled to take, and we should add that we see no reason to interfere with their decision as to the length of the period which was appropriate.

For these reasons we shall refuse the petition and affirm the interlocutor of the Tribunal (*M* v *The Council of the Law Society of Scotland*, Court of Session, unreported, 21.12.90).

In an Appeal to the Court against a sentence set by the Tribunal in which the Tribunal ordered a restriction on the solicitor's practising certificate, the Court in refusing the Appeal said:

So far as this Court is concerned it would require a very strong case to interfere with a competent sentence selected by the Discipline Tribunal for professional misconduct of the character we are concerned with here, for they are the best possible people for weighing the seriousness of such professional misconduct and for deciding what competent orders should be made for the protection of the public interest and the good name of the profession. This was precisely the approach of the *Privy Council* in *McCoan* v *General Medical Council* [1964] 1 WLR 1107 at 1113, agreeing with the opinion of Lord Goddard CJ in *In re a solicitor* [1956] 1 WLR 1312, and if a sentence or part of a sentence is to be set aside it must be shown to be wrong and unjustified (*C* v *The Council of the Law Society of Scotland*, Court of Session, unreported, 27.09.85).

In rejecting an Appeal to the Court against an Order of the Tribunal that the petitioning solicitor's name should be struck off the Roll of Solicitors in Scotland, the Court said:

It was accepted by counsel for the Petitioner that it would require a very strong case to persuade this Court that it should interfere with a competent order made by the Tribunal in the exercise of their powers following a finding of professional misconduct. The various powers which are listed in section 53(2) of the Solicitors (Scotland) Act 1980 are at the discretion of the Tribunal. It has been said many times that they are the best possible people to weigh up the possible consequences of the professional misconduct which has been established to their satisfaction and to decide what should be done to protect the public and preserve the good name of the profession. Lord President Emslie's comments to this effect in *MacColl* v *Council of the Law Society of Scotland* 1987 SLT 524 at p 528 follow closely the words used by Lord Upjohn in *McCoan* v *General Medical Council* [1964] 1 WLR 1107 at p 1113. Lord Keith of Kinkel was making the same point when, in *Finegan* v *General Medical Council* [1987] 1 WLR 121 at p 124 he said:

This is an appeal only against sentence, and in relation to that matter the Board

49

has repeatedly said that professional disciplinary committees are the best possible people to judge of what is appropriate, and that it will interfere only where the sentence is clearly wrong and unjustified.

In some cases such as *Sharp* v *Council of the Law Society of Scotland* 1984 SLT 313 at p 319 the Court has been willing to interfere on matters of detail where it is satisfied that the Tribunal have given insufficient weight to factors of importance in the case. But underlying all the cases where the Court is asked to review a sentence for professional misconduct is the principle that, if the sentence is to be set aside, it must be shown to be plainly wrong and unjustified (*M* v *The Council of Law Society of Scotland*, Court of Session, unreported, 24.05.91).

6

STANDARDS OF CONDUCT

6.01 CODE OF CONDUCT

The preamble to the Code of Conduct promulgated by the Law Society of
Scotland for Solicitors holding Practising Solicitor Certificates issued by the
Law Society of Scotland (October 1989) and now incorporated in the Code of
Conduct (Scotland) Rules 1992 states:

I.   The function of the lawyer in society
*In a society founded on respect for the rule of law lawyers fulfil a special role. Their
duties do not begin and end with the faithful performance of what they are instructed to
do so far as the law permits. Lawyers must serve the interests of justice as well as those
whose rights and liberties they are trusted to assert and defend and it is their duty not only
to plead their clients' cause but also to be their adviser.*

*The function of lawyers therefore imposes on them a variety of legal and moral obli-
gations (sometimes appearing to be in conflict with each other) towards:*
(a) the clients;
*(b) the courts and other authorities before whom the lawyers plead their clients' cause or
     act on their behalf;*
*(c) the public for whom the existence of a free and independent profession, bound
     together by respect for rules made by the profession itself, is an essential means of
     safeguarding human rights in face of the power of the state and other interests in
     society.*
(d) the legal profession in general and each fellow member of it in particular.

II.   The nature of rules of professional conduct
*Rules of professional conduct are designed to ensure the proper performance by the lawyer
of a function which is recognised as essential in all civilised societies. The failure of the
lawyer to observe these rules must in the last resort result in a disciplinary sanction. The
willing acceptance of those rules and of the need for disciplinary sanction ensures the
highest possible standards.*

It is thus important that all solicitors holding practising certificates issued by
the Law Society of Scotland are familiar with and observe the rules of professional conduct which require to be observed by solicitors.

There are Practice Rules (set out in the *Parliament House Book*) promulgated
by the Council of the Law Society, under statutory authority, breach of which
may constitute Professional Misconduct, but not all requirements of conduct
for members of the profession are set out in these written rules. An examination of the Decisions of the Tribunal (and its predecessor the Discipline
Committee) and relative Decisions of the Court of Session will help to clarify
some of these unwritten rules as well as the written ones.

The Tribunal is authorised in terms of section 51 of the 1980 Act to deal with complaints of Professional Misconduct and in terms of section 53A of the 1980 Act with complaints of Inadequate Professional Services. In terms of section 53B of the 1980 Act the Tribunal is given power to adjudicate on Appeals made by solicitors in respect of which the Council of the Law Society under section 42A of the 1980 Act has made a determination or direction in respect of Inadequate Professional Services.

6.02 MEANING OF PROFESSIONAL MISCONDUCT
Professional Misconduct is not defined by statute.

The classic definition of Professional Misconduct most quoted and referred to before the Tribunal is that of Lord President Emslie in the case *Sharp* v *Council of the Law Society of Scotland* 1984 SC 129 at 134, where he said:

> There are certain standards of conduct to be expected of competent and reputable solicitors. A departure from these standards which would be regarded by competent and reputable solicitors as serious and reprehensible may properly be categorised as professional misconduct. Whether or not the conduct complained of is a breach of rules or some other actings or omissions the same question falls to be asked and answered and in every case it will be essential to consider the whole circumstances and the degree of culpability which ought properly to be attached to the individual against whom the complaint is made.

The appeal in *Sharp* followed a Complaint at the instance of the Council of the Law Society of Scotland where the Tribunal had found the partners of a firm of solicitors all guilty of Professional Misconduct in respect of their breaches of rule 4(1) (a) of the Solicitors (Scotland) Accounts Rules 1952, in that there was a shortage of funds on their clients' accounts on 5th November 1979, and additionally finding two junior partners guilty of Professional Misconduct in respect of particular breaches of rules 4(1) (a) and 6.

The Court decided that the Tribunal took the wrong approach in law in two respects.

The first was that the Tribunal appeared to have construed section 20(3) of the Solicitors (Scotland) Act 1949, as amended (now re-enacted as section 35(3) of the Solicitors (Scotland) Act 1980)—which provides that if any solicitor fails to comply with, *inter alia*, any rule of the Accounts Rules, that failure *may* be treated as Professional Misconduct in proceedings before the Discipline Tribunal—to mean that a breach of a rule *shall* be held to constitute Professional Misconduct unless in exceptional circumstances the solicitor concerned is able to satisfy the Tribunal that he took all reasonable steps to prevent it. Putting the matter another way, the Court said the Tribunal appeared to believe that section 20(3) fell to be read as if it declared that failure to comply with the relevant rules 'shall' be treated as Professional Misconduct unless in its discretion the Tribunal is persuaded by the solicitor concerned that he has discharged the onus of showing that it should not be so treated.

The Court said:

> Section 20(3) means precisely what it says. A failure on the part of a solicitor to

comply with a relevant rule *may* be treated as professional misconduct. The sub-section introduces nothing new to the law. Such failure might have been so treated before it was enacted, and it may well be that the true purpose of the subsection is to draw the attention of practitioners to the importance attached to compliance with the rules. However that may be, whether such a failure should be treated as professional misconduct must depend upon the gravity of the failure and a con-sideration of the whole circumstances in which the failure occurred including the part played by the individual solicitor in question.

6.03 PROFESSIONAL NEGLIGENCE/PROFESSIONAL MISCONDUCT

In a Complaint made to the Discipline Committee, the Committee reported the case to the Court with a finding that the solicitor's neglect of the interests of his client and his obstinate delay in carrying out his professional duties amounted to Professional Misconduct. On behalf of the solicitor it was contended that professional negligence could not amount to Professional Misconduct.

The Lord President (Cooper) stated *inter alia*:

> I shall not attempt to define professional misconduct. But if the statutory tribunal, composed as it always is of professional men of the highest repute and competence, stigmatise a course of professional conduct as misconduct, it seems to me that only strong grounds would justify this Court in condoning as innocent that which the Committee have condemned as guilty.

> Two criticisms were addressed to us by counsel against the findings of the Com-mittee. The first was that professional negligence, however crass, can never amount to professional misconduct, a proposition which he supported by reference to two early English cases. What the law of England was, or is, on that matter I do not know. But there is negligence and negligence; and I am certainly not prepared to affirm the proposition that according to Scots law and practice professional negligence cannot amount to professional misconduct . . . (*E* v *T* 1949 SLT 411).

The Tribunal found Professional Misconduct established in a situation where a solicitor failed, or unconscionably delayed, to prosecute a claim for damages for a client. The Tribunal pointed out that by a particular date the Respondent was aware that more than three years had passed since the date of the accident and said:

> By that time, a claimant has ordinarily lost the right to insist on his right of action; but it is a matter for the defender to insist on his plea, and even then, the Court still has an equitable jurisdiction in exceptional circumstances. For this reason, the passing of the triennium did not necessarily give cause for a civil action against the Respondent's firm so as to create a conflict of interest if the Respondent were to continue acting for [the client]. However the passing of time did make it impera-tive for the Respondent to take immediate action and pursue that action without further delay. Regrettably the Respondent did not instruct Counsel for an Opinion [for a further period]. A further month passed before the Opinion was received; and although he instructed his correspondents to proceed with a Summons, the required action had still not been raised when the Respondent met [the client some months later]. Taking the Respondent's initial failure to raise the action within the triennium together with his further delays . . . it [became] apparent that this was

not a simple case of omission but an example of inexcusable neglect extending over a considerable period and in aggregate this undoubtedly require[d] the Tribunal to make a finding of Professional Misconduct (Case 785/90).

6.04 ACTIVE PARTICIPATION MAY NOT BE NECESSARY TO ESTABLISH PROFESSIONAL MISCONDUCT

In a case in 1987 (referred to at para 18.01) the Tribunal, in finding that in the particular circumstances, and having regard to the *dicta* in *Sharp*, *supra*, p 52, the failure of a junior partner fell narrowly short of Professional Misconduct, stated that in its view it may not be necessary for active participation to be proved to establish Professional Misconduct (Case 723/87).

6.05 IGNORANCE OF A PRACTICE RULE NOT AN EXCUSE

In an Appeal to the Court by the Law Society against a Decision of the Tribunal where the Tribunal had, in finding Professional Misconduct not proved, taken into account the fact that a Practice Rule (the Solicitors (Scotland) Practice Rules 1986) had only been in force for a short time before the breach occurred and the solicitor's unexplained ignorance of the rule, the Court said:

> There can be no question of a period of grace being allowed after the coming into force of rules made under the Act [the 1980 Act]. Once they have come into operation they must be taken to have full force and effect, and a solicitor who is in breach of them cannot be heard to say that he is not guilty of professional misconduct simply because they have not been in force for very long. Furthermore a solicitor cannot, at least without explanation, plead ignorance of the rules. Every care is taken before rules are made by the council under s 34 of the Act to see that each member of the society is consulted in advance. This is a requirement in terms of s 34(2) (*a*) of the Act. It is well known that the council goes to considerable lengths to publicise its decisions in regard to the making of such rules by circulation to its members and in the Journal of the Law Society of Scotland before they come into force. Each solicitor must be taken therefore to have seen and read the rules and to be aware of their existence unless an explanation is forthcoming as to why, in his case, this should not be so. In the present case no explanation for ignorance was advanced. All that was put before the tribunal was a statement by the respondent that he had overlooked the precise provisions of the rule, without any reason being given as to why that had occurred. In our opinion the tribunal ought not to have regarded this as a relevant consideration in assessing whether or not professional misconduct had occurred, and their decision insofar as it was based on this consideration cannot stand. They ought to have approached the case upon the basis that the solicitor was obliged by the rules of his profession to comply with rule 5(1) and that no reason had been advanced for absolving him from professional misconduct on the basis that he was ignorant of the provisions of the rule (*Council of the Law Society of Scotland* v *J* 1991 SLT 662 at 665).

See also Case 835/92, referred to at para 9.02, where a solicitor claimed that although he had not overlooked a particular rule he had misconstrued its terms.

6.06 QUALIFIED ASSISTANTS/NEWLY QUALIFIED SOLICITORS

In a case where a qualified assistant was charged before the Tribunal that he was guilty of Professional Misconduct while acting in a conflict of interest situation, the Tribunal observed:

> It is to be expected that a newly qualified assistant will refer any unusual work matter to the partner of the firm to whom he is responsible. Ordinarily the assistant will accept the direction of his superior, particularly as any disagreement could otherwise strike at the employee/employer relationship and possibly even affect his continuing as an assistant with that firm. However, the qualified assistant also has the professional responsibility of a solicitor and this Tribunal cannot accept that by blindly following the directions of the principal solicitor, the assistant can disregard the ethical consequences of any of his actings. Particularly in the case of a qualified assistant who is personally interviewing clients and appearing for them in Court, he has a direct responsibility towards those clients and to the Court. Such assistant must always balance his duties to his employer with his own professional responsibilities; and likewise where a solicitor employs a qualified assistant, he should also respect the professional standing of that assistant and look very carefully if the assistant feels that his obligations to his employer conflict with his professional duties as a solicitor (Case 809/90).

In a case where two partners were charged with breaches of the Accounts Rules and the senior partner had responsibility for running the cashroom, the Tribunal observed *vis-à-vis* the junior partner:

> She was undoubtedly inexperienced, but upon enrolling as a solicitor she accepted the various responsibilities encumbent on all solicitors and this includes compliance with the Accounts Rules. She had not troubled to examine these Rules and it was this failure which materially contributed to the position which she is now in (Case 790/90).

See also Case 857/93 at para 19.05, where the Tribunal did not accept as an excuse for failure, with regard to the Accounts Rules, that the solicitor when he commenced practice was relatively inexperienced.

In a case where a trainee solicitor, holding a restricted practising certificate, framed a fictitious decision of an Industrial Tribunal and communicated the terms of the fictitious decision to his employer's client, the Tribunal in finding Professional Misconduct established said:

> There was no indication that the Respondent's conduct was intended or could have brought about any financial benefit for him. Indeed the suggested outcome might have been the reverse. Nevertheless the mere act of falsifying a document, and thereafter in communicating its terms as if it were genuine, is in itself a grave offence. There was a suggestion that [the client's] application was ill-founded and might not have resulted in a favourable award but this does not in any way minimise the gravity of the Respondent's actings. The Respondent's conduct was inexcusable and reprehensible, and damaging to the good name of the profession. The Respondent may have still only been a trainee in relation to his employers, and was only the holder of a restricted Practising Certificate; but at the relevant time he was a solicitor on the Roll of Solicitors in Scotland and as such he was required to maintain the same standards of integrity as any other solicitor in practice. The

Respondent's course of action displayed crass stupidity and was wholly unbecoming a solicitor. In such circumstances, it was a matter for consideration whether the Respondent should remain on the Roll of Solicitors. In coming under stress, the Respondent acted in an extremely foolish manner and this must reflect on his strength of character and his suitability as a solicitor.

However, it is of relevance to take into account the Respondent's particular situation. He was still a trainee and he ought to have been working under supervision, especially as here in a matter which was completely new to him (Case 747/89).

In Case 673/86 Professional Misconduct was established where a solicitor's employers had made it a condition of his employment that he held a current practising certificate and having asked him to produce his certificate he deceived his employers into believing that he had such a certificate, which he did not in fact have.

6.07 DISHONESTY

Solicitors must act honestly at all times and in such a way as to put their personal integrity beyond question (Code of Conduct, para 7).

Dishonesty may take an almost infinite variety of forms, but among the instances of dishonesty which the Tribunal have had to consider and which resulted in a finding of Professional Misconduct have been:

Misleading a partner by concealing from the partner material matters in relation to a transaction which the partner was carrying out with a professional colleague (Case 829/92).

The Tribunal took a particularly serious view of a case where a solicitor, who had been involved in embezzling money belonging to a client for whom he held a Power of Attorney, in his endeavours to obscure the true nature of his actings involved a third party and persuaded him to make false statements which were not only misleading to the Law Society but would have resulted in perjury in the event of the statements being repeated before the Court (Case 810/91).

Embezzling money belonging to a client, while acting as solicitor and exercising Power of Attorney over the financial affairs of that client. The Tribunal took the view that the solicitor was in a position of trust and had a duty to act with utmost propriety in all his dealings with his client's money (Case 810/91).

Diverting substantial sums of money which the solicitor received for clients for his own personal benefit (Case 844/93).

Withdrawing money from a client's account in such a way as to deprive his partners of a share of fees to which they were entitled and reducing the figures upon which his firm's liability for VAT and Income Tax should be computed (Case 844/93).

Misleading clients by writing to them and falsely representing what had happened to money which the solicitor had misappropriated (Case 823/92).

Misleading a client by allowing the client to believe that his application for legal aid was being processed, the truth being that it was not (Case 822/91).

Deceiving partners and other parties by writing letters to and from, and framing fictitious documents purporting to be by, a person (fictitious); and operating a bank account in a fictitious name with the intention of concealing that the solicitor was the true operator of the account (Case 823/92).

Forging the signature of the granter of a Disposition and falsifying the testing clause (Case 829/92).

Deliberately debiting excessive fees against clients (Case 723/87).

Where a partner in a firm of solicitors in conveyancing transactions provided clients with an accounting which included an item in respect of his firm's fees but no fee note was prepared, and he thereafter intimated to the firm's cashier that no fee would be charged, and he withdrew the amount representing his firm's fees from his firm's client account and misappropriated the money (Case 756/89).

Giving evidence on oath at a hearing on an Open Commission that was incorrect and amounted to a careless misstatement (Case 782/90).

Carrying through a conveyancing transaction in the name of a fictitious person, when the conveyance was to the same person using his real name, thereby giving the impression that the transaction was at arm's length (Case 817/91).

6.08 INADEQUATE PROFESSIONAL SERVICES
Section 65 of the 1980 Act defines Inadequate Professional Services as

> [P]rofessional services which are in any respect not of the quality which could reasonably be expected of a competent solicitor, and cognate expressions shall be construed accordingly; . . .

The following are examples of circumstances in which the Tribunal has found Inadequate Professional Services established.

Failure to progress a matter with any expedition on behalf of a client over a period of time and over the same period of time failing to keep the client informed regarding the lack of progress (Case 842/93).

In a Court case where the client (defender) suffered no financial loss, in that monies which were the subject-matter of the Court action were undoubtedly due, the failure of the solicitor to advise the client that he had been unable to obtain any adequate response from the pursuer's solicitors and to advise the client of the potential consequences of the action (Case 842/93).

6.08 INADEQUATE PROFESSIONAL SERVICES

Failure timeously to record a Disposition and likewise to record a Standard Security (Case 831/92).

Failure to inform a lender of problems which had arisen with the obtaining of a heritable security and to respond to the lender's reasonable inquiries by letter and by telephone (Case 831/92).

Failure to implement instructions to take proceedings to recover a debt (Case 831/92).

Failure to advise a client adequately prior to making an offer to purchase heritable property on behalf of the client. In the particular case the client had apparently 'only limited knowledge' relating to the purchase and sale of house property in Scotland and the solicitor left it to a relatively inexperienced assistant to explain the whole procedure to the client; and in that prior to entering into missives to purchase the property no advice was given as to the necessity of securing bridging finance should the client not have sold and obtained the price of his existing house prior to the date of entry of the property he was purchasing (Case 835/92).

A lack of care by a solicitor in purporting to conclude missives which did not in fact effect a concluded bargain (Case 835/92).

Not advising a client properly that a fee which had been quoted was not inclusive of all outlays. In deciding this case the Tribunal said *inter alia*:

> ... It is significant that in the Code of Conduct for Scottish Solicitors published by the Law Society of Scotland, it is provided at paragraph 5(*e*):
>
>> Solicitors are required to try to ensure that their communications with their clients and others on behalf of their clients are effective. This includes providing clients with relevant information regarding the matter in hand and the actions taken on their behalf. Solicitors should advise their clients of any significant development in relation to their case or transaction and explain matters to the extent reasonably necessary to permit informed decisions by clients regarding the instructions which require to be given by them. Information should be clear and comprehensive and where necessary or appropriate confirmed in writing.
>
> Whilst it is always desirable that any quotation of fees by a solicitor should be set down or at least confirmed in writing, the failure of a solicitor to confirm the position does not necessarily give rise to the provision of an inadequate professional service; but it does leave a quotation open to challenge at a later date. It is significant that in this case, the Law Society's Committee recorded in the Disposal Schedule
>
>> that in failing to explain the situation to [the complainer] properly, there was an inadequate professional service
>
> and in the following paragraph there was a reference to the actings of the Appellant's firm
>
>> in not advising their client properly.

The failure of a solicitor to advise the client properly can undoubtedly amount to an inadequate professional service. The overall cost of a conveyancing transaction is a very significant element in the client's financial considerations and it is reasonable for a client to expect the solicitor to advise the client properly in regard to the whole charges to be incurred. Whatever may have actually been said to [the complainer] by [the solicitor's assistant], the essential matter was that the extent of the whole charges were not properly explained to her and on the basis of this finding, there were reasonable grounds for the Council of the Law Society to determine that there had been an inadequate professional service (Case 860/93).

Failure to progress a conveyancing transaction and supply the client with a completion statement and to respond timeously and accurately (Case 868/93).

Failure to respond to reasonable requests from clients for information and to account timeously for sums received (Case 868/93).

6.09 UNPROFESSIONAL CONDUCT
The Tribunal in a case decided in 1981 said:

Unprofessional conduct has been described as being conduct which, while not quite amounting to professional misconduct, is not approved—where for example, the court or the Disciplinary Committee may not have been prepared to find professional misconduct on the facts of some case, but have decided that the solicitor has no one but himself to blame for having been charged with the offence. The foregoing aptly describes the conduct of the Respondents in this matter and it is for this reason that the Tribunal has resolved that there shall be no liability for expenses to or by either party (Case 493/81).

7

DUTIES TO CLIENTS

7.01 DUTY OF CONFIDENTIALITY

The observance of client confidentiality is a fundamental duty of solicitors (Code of Conduct, para 4).

A solicitor (the Respondent) was found guilty of Professional Misconduct in respect that *inter alia*:

(1) in the knowledge that a conflict of interest had arisen in that Mr [A] was making accusations of a criminal nature against Mr [B] he accepted instructions to act for both parties in Mr [B's] purchase of Mr [A's] house in [. . . .]; and during the course of the conveyancing transaction, he continued to advise Mr [A] on the subject matter of these accusations; (2) he informed Mr [A] about Mr [B's] travel arrangements although he ought to have known that this information would be transmitted to the Police, as a result of which Mr [B] was arrested by the Police and charged as aforesaid; and thereby committed a gross breach of confidentiality to the serious prejudice of his client, Mr [B]. . . .

In its Decision the Tribunal said:

The circumstances of this Complaint relate to the Respondent's acting for Mr [B]. The Respondent also acted for the seller of the property which Mr [B] was purchasing and although this in itself was acceptable, the Respondent was in an exceptional position in that he was already aware of a charge of bribery which had been made by the seller against Mr [B]. The Respondent's awareness of this charge should in itself have been sufficient to dissuade him from acting for Mr [B] but instead the Respondent persisted in acting even after he attended a meeting in London in furtherance of the enquiry into the bribery charge.

The prudence of not acting in a conflict situation patently demonstrated itself in this matter in that at a later stage, the Respondent was made aware of Mr [B's] movements in this country; and to his gross prejudice, he disclosed Mr [B's] movements to the other party. A solicitor has a high duty of confidentiality towards his client and he must not disclose his client's address under any circumstances without that client's permission; and it matters not that the client's whereabouts might ultimately be passed to the Police in connection with an intended prosecution.

. . . It is acknowledged that the conflict which arose between the seller of the property and Mr [B] did not arise out of a professional matter. However, the Respondent continued to act and passed information to the seller which was grossly prejudicial to Mr [B] and for this reason the Tribunal must take a particularly serious view of the Respondent's actings. . . . (Case 496/81).

In a case brought by a lay complainer against a solicitor alleging Professional

Misconduct in relation to a number of matters, the Tribunal in dismissing the Complaint said:

> The circumstances noted from the Complainer's Affidavit are that up until 1978 the Respondents' firm acted for the Complainer and that after the breakdown of the marriage in that year, the Respondents' firm accepted instructions from the Complainer's wife in the subsequent matrimonial proceedings. It is not stated by the Complainer that the Respondents' firm also acted for the Complainer's wife prior to 1978 but it is apparent from the file produced by the Complainer that the Respondents' firm acted for both the Complainer and his wife in regard to certain transactions. Upon the breakdown of a marriage, it is not uncommon for a firm of Solicitors to accept continuing instructions from one of the spouses and for the other party to be separately represented. In this case, the Respondents' firm accepted instructions on the breakdown of the marriage from the Complainer's wife and the Complainer instructed another firm to act for him in the subsequent Court of Session proceedings for divorce.
>
> It is noted from the print of the Record which was produced by the Complainer that the Court of Session action was by the Complainer's wife and that the conclusions were for Decree of Divorce and awards of a capital sum and periodical allowance. The authority for claiming such financial sums in divorce is contained in section 5 of the Divorce (Scotland) Act 1976, and subsection (2) of that section provides that
>
> > . . the Court on granting Decree . . . shall make . . . such Order, if any, as it thinks fit, having regard to the respective means of the parties to the marriage and to all the circumstances of the case. . . .
>
> In such matter, it is appropriate that each party should therefore have the fullest information about the other party's financial circumstances before any award is made by the Court and the Court will normally require each party to disclose their whole financial circumstances in the course of such proceedings.
>
> It is apparent from the Complainer's Affidavit that the Respondents' firm had some information in regard to Life Policies taken out by the Complainer and that the Respondents' firm sought to obtain further information direct from the Insurance Company concerned. Standing the nature of the action between the Complainer and his wife and the desirability of the fullest information being made available, the Tribunal is of the opinion that the Respondents' firm in their capacity as Agents for the Complainer's wife in the said action, were entitled to seek relevant information regarding the Complainer's financial affairs and that accordingly the use of any information available as a result of their prior actings for the Complainer or any subsequent attempt to obtain relevant information from a third party could not be open to such criticism as might be stigmatised as professional misconduct (Case 557/82).

See also case 462/80, referred to at para 9.01, which also deals with issues of conflict of interest arising where a husband and wife, for whom a solicitor has acted/is acting, are in dispute.

7.02 INSTRUCTIONS THROUGH AN INTERMEDIARY

Solicitors act as agents of the clients and must have the authority of the clients for their actions (Code of Conduct, para 5(a)).

7.02 INSTRUCTIONS THROUGH AN INTERMEDIARY

The Tribunal has said:

> In attending to the sale of a client's property, the solicitor's duty is to inform his client fully in regard to any written offer received, advise him in regard to that offer and all other related circumstances and when he is satisfied that the client comprehends the whole position, to take the client's clear and unequivocal instructions whether or not the offer is to be accepted and whether any qualifications are to be added to the acceptance. It is always preferable that such instructions are taken personally whether at a meeting, or by telephone or by letter, but it is accepted that there are circumstances where such instructions may be given through a third party. An obvious example is where one spouse gives instructions in relation to a property in joint names. But if instructions are conveyed through a third party, the solicitor must be satisfied that his client has been fully informed and advised and that the instructions given are on the basis of the client's complete understanding of the position (Case 607/85).

The Tribunal found a solicitor not guilty of a charge that 'he accepted unauthorised instructions from an estate agent to act and did act for a new client in the conclusion of missives of sale and the conveyancing transaction following thereon'. The Tribunal found that the solicitor had accepted instructions on behalf of the new client directly from the estate agent in circumstances where the client already had a solicitor and that the solicitor had accepted an offer for the property without checking the title which turned out later to be leasehold. In its Decision the Tribunal said:

> This charge gave the Tribunal considerable difficulty in that the acceptance of unauthorised instructions would not in itself support a charge unless it might be established that the Solicitor knew that the instructions were issued without authority or if the Solicitor recklessly accepted the instructions without considering whether the client had given his approval. . . .

However

> . . . The Respondent was further charged that 'he gave entry to the purchaser without authority from the seller and without taking proper safeguards regarding the availability of the price'. The Respondent, by his own admission, knew nothing of the arrangements for entry and at no time did he make any enquiries into the same. It is an essential duty of a Solicitor in a conveyancing transaction to ensure that a purchaser does not take entry and that the keys are only handed over in exchange for the purchase price. In this case the Respondent allowed the purchasers to take entry without authority from the seller and without proper safeguards regarding availability of the price and the Tribunal are satisfied that this in itself amounted to professional misconduct. . . . (Case 481/80).

See also Case 701/87, referred to at para 9.01, and Case 612/85 at para. 10.01.

7.03 KEEPING CLIENT INFORMED

Solicitors are under a professional obligation to provide adequate professional services to their clients (Code of Conduct, para 5).

Failure to provide an adequate professional service as well as making a solicitor liable to a charge of Inadequate Professional Services may also result in a finding of Professional Misconduct.

The Tribunal in finding a solicitor guilty of Professional Misconduct has observed:

> Regarding the Respondent's admitted failure to reply to the reasonable enquiries of Mr [. . .], Counsel pointed to the fact that much of the correspondence had been dealt with by the Respondent's then assistant and that Mr [. . .] had from time to time spoken to the Respondent on the telephone. Nevertheless it is of cardinal importance that a solicitor should at all times keep his client fully informed regarding his progress in dealing with his client's business and to respond to any enquiries which are received by him from his client. It is accepted that in this case, a number of the enquiries were addressed to the Respondent's firm coupled with the name of his assistant but nevertheless the Respondent had an overriding duty of supervision and the Respondent must accordingly accept personal responsibility for the delay in replying to all the specified correspondence (Case 751/89).

Failure to keep clients informed as to developments, particularly adverse developments, in the sale of their property, thereby depriving the clients of the opportunity to consider separate representation or taking other steps to safeguard their interests, has been found to constitute Professional Misconduct (Cases 828/92; 831/92 and 834/92).

Although it did not make a finding of Professional Misconduct in this regard, the Tribunal has said:

> In the opinion of the Tribunal, a solicitor has a professional duty to ensure that his client is fully aware of the terms of missives or any other contract which may be concluded on his behalf and in such circumstances, it is usually prudent for the solicitor to provide the client with a copy of such missives. This is particularly so if the solicitor is acting for both parties; and the solicitor must accept responsibility for any misunderstanding or confusion that might subsequently arise if he has indeed failed to provide such information to his clients (Case 660/86).

In dismissing charges of alleged Professional Misconduct made against two solicitors, the Tribunal said:

> It would appear from the foregoing that the Respondent, Mr [A], had been instructed by the Complainer to make enquiries relative to the paternity of her child. Where a Solicitor is instructed to carry out investigations, he is entitled to a wide discretion as to the potential witnesses he might precognosce and it is a matter for the judgement of the Solicitor to assess the relative value and importance of each item of information which might be obtained. Furthermore although a Solicitor has a general duty to keep his client informed, such obligation does not extend to each and every action or item of information which is obtained; and in the opinion of the Tribunal the averments as stated above do not contain any averment or sufficient specification as might indicate that the Respondent, Mr [A], could have been guilty of such serious conduct as could support a finding of professional misconduct. . . .
>
> . . . As stated above, a Solicitor is entitled to the widest discretion in regard to pursuing investigations which he is instructed to carry out and it would place an intolerable burden on a Solicitor if he were under a general obligation to seek the consent of his client before making each and every enquiry (Case 567/82).

In dismissing a Complaint brought by a lay complainer (A) against a solicitor (the Respondent), the Tribunal said:

> Being a statutory Tribunal, the Scottish Solicitors' Discipline Tribunal is limited to exercising the powers contained in statute and as these powers do not extend to matters of negligence and incompetence, charges under these headings are only relevant in so far as any such negligence or incompetence might in themselves amount to professional misconduct.

> [A's] letter contains seven separate charges. Four of these charges relate to particular witnesses not being cited or called to give evidence, further charges relate to a witness not being asked a specific question, the precognitions of Crown witnesses not being shown to [A] and finally that [the Respondent] or [Counsel instructed by the Respondent] were also working on three other serious criminal cases at the same time.

> Where a Solicitor is instructed to act in Court proceedings it is an essential part of those instructions that he should have the widest discretion in deciding which witnesses, if any, should be called to give evidence and this discretion will only be open to challenge if it can be shown that the Solicitor acted maliciously, recklessly or with a total disregard for the interests of his client. It is not apparent from [A's] letter whether the decision not to cite or call particular witnesses was determined by [the Respondent] or [Counsel] but in any event there is no suggestion in [A's] letter that [the Respondent] acted maliciously, recklessly or with a total disregard of the interests of [A] and in the absence of such averments, the Tribunal is of the opinion that no further action is called for in relation to these charges.

> Whether a witness should be asked particular questions is similarly a matter for the discretion of the party conducting the proceedings. It is only a member of the Faculty of Advocates who may represent a party before the High Court. It was accordingly [Counsel's] decision whether to ask particular questions of witnesses and any charge of this nature cannot therefore be relevantly made against a Solicitor in such circumstances.

> While a Solicitor is expected to work closely with his client and keep him fully informed, there is no absolute duty on a Solicitor to show every document to his client and this Tribunal is of the opinion that an allegation of failing to show a client two precognitions would not in itself constitute a relevant charge of professional misconduct. ... (Case 583/83).

7.04 DUTY NOT TO MISLEAD CLIENT

In a case where a solicitor, who was responsible for a delay in recording a Disposition following settlement of a transaction, implied in letters to another firm of solicitors, acting on behalf of a lending Building Society, that a firm of solicitors, other than his own, was responsible for the delay in recording the deed, the Tribunal found that the solicitor's explanations to the solicitors acting for the Building Society were inaccurate, evasive and misleading and were tendered recklessly in an attempt to mislead the solicitors acting for the Building Society and that this constituted Professional Misconduct (Case 711/87).

The Tribunal had little sympathy with a solicitor's excuse that he did not inform his clients of a delay in recording their title in circumstances where, at the date of entry, he had paid over the price to the sellers (a substantial institution which had little or no chance of going into liquidation) on a Letter of Undertaking because the solicitor said he did not wish to worry the clients. The Tribunal said:

> It is an essential feature of the relationship between a solicitor and a client that there is absolute trust between them and this can only be achieved if the solicitor is frank and open with his client and keeps his client fully informed in relation to the transaction in which the solicitor is engaged on behalf of the client, particularly if any difficulty arises (Case 815/91).

The solicitor has a duty to advise his client if a transaction is taking an unusual turn, detrimental to the interests of the client. In addition to keeping the client informed of the position, such communication permits the client to consider any steps he should take to safeguard his interests.

Professional Misconduct was established where a solicitor misinformed a client in circumstances where out of his own funds he paid her £440 and conveyed the impression that these funds had been recovered from her former husband by way of maintenance (Case 766/89).

On a number of occasions the Tribunal has found a solicitor guilty of Professional Misconduct when the solicitor failed to inform a Building Society for whom the solicitor was acting, of a material change in circumstances in a loan transaction, as for instance where, after encashing the loan cheque, a problem occurs which prevents the immediate recording of the Standard Security in favour of the Building Society (Case 831/92).

Solicitors must act on the basis of their clients' proper instructions or on the instructions of another solicitor who acts for the client (Code of Conduct, para 5(a)).

As is said below at para. 7.06, a solicitor has a duty to implement timeously a mandate from a new solicitor for a client and forward the client's papers to the new solicitor as well as to deal with the reasonable inquiries of that solicitor (Case 822/91).

In another case the Tribunal said:

The implementation of a Mandate was a head of complaint in relation to [A] and also in the remaining three matters which were the subject of this Complaint. In regard to [A] the circumstances were somewhat unusual in that the Respondent claimed that there was no enclosure with the letter from [A's] new Solicitors, Messrs [C], dated 27th January 1983 which purported to enclose 'a Mandate from [A] of [.....], authorising you to release all the papers and documents which you hold in connection with her tenancy of [.....]'. Whether or not any Mandate was enclosed with that letter, it was clear that [A] had consulted [C] and that it was her wish that the Respondent should deliver all the relevant papers to her new Solicitors. Even without the Mandate, it would have been correct for the Respondent to have forwarded to [C] all the relevant papers relating to [A's] affairs. Alternatively if the Respondent had any doubt regarding the authority of [C] in view of the fact that the Mandate was not enclosed, it would have been appropriate for him to have replied immediately to this letter pointing out that the Mandate had not been enclosed and requesting a substitute Mandate to be sent. What was not acceptable, standing the clear terms of [C's] letter, was for the Respondent to take no action

65

> whatsoever for a period in excess of two weeks, and it is in such circumstances that the Tribunal find the alternative charge established (Case 636/84).

The Tribunal has said that it was quite improper for a solicitor, having received a mandate from a firm of solicitors acting for a former client, to write to the former client in the following terms: 'We require to meet with you as a matter of urgency to discuss this position and the proposed transfer by you to Messrs [.....]', and failure of the former client to reply to such a letter provided no excuse for delay in implementation of the mandate (Case 636/84).

The Tribunal has also said in relation to termination of agency:

> It is the privilege of a client that he can terminate his Solicitor's Agency at any time and, subject to any matter of outstanding fees, it is the former Solicitor's duty in such circumstances to comply without question and as soon as practicable with any request or instruction by that client for the delivery of papers which might be regarded as belonging to that client. In none of the cases considered in this Complaint did the respondent claim any lien. Where there is a change of Solicitor and papers require to be delivered, it is most common for the new Solicitor to prepare a Mandate which is signed by the client and sent on to the former Solicitor for implementation. On many occasions, however, the authority of the new Solicitor is respected without the formality of a Mandate or alternatively the client's request for delivery of papers is contained in a simple letter written direct to the former Solicitor. Whatever the circumstances, the former Solicitor is retaining papers which are no longer those of a client and provided that there is sufficient evidence of the client's authority, it is his duty to comply with any relevant request. Furthermore it is the Solicitor's duty to effect delivery as soon as practicable. The new Solicitor will not have the same knowledge of the client's affairs and it is appropriate that he should have access to such papers as may be available in order to assist him in advising the client. In the interests of the relationship between the new Solicitor and the client, it is essential that the papers should be transmitted as soon as possible in order that the client can be adequately advised by the new Solicitor and it is quite inappropriate for the former Solicitor himself to determine whether or not the delivery of papers should be effected with any degree of urgency (Case 636/84).

7.05 INSTRUCTIONS TO BE PERFORMED DILIGENTLY

Failure to progress a conveyancing transaction with reasonable expedition can amount to Inadequate Professional Services and it has also been found to constitute Professional Misconduct (Case 828/92).

See also Case 831/92, referred to at para 12.08.

Failure to attend with reasonable diligence to a Court case in which the solicitor was acting for defenders in that he failed to appear in Court on one occasion and to take steps to safeguard the position of his clients for some time thereafter, to serve a reponing note timeously and attend a debate in consequence of which a decree of default was pronounced against the clients was found to constitute Professional Misconduct (Case 806/90).

Professional Misconduct was established where a solicitor failed to check that a claim form had been lodged with the Criminal Injuries Compensation Board and failed to make inquiries regarding the same, where the claim form was inadvertently placed in the wrong file. When the client repeatedly pressed for progress reports the solicitor paid the client sums of money from his own funds and failed to check that the claim had been lodged or to make any inquiry as to what might have been happening to it. In the same case Professional Misconduct was also found proved where it was shown that the solicitor had failed to communicate with his client when his client's wife applied to the Court of Session for variation of interim aliment and, accordingly, he failed to instruct the Edinburgh agents with his client's latest financial position and his comments on the motion (Case 682/86).

The Tribunal in a Decision in October 1980 said:

> In this Complaint, the Respondent was charged with professional misconduct in that he
>
> > was in 1972 charged with the professional duty of administering the Estate of the late Mrs [A] and of distributing the residue thereof to or for behoof of her orphaned daughter [B]; and that in connection therewith he failed to take any steps to wind up the Estate between 1972 and 1978, he failed to keep [B's relatives, X and Y] informed. . . .
>
> It is appropriate that the first and second parts of this charge should be separately considered.
>
> It was established that the Respondent commenced the administration of Mrs [A's] Estate and that between 1972 and early 1973 he investigated the estate and made enquiries to ascertain [B's] next of kin for the purpose of presenting a Petition for the appointment of a *Curator Bonis*. During the course of the foregoing, he met [X and Y] on several occasions during 1972 and February 1973 and during this period he informed them of his progress. He also met [B] at this time.
>
> The Respondent explained in evidence that he became apprehensive that if a title was taken to the Estate, [X and Y] would endeavour to have the funds handed over to them, even if a *Curator Bonis* were to be appointed; and accordingly he decided that it was in the interests of [B] not to proceed with the appointment of a *Curator* and the winding up of the Estate. In support of this he pointed to the [X and Y's] financial difficulties about this time, although they stated in evidence that these had been resolved. The Respondent also made reference to the substantial withdrawals from the [.....] in 1972 and he expressed the opinion from meeting [B] that she was lacking in intelligence. The Respondent did not convey to [X and Y] his decision not to proceed with the Estate or his reasons for not doing so.
>
> It was not disputed that the Respondent had accepted instructions to act in the winding up of Mrs [A's] Estate. Begg in 'Treatise on the Law of Scotland Relating to Law Agents', second edition, page 233, states that
>
> > By the mere acceptance of employment, a Law Agent undertakes to perform, with due diligence and the requisite skill, the business committed to his charge. . . .
>
> The Respondent's explanation did not excuse himself from his duty to wind up Mrs [A's] affairs; and the Tribunal cannot condone the Respondent's measures in acting outwith normal procedure and in conflict with his professional duty, even although the outcome might have been to the ultimate financial advantage of the particular beneficiary. Nevertheless the Tribunal does, with some hesitation, accept that the Respondent's explanation was genuine, and that accordingly his

> failure to proceed with the Executry and to keep [X and Y] informed, fell short of professional misconduct. . . . (Case 470/80).

7.06 DELAY

In a case where the Tribunal found that the facts and circumstances established were insufficient to justify a finding of Professional Misconduct on the ground of *inter alia* 'delay', the Tribunal said:

> It was admitted in the Answers that the Respondent was instructed by [A Ltd] in 1974 and that the Disposition was executed in 1979. But to establish professional misconduct it is necessary to show that there was unconscionable delay on the part of the Respondent and the Tribunal does not accept that the mere lapse of time *per se* transfers the onus to the Respondent to show that there was an acceptable explanation for the delay. There was no evidence that the Respondent had received complaints from [A Ltd] about the delay. Furthermore the Tribunal did not hear the evidence of any of the Directors of [A Ltd], [the seller] or his Agents; and any of those parties could have contributed to the delay. Indeed [A Ltd] might have encouraged delay. There was no attempt to develop the ground and the balance of the purchase price was unpaid. Professional misconduct is always a serious matter, and in the opinion of the Tribunal, substantial evidence on these matters would require to have been led before there could be any finding of material delay on the part of the Respondent (Case 502/81).

Instances of delay which have been found by the Tribunal to constitute Professional Misconduct have included the following:

Failure to implement timeously a mandate from a new solicitor for a client and forward the client's papers to the new solicitor as well as to deal with the reasonable inquiries of that solicitor (Case 822/91).

Where a client had instructed a solicitor to appear in Court on his behalf in connection with a criminal charge but the solicitor failed to do so (Case 822/91).

A culpable failure to respond to reasonable enquiries of the Accountant of Court (Case 671/86; Case 697/87).

Gross and persistent failure to wind up an Executry timeously (Case 786/90).

Gross and persistent failure to render accounts timeously in various matters e.g. conveyancing and executries (Case 786/90).

Failing to carry through the necessary conveyancing for the sale of a property belonging to a client resulting in the date of entry passing without any acceptable explanation for the failure to complete the business timeously (Case 822/91).

Failing for a period of fourteen months to prosecute a client's claim for personal injuries with reasonable diligence (Case 671/86).

Failing to look after the interests of a client in an action for payment served on the client in that he allowed an undefended decree to pass against the client (Case 671/86).

In a case where a solicitor who had been instructed by a client in relation to a claim for personal injury, allowed the triennium to expire without raising an action and then took Counsel's Opinion as to the position, but failed over a period of several months to inform his client as to the contents of that Opinion, and thereby deprived the client of the advice she was entitled to receive on the basis of the Opinion, the Tribunal found Professional Misconduct established because by withholding this information the solicitor had in effect deceived his client into believing that matters were taking their ordinary course (Case 785/90).

Delay in carrying out instructions of a client to enforce a decree for aliment (Case 778/89).

Delay in progressing an action of divorce (Case 778/89).

Failing or delaying inordinately in the compilation of proper and accurate accounts in a trust (Case 734/88).

Unreasonable delay in the procedure for appointment of a *curator bonis* (Case 713/87).

Delaying unreasonably in paying to a client a sum of money recovered on behalf of the client from the Criminal Injuries Board for a period of some 17 days (Case 822/91).

Gross and persistent failure to communicate with Messrs [X & Y] who had a legitimate interest on behalf of their client [A] to have judicial expenses ascertained, and gross and persistent failure to prepare, lodge and tax an account of expenses, despite repeated reminders (Case 632/85).

See also the cases cited in para 6.08.

7.07 WITHDRAWAL OF INSTRUCTIONS

A Bank instructed a solicitor to prepare security documents on its behalf. After considerable delay on the part of the solicitor, the Law Department of the Bank carried out a search and found that no Disposition in favour of the borrowers, and no Standard Security in favour of the Bank, had been recorded. On [. . .] 1983 the Law Department wrote to the Respondent's firm withdrawing their instructions to the Respondent's firm to act on behalf of the Bank and intimating that they would instruct other solicitors to do so. Seven days later the solicitor recorded the Disposition in favour of the borrowers and the Standard Security in favour of the Bank, having signed the warrant of registration as agents for the Bank, contrary to the instructions contained in the Law Department's letter of [. . .] 1983.

In finding the solicitor guilty of Professional Misconduct in his continuing to act for the Bank notwithstanding the withdrawal of their instructions, the Tribunal said:

> After the Respondent received the letter of [. . .] 1983 from the Bank which withdrew his instructions, he had a duty to cease acting forthwith. In his evidence, the Respondent claimed that he gained the impression from a telephone call to a member of the staff of the Bank that it would have been in order to proceed and record the Standard Security; but this confusion only arose because the Respondent did not have due regard to the written instructions from the Bank instructing him to withdraw from acting (Case 646/84).

See also Case 660/86, para 10.03, and Case 611/85, para 12.02.

7.08 TERMINATION OF AGENCY

> *Solicitors shall not act, nor shall they cease to act for clients summarily or without just cause, in a manner which would prejudice the course of justice* (Code of Conduct, para 5(f)).

In a case where a solicitor had arranged to represent two clients in a Trial in the Sheriff Court on 29th April, the Tribunal said:

> . . . The Respondent was representing two accused in the Sheriff Court trial, there was no Medical Certificate for [client A] and there remained the possibility that [client B's] trial might proceed.
>
> Even if the Respondent had intended to cease acting for [client B] on the following day, he had misdirected himself on that matter. In certain circumstances, a Solicitor undoubtedly has the right to withdraw from acting. Indeed in *Monteith v HM Advocate* 1965 SLT (N) 41, Lord Clyde (with whom Lord Carmont and Lord Migdale agreed) observed:
>
>> We should take the opportunity of dispelling the idea that any professional adviser acting under this Legal Aid Scheme is bound to carry on the defence even though he is satisfied that the defence is a dishonest one or that any Judge is bound automatically to grant a postponement of the case whenever the professional adviser retires from the case because his client refuses to take his advice.
>
> But a solicitor may only exercise his right to withdraw provided he has good cause, and on giving reasonable notice. Where appropriate the solicitor should also obtain the consent of the relevant Legal Aid Committee and the Court. What constitutes 'good cause' may be largely subjective on the part of the Solicitor and this Tribunal hesitates to comment on whether the Respondent might have had good cause to withdraw at any time from acting for one of the co-accused, but if it had been his intention so to withdraw from acting for [client B], the Respondent ought to have given reasonable notice of his intention. There was no evidence that the Respondent forewarned [client B], of his intention prior to 29th April; and by leaving [client B] to renew the motion [for an adjournment] he did not provide himself with the opportunity to obtain the consent of the Court to his withdrawal in the event of the motion being refused.
>
> In leaving [client B] to renew the motion, the Respondent not only neglected the interest of his client, but showed gross disrespect to the Court (Case 636/84).

7.09 RESPONSIBILITY FOLLOWING DEATH OF PARTNER

Where a solicitor (X) who had acted as *curator bonis* for a number of wards, died, the Respondent, who had been one of two partners of X before his death, was found guilty of Professional Misconduct *inter alia* on the grounds of delaying unreasonably to give attention to the wards. The Tribunal said:

> It was apparent that prior to Mr [X's] death, the Respondent's firm acted for each of the wards with the instructions coming from Mr [X] in his capacity as curator. Upon Mr [X's] death the wards did not necessarily cease to be clients of the firm. It is significant that for the purposes of section 53A, subsection (8) provides that 'solicitor' and 'client' have the same meaning as in section 42A(8) and that the term 'solicitor' is defined therein as to include a firm of solicitors, whether or not there has been any change in the partnership of that firm. Accordingly the Respondent must accept that as an ongoing partner of his firm, he continued to be in a solicitor/client relationship with each of the wards and that the provisions relating to inadequate professional services could accordingly relate to the Respondent even after Mr [X's] death (Case 880/94).

8

SOLICITOR'S PERSONAL INTERESTS

8.01 IMPARTIAL ADVICE

Solicitors must not permit their own personal interests or those of the legal profession in general to influence their actings on behalf of clients; . . .

Where solicitors are consulted about matters in which they have a personal or a financial interest the position should be made clear to the clients and where appropriate solicitors should insist that the clients consult other solicitors (Code of Conduct, para 2).

In a situation where a solicitor was acting for a lender, and he himself was the borrower and had recorded a Discharge of a security prior to repaying the loan, the Tribunal stated that any variation of the normal procedure whereby the solicitor should only record the Discharge after the loan had been repaid, even for a relatively brief period would require that the lender should be given independent advice so that he was fully appraised of the risks in such an arrangement. Since in the particular transaction being considered the solicitor was acting not only for the lender but was also himself the borrower, and consequently the prospective beneficiary of any benefit accruing from the arrangement, he was not in a position to give such independent advice (Case 832/92).

The Tribunal had to consider a case where a solicitor approached a personal friend/client for financial assistance for his own business and the client agreed to help. The solicitor negotiated a loan which was secured over the client's property and the loan money was retained by the solicitor. The Tribunal found the solicitor guilty of acting in a conflict of interest situation in that he acted as a solicitor in a transaction where he was unable to give, and knew that he was unable to give, impartial advice to his client, having regard to his own distinct separate and material financial interest, and when he found himself unable to maintain payments to the creditor he made no attempt to advise the client about the situation nor to insist that the client obtain independent legal advice and that the foregoing amounted to Professional Misconduct. In its Decision the Tribunal stated:

> It is a long-established principle that a solicitor should not act for more than one party to a transaction where the interests of parties conflict, and this particularly applies where one of the interests is that of the solicitor himself; and in Begg on Law Agents, 2nd edition, page 295, it is observed that
>
>> Where a law agent proposes to enter into a contract with a client or to obtain from him a conveyance or other deed in his own favour, his proper course is, in the first place, to see that the client's interests are committed to the charge of

72

another and independent law agent, and in the second place to supply the new agent with all the information possessed by himself.

In this transaction, the matter ought to have been abundantly clear to the Respondent as he was acting for [the client] in relation to a transaction in which between them he was the only party to receive any benefit. The Respondent had an absolute duty to advise his client to be separately represented. He failed to do so and it is in these circumstances that the Tribunal takes a most serious view of the events which occurred in June 1985, even if the Respondent had subsequently been in [a] position to repay the loan monies in full and discharge the security. By his own actings, he put his client financially at risk: the effect of the Standard Security was to expose the particular property in the event of the Respondent defaulting on the loan and [the client] was given no protection if these circumstances were to arise.

[The client] was entitled to separate legal representation and the Respondent had an overriding professional responsibility to direct [the client] to seek independent advice. That requirement exists not only in the interests of the client but also to protect the solicitor from any suggestion that there was undue influence or that the client was not adequately advised. Counsel suggested that [the client] might still have been prepared to enter into the arrangement even if [the client] had been separately advised—which would imply that the standard of advice given by the Respondent was not less than what would have been conveyed by another solicitor, but the strength of the principle requiring the client to be separately advised is such that it is unnecessary for the Tribunal to contemplate what was speculated by Counsel, and the Respondent must accept the full consequences of failing to respect his client's position and ensure that [the client] had the independent advice to which [the client] was entitled.

The second stage of the matter began ... when the Respondent found himself unable to service the loan. At that point, it became inevitable that the finance company would take steps to call up the loan and this course of action would be against [the client] or [the client's] property. With this background, [the client] should have been advised to consider [the] position in relation to the Respondent and, given that the Respondent was still acting for [the client], his duty was to terminate his solicitor/client relationship and to advise [the client] to seek independent legal advice. An independent solicitor would have been able to take immediate steps in an endeavour to protect [the client's] financial position in relation to the Respondent and seek to negotiate even in the short term, an acceptable arrangement with the Finance Company (Case 783/90).

In a case where a solicitor was charged that he acted in the preparation, signature and recording of a Standard Security in circumstances where he knew that he was unable to give impartial advice to the granters because of his own separate interests in the transaction, the Tribunal stated:

Even before the introduction of the Solicitors (Scotland) Practice Rules 1986, it has always been recognised that a client should be in a position to look to his solicitor for advice and obtain advice, which is not only independent and impartial but can be seen to be independent and impartial in that the solicitor is not representing the interests of any other connected party. Where the solicitor is himself a connected party, the client is unable to look to the solicitor for the independent advice to which he is entitled and there is a resultant conflict of interest situation in which the solicitor should not act for the client. The emphasis must be on the conflict of interest and a solicitor is not entitled to act or continue to act until an actual dispute arises, as the essence of the conflict of interest principle is to prevent the solicitor from acting in circumstances which could result in a conflict between the solicitor and his client or two clients of the same solicitor.

Later in the same case the Tribunal said:

> The Profession condemns any course of action by a solicitor which is for his own personal benefit and adverse to the interests of his client; and this applies even although there is a degree of relationship, as the members of a solicitor's family are entitled to the same protection as any other clients. The public are entitled to know that the solicitors' profession regards it as an important principle that every client has a right to independent advice and that a solicitor has a duty to ensure that his client is separately advised where the solicitor's personal interests are involved (Case 789/90).

The solicitor was found guilty of Professional Misconduct by the Tribunal and appealed against the conviction. The Court in refusing the Appeal said *inter alia*:

> There was some discussion as to the relevance of a passage in Begg on Law Agents (2nd ed), p 295, to which the Tribunal were referred. It is in these terms: 'Where a law agent proposes to enter into a contract with a client or to obtain from him a conveyance or other deed in his own favour, his proper course is, in the first place, to see that the client's interests are committed to the charge of another and independent law agent, and in the second place to supply the new agent with all the information possessed by himself.' Counsel for the petitioner submitted that this passage had been taken out of context, since the introduction to it on p 294 shows that it is concerned with the disabilities which arise from the existence of a fiduciary relationship which disqualifies the dominant party from dealing or transacting as freely as with a stranger. It was said that, in so far as the passage may be taken as a warning to solicitors, it provides a warning of the risk that transactions of this character may be unenforceable or reduced, not that the solicitor may be exposed to a finding of misconduct. But the significance of the passage in the present context is that it recognises the underlying principle that a solicitor ought not to enter into any contracts or transactions with his client where his own personal interests may be in conflict. The fact that such contracts may be set aside on grounds of public policy is merely one aspect of the effects of that principle. Another is that actings of that character are now capable of being dealt with as professional misconduct by the Tribunal, irrespective of whether resort to litigation of the kind envisaged by Begg has become necessary (*Doran v Council of the Law Society of Scotland* 1992 SLT 456 at 459).

The Tribunal found a solicitor (A) guilty of professional misconduct in that he failed to disclose to his clients the fact that the person making the offer to purchase from his clients was one of his partners and failed to require or recommend to them to seek independent advice and took their instructions to conclude the bargain by accepting the offer. The Tribunal further found [B, C and D who were all partners of A] guilty of professional misconduct in that they failed in their professional duty to make appropriate enquiries in order to ensure that their clients were fully conversant with their personal interest in the transaction and were advised accordingly.

The property in question had been specifically bequeathed to the sellers by a testator whose executors were A and B; the sellers gave instructions to the Respondents' firm to sell the property. In its Decision, the Tribunal said:

On behalf of the complainers, [the Fiscal] referred to the following authorities:

McPherson's Trustees v *Watt* 1877 5 R(HL) 9
Clelland v *Morrison* 1878 6 R 156
Aitken v Campbell 1909 SC 1217
Spector v *Ageda* [1971] 3 All ER 417
RS and Others v *Law Society of Scotland*, unreported
Begg on Law Agent[s], 2nd edition, pages 295, 300, 345
Gloag on Contract, pages 524–526
Walker on Contract, pages 294/5
A Guide to the Professional Conduct of Solicitors, 1974
Webster: *Professional Ethics and Practice*

and [Counsel for one of the Respondents] also referred to the case of *Mair* v *Wood* 1948 SC 83.

The first Charge as amended related only to [A] and averred that in circumstances where a clear conflict of interest had arisen, he failed to disclose to his clients the fact that the person making the offer to purchase was one of his partners. He failed to require or recommend to them to seek independent advice and took their instructions to conclude the bargain.

The relationship between [C] and [the sellers] in itself requires examination. Lord Gifford in *Clelland* v *Morrison* at page 169 observed that 'employment of a firm is employment of all the partners' and the effect of this is that it was as if [A] had submitted an offer in his own name to [the sellers]. In such circumstances [A] had an absolute duty to disclose this interest to [the sellers] and on the authority of *McPherson's Trustees* v *Watt* his failure to disclose was fatal to the validity of the transaction.

[A] himself conceded in evidence that in submitting [C's] offer to [the sellers], a conflict of interest situation had arisen and on his behalf [his Counsel] acknowledged that he failed in his duty to inform them that the offer came from one of his partners. The question before the Tribunal was whether such failure to disclose [C's] interest and the consequent failure to direct his clients to seek independent legal advice and his action in taking instructions to conceal the bargain amounted to professional misconduct.

It was observed by [Counsel for A] that there was no evidence that [the sellers] had been prejudiced, that [the sellers] had received the difference between the respective sale prices together with interest, that there was no charge of conspiracy or dishonesty and that there was no complaint from [the sellers].*

These factors have been taken into consideration but it is significant that judicial authority has been strongly critical in cases where a Solicitor has failed to disclose his personal interest or that of his partner, Lord O'Hagan in *McPherson's Trustees* v *Watt* at page 17 observing:

if the purchase be made covertly . . . the law condemns and invalidates it utterly.

In the particular circumstances, [A] had a duty not only to disclose that the offer had been submitted by his partner but also to direct his client to seek separate legal advice. In failing to fulfil these duties, and in proceeding to accept instructions to conclude the bargain, [A] acted reprehensibly and in the opinion of this Tribunal that amounted to professional misconduct. . . .

8.01 IMPARTIAL ADVICE

The Tribunal found that two further charges were not established and then said:

> ... The final charge was that [B, D and C] failed to make appropriate enquiries to ensure that their clients were fully conversant with their personal interest in the transaction and advise accordingly. On the basis of the observation by Lord Gifford (*supra*) [the sellers] were clients of each of them. [C] knew that the offer was addressed to clients of his firm and in the opinion of this Tribunal it was not sufficient for him to leave the offer with [A]. He had a duty at least to enquire from [A] whether [the sellers] had been informed of his personal interest. [D] and [B] had similarly a duty when they each became aware of the transaction between a partner of their firm and [the sellers]. [B] may only have become aware of his partners' interest when he signed the conveyance but the circumstances whereby one of his partners was purchasing a property from clients were exceptional and even at the stage of signing the deed, [B] should immediately have enquired whether [the sellers] had been fully informed and suitably advised. This was not a matter of [B D and C] 'checking on' their partner but merely fulfilling a duty incumbent on each of them personally because of their separate involvement in the transaction. Their failure to make such enquiry was in itself inexcusable and reprehensible and amounted to professional misconduct. . . . (Case 568/82).

* Following the initial purchase the property had been resold at a higher price than that originally paid to the sellers and it was the subsequent purchaser who brought the matter to the attention of the Complainers.

8.02 BEQUESTS TO SOLICITOR

> *[N]either a solicitor, nor a partner of that solicitor, is generally permitted to prepare a will for a client where the solicitor is to receive a significant legacy or share of the estate* (Code of Conduct, para 2)

The Tribunal had to consider a case where a solicitor had prepared wills for four clients which contained legacies in his favour. All the testators were still alive at the time a Complaint alleging Professional Misconduct was brought against the solicitor. The solicitor for the Respondent suggested that the present rule was largely there to protect solicitors from a charge arising out of facility and circumvention. He claimed that the particular legacies were relatively small having regard to the value of the respective estates and that in any event the Respondent's actings did not justify being stigmatised with a finding of Professional Misconduct. The Tribunal said:

> [I]f a client seeks to leave a solicitor more than a token legacy the client must be sent to another solicitor for independent advice; and it follows that if the client is unwilling to consult another solicitor then the proposed legacy must be excluded from the Will.

> The solicitor for the Respondent attempted to put the particular legacies into perspective by having regard to the present-day value of each testator's estate but in times of high inflation or in the event of a lengthy period of incapacity, the eventual value of a testator's estate may increase or decrease significantly between the making of a Will and the date of death. In any event, it would be wholly

inappropriate for the Tribunal to set down what figure or what proportion of a testator's estate would constitute the upper limit of a 'token' legacy. . . .

Later in the same case the Tribunal said:

> In considering the gravity of the Respondent's conduct, it requires to be taken into account that he had prepared Wills for four separate clients containing substantial legacies in his own favour. The profession has been frequently reminded of the particular principle and it is not accepted as an excuse that the Respondent only thought that the principle applied to bequests of residue and that the various testators insisted on the particular bequests. In relation to a client's instructions, the principle is absolute; and if the client insists on making such a bequest he must be directed to another firm. The solicitor cannot under any circumstances continue to act for the testator in relation to such Will (Case 780/90).

In 1972 a solicitor (the Respondent) accepted instructions from his client, Miss D, to prepare a Will for her in terms of which she bequeathed the residue of her estate equally between the Respondent and her medical practitioner, whom failing to members of their respective families. Miss D did not receive independent legal advice in relation to the Will and the Respondent did not advise Miss D to seek such advice. In 1975 the Respondent advised Miss D that the Will was open to question and that another solicitor would require to be instructed. Miss D accepted the Respondent's advice and she instructed him to prepare a new Will. The Respondent approached another solicitor, Mr M, of another firm (X & Y) who agreed to assist and the Respondent prepared and typed the new Will and at the suggestion of Mr M added the name X & Y on the backing in place of the Respondent's own firm's name. The new Will was in identical terms to the 1972 Will. Mr M went over the terms of the 1975 Will with Miss D, which she understood, and she signed the Will in the presence of Mr M and another party outwith the presence of the Respondent. There were two subsequent Codicils signed by Miss D and the Respondent explained that he deliberately decided not to involve another solicitor because it was apparent that the effect of the Codicils was to diminish the Respondent's prospective benefit. The Tribunal in finding the Respondent guilty of Professional Misconduct said:

> The Respondent was charged with professional misconduct in that:
>
> > [I]n gross breach of well-established proper professional practice, he [the Respondent] accepted instructions from his client, Miss [D], for the preparation of the testamentary writings and prepared said deeds, and caused said deeds to be executed by her, when he knew that by their terms she made and intended to make a substantial testamentary gift to himself, whom failing to members of his family, and that she had not obtained independent legal advice on the matter;
>
> In his Answers, the Respondent admitted Professional Misconduct in relation to the original Will in 1972 but the remainder of the charge was resisted.
>
> The Fiscal for the Complainers submitted that although the 1975 Will *ex facie* appeared to have been prepared by an independent solicitor, the Respondent had not sufficiently distanced himself from Mr M. He argued that the Respondent was also culpable in relation to the two Codicils. The effect of each Codicil was to

confirm the provisions of the relevant Will, and in particular the second Codicil actually dealt with the residue. The testamentary provisions still left to the Respondent a major share of Miss [D's] estate. The Respondent's benefit was indeed substantial, amounting to some £65,000.

The Fiscal referred to the advice in Begg on *Law Agents*, second edition, 1883:

> Where a law agent proposes to enter into a contract with a client or to obtain from him a conveyance or other deed in his own favour, his proper course is, in the first place, to see that the client's interests are committed to the charge of another and independent law agent, and in the second place to supply the new agent with all the information possessed by himself.

And at page 306, quoting from *Grieve* v *Cunningham* 8 M 317:

> In many, perhaps most cases, the presumption against the deed created by the mere circumstance that the party favoured is the law agent who prepared it, will supply the want of all other element of fraudulent impetration. It never can be the proper course, in any ordinary circumstances, for a law agent so to act, and it will always be upon him to show that the making of the settlement in his favour was the free and uninfluenced act of the testator, deliberately entertained and carried through with an entire knowledge of its effect.

These cases were only concerned with the validity of the particular testamentary writings but in *Re a Solicitor* [1975] QB 475 at 483 Lord Widgery observed:

> The question of how far the Solicitor is bound to see that his client is separately advised, and what are the consequences of a failure in that duty, can arise in two different spheres and be judged by two different sets of rules. Often enough, as indeed in this case, a will is challenged on the basis that a beneficiary is a solicitor and that the solicitor did not take the steps which the law regards as necessary to protect the client against undue influence. When those cases arise of course they arise in the ordinary courts of the land, and the law has laid down the standards with which a solicitor is required to comply. The second way in which the question may arise is in disciplinary proceedings such as the present. In disciplinary proceedings the standards are not necessarily the same as they are in a probate action and they are far less well defined, because, whereas judgements of the courts find their way into the law reports, it cannot always be said that the same thing happens about expressions of opinion by the Law Society.

The Fiscal also referred to the advice contained in *A Guide to the Professional Conduct of Solicitors*, 1974, p 23:

> Where the testator intends to make a gift by his Will to his solicitor or a partner of his or a member of the solicitor's staff or to the families of any of them and the gift is of a significant amount, either in itself or having regard to the size of the testator's estate and to other normal claims on his bounty, then the solicitor should advise the testator to be independently advised as to that bequest. If the testator refuses to be independently advised and presses the solicitor to act, the solicitor must persist in his refusal to act. It is not sufficient for the will merely to be attested by an independent solicitor.

This advice was repeated in the *Journal of the Law Society of Scotland*, June 1983, p 277. R. M. Webster in his *Professional Ethics and Practice for Scottish Solicitors*, first edition (1976), similarly advised:

> [T]here is no reason why a client should not leave money in his will to a solicitor, who may have given much help and friendship exceeding the bounds of pro-

fessional duty over the years, but if a client wants to do this you *must* send him to another solicitor for independent advice,

and this advice is largely repeated in the second edition (1984), p 13.

The Fiscal distinguished the present case from the circumstances in *Weir* v *Grace* 1898 1F 253 and 1899 2 F (HL) 30. In that case the Solicitor had brought in his Edinburgh correspondent. It was that solicitor who prepared the Will and it was his clerk who attended on the testator. The Fiscal submitted that the Respondent had not sufficiently distanced himself in the making of either of the Wills or the Codicils. The Respondent had apparently never considered the professional propriety of his actings and his active involvement in the preparation of the various testamentary writings constituted a gross breach of proper professional practice.

The Solicitor for the Respondent accepted the Fiscal's statement of the law. However, he pointed out that in the particular circumstances the onus was on the solicitor to establish that there had been no undue influence on the testator and that the purpose of the professional obligation was to protect the solicitor from such a charge. The Respondent had advised Miss [D] that another solicitor had to be instructed. The Will had been typed within the Respondent's office, but the typing of [X & Y's] name on the backing (at Mr [M's] suggestion) demonstrated that Mr [M] was taking responsibility for the Will. When he called at Miss [D's] house, the Respondent's participation had only been to introduce Mr [M] to Miss [D]. He then withdrew, the reason being that it might otherwise have been more difficult to repel a charge of undue influence. It was accepted that the measures adopted by the Respondent in 1975 had been misconceived, but it was submitted that he had done enough to distance himself to the extent that his actings fell short of being 'serious and reprehensible' such as might constitute Professional Misconduct. The Solicitor for the Respondent added that if the Tribunal did not make any finding in relation to the 1975 Will, then the Tribunal should accept that the Codicils, having the effect of lessening the Respondent's benefit, could not in themselves take the Respondent into the area of Professional Misconduct.

The procedures to be followed by a solicitor in preparing a will for a client are firstly to take instructions and to advise the client in relation to these instructions, thereafter to prepare the will in accordance with these instructions and finally to arrange for the will to be executed. These procedures are closely interlinked and throughout the solicitor must be satisfied that the proposed will is in accordance with the testator's wishes. However, in the event of the solicitor ascertaining that it is the testator's wish to confer a significant benefit on the solicitor or indeed to the solicitor's partner or member of staff or to the families of any of them, then the solicitor has a duty not to proceed further but to advise his client to be separately represented. It is then for the independent solicitor to take instructions and advise the testator, prepare the testamentary deed and have the same executed. The purpose of this rule is not simply to protect the solicitor in the event of a charge of undue influence. As appears from the authorities quoted by the Fiscal, the rule is of long standing and is based on the principle that the employment of a solicitor involves a very high degree of trust and influence. As Lord Widgery pointed out, the propriety of a solicitor's actings is an entirely separate matter from the validity of the testamentary writing or the particular bequest. At no time during the Hearing was it suggested that the Respondent might have exercised undue influence on Miss [D], and it is outwith the jurisdiction of this Tribunal to consider the validity of Miss [D's] testamentary writings. The Respondent acknowledged that when he arranged for the substitute Will in 1975 and thereafter prepared the Codicils in 1978 and 1981, he had only been concerned that there might subsequently be a suggestion of undue influence, and the arrangements which he made in 1975 were merely to protect himself from any such charge. There was no suggestion in the Complaint nor was it averred by the Fiscal that there was anything improper in having the name of Mr [M's] firm placed on the backing of the 1975 Will; and the Tribunal accepts that this was done on the suggestion of Mr [M].

In considering the propriety of the Respondent's actings in 1975, it is appropriate to have regard to the separate participation of the Respondent and Mr [M]. The Respondent initially advised Miss [D] that an independent solicitor would require to be instructed but as was emphasised in *Re a Solicitor* [1975] QB at 484:

> It is not sufficient from a disciplinary point of view for a solicitor to tell his client that she ought to be separately advised. This standard requires that he should tell her that she must be separately advised, and if she refuses to accept that advice and refuses to go to another solicitor, then the standard laid down requires that the solicitor beneficiary should forego his benefit.

In the preparation of a Will, there is a close relationship between the advice which may be given by the solicitor and the instructions given to the solicitor by the client, and the preparation of the Will is largely dependent on the outcome of such instructions. It is particularly significant that in 1975, Miss [D's] instructions to prepare a substitute Will were given to the Respondent outwith Mr [M's] presence and it was the Respondent who proceeded to have the Will prepared on the basis of these instructions. In the opinion of the Tribunal, the circumstances of these instructions are critical and if the Respondent had genuinely sought to distance himself he ought to have arranged for Mr [M] to meet with Miss [D] and for Mr [M] to take her instructions before the Will was prepared. It was only at that stage that Mr [M] could properly have advised Miss [D] in relation to her proposed testamentary provisions. As it happened, Mr [M] only met Miss [D] on a visit which had been arranged for the signing of the new Will. The Tribunal accepted the evidence of Miss [B] to the effect that Mr [M] went over the terms of the new Will carefully with Miss [D] and that he was satisfied that she fully understood the provisions of the same; but such procedures fall short of advising the testator at the time when the instructions were being given. At the visit on 12th March 1975, Miss [D] would have known that the new Will had been extended for her signature. The stage had passed when she might ordinarily have given instructions *de novo* and to put it no higher, there would be a certain expectation on Miss [D] to sign the new Will as prepared. In the opinion of the Tribunal, the Respondent was culpable in taking matters to that stage before introducing Mr [M] to Miss [D]. Whilst he advised Miss [D] that an independent solicitor was required, he did not ensure that Miss [D] was independently advised in relation to the preparation of the Will. The Respondent continued to act for Miss [D] in relation to the Will and it was solely in relation to the execution of the Will that Mr [M] was involved. In effect, the Respondent continued to act as Miss [D's] solicitor during the whole process of the making of this Will. This was in direct contravention of the established rule, and in the opinion of the Tribunal the participation of Mr [M] at the time of execution did not materially diminish the Respondent's culpability. On his own admission, the propriety of his actings had not occurred to him. Even for an inexperienced solicitor, this conduct would have been inexcusable. Solicitors are privileged to enjoy a close position of trust with their clients and this Tribunal will always take a very serious view of any circumstances where that relationship of trust has not been respected.

The Respondent did not trouble to involve an outside solicitor in the preparation of either of the Codicils in 1978 and 1981. It is accepted that each of these Codicils had the effect of diminishing the Respondent's testamentary benefit; but nevertheless even in preparing a Codicil, it is a solicitor's duty to review the prior extant testamentary writing. In taking instructions for a Codicil the proposed variations cannot be taken in isolation and it is necessary for the solicitor to advise the testator in relation to her whole testamentary provisions. On each occasion, the intended benefit to the Respondent ought to have been a matter which was the subject of consideration in relation to the testamentary provisions as a whole, and in the opinion of the Tribunal, the Respondent was again culpable in failing to advise Miss [D] to be separately advised and thereafter in continuing to take instructions and proceed with the preparation and execution of each Codicil. It was also pointed out that each Codicil contained the phrase 'and except in so far as hereby altered I confirm my (said Will and Codicil) and direct that (they and this additional Codicil) shall be read together and construed as forming one document,' but these words in themselves are largely words of style.

In terms of Miss [D's] Will, the Respondent and the other executors were bequeathed a legacy of £100 each. This was not the subject of any specific averment in the Complaint. However, it is not uncommon for such a bequest to be made to an executor and the Tribunal would have had no criticism of the Respondent's actings if his benefit under the Will had been confined to such bequest (Case 699/87).

In a later case the Tribunal said:

The Rule that a solicitor should not take instructions to prepare a Will containing a substantial benefit in his own favour, is long established, and from time to time the profession has been reminded of the importance of involving another solicitor in the whole process from the point when the instructions are taken through to the execution of the Will itself.

There are two recognised exceptions. It is accepted that a solicitor may ordinarily make a Will for his spouse, his parents or children and perhaps his collaterals on the understanding that any potential beneficiary is not materially disadvantaged but this Tribunal would be slow to accept that this exception might apply to more remote relations or those for whom there is no direct family connection.

The other exception concerns the amount of the legacy. There can ordinarily be no objection to a solicitor preparing a Will which contains the specific bequest of a small item in the testator's estate or a relatively small pecuniary legacy. However, it has never been suggested that this principle should extend to a share of the residue, however small a proportion that might be, and a possible reason for this is illustrated by the fact that the value of [. . . . .]'s estate practically doubled between the time when she had made her last Will and her death.

The Tribunal then considered the test in *Sharp* v *Council of the Law Society of Scotland* 1984 SC 129 as to whether Professional Misconduct had been established and said:

The rule that a solicitor should not take instructions to make a Will containing a substantial bequest in his favour has its foundation at common law and is not covered by any statutory provision or Practice Rule. Nevertheless in the opinion of the Tribunal, it is appropriate that the same test should apply to the breach of a common law rule in determining whether there has been professional misconduct.

In accordance with the test set out by the Lord President in *Sharp* the Tribunal proceeded to consider the gravity of the solicitor's actings and found in the particular case:

> [H]aving regard to the whole circumstances, and in particular his close relationship with the deceased, his actings on this occasion fell marginally short of what might be stigmatised as serious and reprehensible. Nevertheless having regard to the importance of the Rule, it was right and proper that the Law Society should have brought this Complaint to the Tribunal and this recognition is reflected in the finding of expenses against the Respondent.

The Tribunal also said:

> It was also mentioned that when the matter was drawn to the Respondent's attention by the Law Society, he renounced the residuary bequest, but this took place about a year after the testator's death. The essential part of the rule is that the solicitor should not take instructions or make such a Will and if *per incuriam* such a Will is made outwith the solicitor's knowledge, it is his duty to renounce the bequest at the earliest possible date (Case 755/89. See also Case 559/82).

9

CONFLICT OF INTEREST

9.01 CONFLICT OF INTEREST

Solicitors (including firms of solicitors) shall not act for two or more clients in matters where there is a conflict of interest between the clients or for any client where there is a conflict between the interest of the client and that of the solicitor or the solicitor's firm (Code of Conduct, para 3).

In a case heard by the Tribunal in 1987, the Tribunal said:

In recent years the question of solicitors acting in a conflict of interest situation has been a matter of increasing concern and solicitors are now expected to adopt a strict approach whenever a conflict situation arises (Case 690/86).

A solicitor (the Respondent) acting for Trustees also acted for the purchaser of ground from the Trustees and attended to the recording of a Disposition to the purchaser. It later became apparent that the Disposition to the purchaser included an area of ground to which a neighbour already had a title and on which the neighbour had constructed an annexe to his property, and there was no prospect of the neighbour conveying the area in question to the purchaser. At a meeting between the Respondent and the purchaser, the purchaser insisted that he was entitled to the whole ground in the Disposition and in finding the solicitor guilty of Professional Misconduct in continuing to act for the purchaser and the Trustees after a conflict of interest had arisen, the Tribunal said:

At that point there was a clear conflict between the Trustees of [. . . . .] and [the purchaser] and it was the Respondent's duty at that time to cease acting for both parties. The Respondent explained that he continued to act in an endeavour to achieve an acceptable solution, and whereas this might have been permissible in circumstances where there was a defect in the title which could be overcome, this was not the situation here in that there was no possibility of [the Trustees] conveying the remaining ground to [the purchaser] . . . (Case 491/80).

In a case where a solicitor was found guilty of Professional Misconduct in that *inter alia* he continued to act on behalf of both a husband and wife (Mr and Mrs X) when a conflict of interest had arisen between them, the Tribunal said:

The Respondent accepted instructions from his clients Mr and Mrs [X] to attend to the sale of [House A] and [House B]. Subsequently Mrs [X] instructed the Respondent to commence divorce proceedings against Mr [X] and the divorce summons was served on Mr [X] on [. . . .] 1978. The Respondent settled the sale of [House A] on [. . . .] February 1979 and the sale of [House B] on [. . .] April 1979.

It was submitted by the Fiscal for the Complainers in the circumstances where there is a matrimonial dispute between parties who have jointly instructed a Solicitor in a conveyancing matter then the Solicitor should decline to accept any instructions to proceed with a divorce action and should cease acting for either party in the conveyancing transaction. The Fiscal did not claim that the Solicitor was obliged to proceed on the foregoing basis; but he did submit that in such circumstances a Solicitor was under the highest duty to account to the parties expeditiously and remit the proceeds of sale under deduction only of such items as had been authorised by the parties. Between [. . .] February and [. . .] March the Respondent made various payments to Mr [X] from the proceeds of sale of [House A] but it was not until [. . .] April 1979 that the Respondent sent a Cash Statement in connection with the sale of the property. The Respondent did not provide any detailed accounting in respect of the sale of [House B] (other than to state that a specific sum had been placed on deposit receipt) and he did not make any payment prior to the funds in the Respondent's hands being arrested on [. . .] May 1979.

The Tribunal are satisfied in these circumstances that the delay on the part of the Respondent in providing an accounting to Mr [X], amounted to professional misconduct.

The divorce proceedings raised against Mr [X] concluded for aliment for the children of the marriage, a capital sum of [. . .] and periodical allowance for Mrs [X]. In such circumstances, it is likely to have been in Mrs [X's] interest to have any capital monies belonging to Mr [X] retained whereas at the time Mr [X] was anxious to receive early payment of his share of the proceeds of sale of the two heritable properties. The conflicting interest in such circumstances should have caused the Respondent to cease acting for both parties and the Tribunal are satisfied that he was failing in his duties as a Solicitor when he continued to act.

The gravity of this conduct is demonstrated with reference to various debts (including an account to Messrs [Y]) which the Respondent treated as being the joint liability of the parties; and without seeking instructions, he debited these debts from the joint funds before making a division between the parties. By intromitting with funds without authority, the Respondent acted improperly. It was submitted in the Respondent's Answers that the account of [Y] was in fact a joint liability but there was no suggestion that this had been accepted by Mr [X], and in the absence of any authority it was the duty of the Respondent not to deduct any such item (Case 462/80).

See also Case 557/82, referred to at para 7.01, which also deals with issues of conflict of interest arising where a husband and wife, for whom a solicitor has acted, are in dispute.

The Tribunal has said in a case where a solicitor was found guilty of Professional Misconduct when he continued to act for a seller and purchaser in a conveyancing transaction after a conflict had arisen between the clients:

As mentioned above, the Complainers withdrew the charge that the Respondent failed to require the purchasers to seek independent legal advice; but in a conflict situation, a solicitor's duty goes beyond the stage of merely advising one of his clients to be separately represented. It is an established principle within the profession that where a conflict arises, mere advice is not enough and it is always the solicitor's duty forthwith to cease acting for at least one of the parties; and where as a consequence of his previous representation the solicitor is aware of circumstances which might prejudice the interests of that former client then the solicitor must also cease acting for the other client (Case 669/86).

The Tribunal had to consider a case, prior to the introduction of the Solicitors (Scotland) Practice Rules 1986 (which introduced a specific rule regarding Conflict of Interest) where a solicitor (the Respondent) had acted on behalf of both the seller and the purchasers in connection with the sale/purchase of a dwellinghouse. The Tribunal found the Respondent not guilty of Professional Misconduct in respect of the charge that he negotiated and adjusted the price of the house while acting for both the seller and purchasers in circumstances where the parties had adverse and opposite interests, but guilty of Professional Misconduct in respect of the charge that prior to submitting an offer for the purchasers, he failed to inform them of circumstances known to him, namely a history of complaints of serious structural and other defects in the house and that these were still giving cause for concern and to advise them to instruct a suitable expert to inspect and report on the property and in particular to report on the structural stability of the same. In the Note to its Decision the Tribunal said *inter alia*:

The terms of the first charge were that the Respondent

negotiated and adjusted the price of said house while acting for both the seller and the purchasers, notwithstanding the fact that the parties had adverse and opposite interest.

The Fiscal for the Complainers pointed out that this was not a case in which the parties had agreed a price and had jointly come to the Respondent with instructions to conclude missives. In this case [the purchaser] had told the Respondent that he would go up to £X whereas the Respondent had apparently advised [the seller] that the house should fetch between ['£X–£5,000' and '£X']. The Fiscal submitted that the Respondent had 'special knowledge' in respect of each client and that it was accordingly improper for him to continue to act for both clients. Counsel for the Respondent contended that the Respondent had merely acted as a 'conduit' conveying offer and counter-offer between the parties. The Respondent had provided a service, introducing the parties to each other and he had merely carried out the wishes of each party.

Where a bargain is successfully concluded for the sale of heritable property, the actual price is determined partly from objective considerations, namely what similar property is likely to fetch given a willing buyer and a willing seller, but the agreed price for any particular property is also affected by the highest figure which the prospective buyer is willing to offer and the lowest figure which the seller is willing to accept.

The relationship between a solicitor and his buying or selling client may vary considerably depending on the type of property and the particular client involved. In regard to domestic property, it is more common for the client to look to his solicitor for advice. Indeed it was [the purchaser's] evidence that he never had any intention of discussing the matter of price direct with [the] seller and that he was relying on the Respondent to carry out negotiations on his behalf.

Throughout the relevant period, it was accepted that the Respondent was acting as solicitor for both [the seller] and [the purchasers] and it is perhaps appropriate to look at his relationship with each of them at the various stages leading up to the conclusion of the missives.

The Tribunal then proceeded to review and analyse each of the stages leading up to the conclusion of the missives and the Tribunal's Note continued:

Considering the foregoing in relation to the charge, the Respondent was clearly acting for both parties and they undoubtedly had conflicting interests in that each party wished to secure a bargain at the most beneficial price. But was there 'negotiation' of the price by the Respondent? The Respondent transmitted differing figures between the parties but did he give advice to each party in relation to the other party's figure? Taking that question, there was no evidence before the Tribunal that the Respondent actually advised either party in relation to the other party's figures and accordingly on this narrow point, the charge must fall. Nevertheless the Respondent must accept considerable criticism for allowing himself to be put into a position on two separate occasions when he was unable to advise his respective clients when taking instructions from them. If a solicitor requires to take instructions from his client and is not in a position to give his client full and independent advice because of the conflicting interests of another client it is the solicitor's duty immediately to withdraw from acting for that client and to advise that client to be separately represented.

It should be added that the Fiscal very properly referred the Tribunal to the dissenting opinion of Lord Shand in *Watt* v *McPherson's Trustees* 1876 4R 601 at 617/618, which opinion was subsequently upheld on appeal, that decision being reported as *McPherson's Trustees* v *Watt* 1877 5R (HL) 9. In his opinion, Lord Shand observed:

I find no difficulty in realising the position of an agent acting for both buyer and seller in a contract of sale. It is a thing, I apprehend, of daily occurrence. He brings seller and purchaser together; he assists in adjusting the price by telling one what he thinks he should take and the other what he thinks he should give. In doing so he does not act or profess to act as an Arbiter but as an agent giving information and disinterested advice to each party.

Counsel for the Respondent also referred to this passage but did not rely heavily on it. Looking at the decision as a whole, the foregoing was *obiter* and had no direct bearing on the merits of the case which concerned the reduction of missives where the solicitor for the sellers had in fact also been the true purchaser. In the opinion of the Tribunal, the statement by Lord Shand no longer reflects what would be now acceptable practice for a solicitor.

The second charge was

that despite being aware of the history of complaints of serious structural and other defects in said house, and of the fact that these were still giving cause for concern ... the Respondent culpably failed to inform [the purchasers] of the existence of these complaints and to advise them to instruct a suitable expert to inspect and report on the property, and in particular, to report on the structural stability of said house, prior to their submitting said offer.

The Fiscal submitted that the Respondent knew the history of the property and that his failure to inform [the purchasers] was either wilful or as a result of 'shutting his eyes' to the previous circumstances and the Fiscal referred to the observation by Lord President Boyle in *Gray* v *Wardrop's Trustees* 1851 13D 963 at 970.

> When an agent undertakes the solemn duty of acting for both lender and borrower he must never lose sight of the delicacy of his position and he is bound to make the fullest disclosure to the lender of everything that affects the security.

The Tribunal was also referred to the decision in *Spector* v *Ageda* [1971] 3 All ER 417 in which Mr Justice Megarry observed at 430: 'A Solicitor must put at his client's disposal not only his skill but also his knowledge, so far as it is relevant; and if he is unwilling to reveal his knowledge to his client, he should not act for him. What he cannot do is to act for the client and at the same time withhold any relevant knowledge that he has' . . .

The Tribunal's Note later continued:

> There remains the question of the gravity of the Respondent's failure. The Tribunal is satisfied that there was no deliberate intention on the part of the Respondent to withhold information from [the purchasers] but on the basis of the decision in the case of *E* v *T* 1949 SLT 411 Lord President Cooper observed that
>
> > there is negligence and negligence; and I am certainly not prepared to affirm the proposition that according to Scots law and practice professional negligence cannot amount to professional misconduct.
>
> On the basis of the evidence before the Tribunal, there was undoubtedly negligence on the part of the Respondent in failing to disclose the whole circumstances to [the purchasers], and the question before the Tribunal is whether such failure was serious and reprehensible such as might be regarded as professional misconduct. The Respondent has considerable experience and expertise in the sale and purchase of houses. House purchase is an activity which the average person only engages in on a few occasions during his lifetime and it is of critical importance for such purchaser to ensure that he makes a sound investment. In such circumstances there is usually a very great reliance by the client on the professional knowledge and services of the solicitor. This was particularly so in regard to [the purchasers]. They had no previous experience of house purchase in Scotland, they were purchasing a substantial dwellinghouse and as is evidenced by [the purchasers'] insistence on a survey, they were anxious to ensure that the purchase was carefully carried through. The Respondent had recent knowledge of continuing difficulties affecting this property. In so far as there was a possibility of settlement, these difficulties were of a potentially serious nature and if the Respondent had been acting responsibly for his clients, he would have provided them with more than an inspection report carried out for security purposes only. It is in the light of these circumstances that the Tribunal considers the Respondent's omission to have been grave and culpable such as to justify a finding of professional misconduct (Case 630/85).

NB. In Case 663/86 the Tribunal again said in relation to the observation of Lord Shand in *Watt* v *McPherson's Trustees*, quoted in Case 630/85 above, 'that it is no longer accepted practice for a solicitor to advise one party on what is acceptable and the other party on what should be offered'.

In a case heard by the Tribunal in 1989 the Tribunal said:

> It is open to a solicitor to act for two or more parties who may have related interests but in these circumstances, it is the solicitor's duty not only to act with scrupulous

fairness to each party but also to ensure that each client receives the same advice and guidance which they would [have] had if they had been separately advised. However a solicitor should recognise a conflict of interest when the interests of one of the clients are at variance with the interests of another and in such circumstances, it is less [than] responsible for the solicitor to continue acting for both parties, with the excuse that he is merely doing what he has been instructed to do. The solicitor must ensure that the interests of each party are wholly respected at all times. A solicitor should never put himself into a position that he is unable to advise any of his clients when taking instructions from them and if there are significant legal questions to be considered, the solicitor ought to be in a position to give each client independent advice, whether or not either of the clients has consulted the solicitor in respect of any of the outstanding matters. Where a solicitor persists in acting in such circumstances, he puts himself in the position of being unable to give each of his clients the independent advice to which they are entitled.

It is for these reasons that there is the well established principle that where a conflict of interest arises between two clients of a solicitor, it is the solicitor's duty forthwith to cease acting for at least one of the clients and advise that client to be separately represented. In such circumstances, merely advising the client to be separately represented is not enough because each client is entitled to the independent advice of the solicitor and he is unable to provide impartial guidance if he continues to act for the other client even although he is not required to advise the other client in relation to the disputed matter. It is a solicitor's duty to act with scrupulous fairness to each client and it is not open to the solicitor to seek a basis or a formula for a mutually acceptable compromise, for a prerequisite of compromise must be that each client is separately advised on the merits of accepting any such arrangement.

Outwith his professional responsibilities, a solicitor is ordinarily [as] entitled as any other member of the public to enter into commercial ventures but in these circumstances, the solicitor must take particular care if he already has a solicitor/client relationship with another party to such venture or if his professional services are to be provided in relation to the venture. The principle is clearly laid down in the second edition of Begg on Law Agents (page 295):

> Where a law agent proposes to enter into a contract with a client or to obtain from him a conveyance or other deed in his own favour, his proper course is, in the first place, to see that the client's interests are committed to the charge of another and independent law agent, and in the second place to supply the new agent with all the information possessed by himself.

A contract entered into between a solicitor and a client who is not separately represented may be voidable, but in any event a solicitor must not act for a client in a matter in which the solicitor has a personal interest for the obvious reason that in such circumstances the client cannot expect the independent advice to which he is entitled. A solicitor should look carefully at any finance which is provided for his client. It is of course normal for a solicitor to fund a client's outlays in the course of legal business for a client and it is also common practice for bridging loans to be arranged in the solicitor's own name. These arrangements are wholly acceptable. It used to be common, before the advent of Building Societies and the general availability of funds, for solicitors to advance on a long term basis not only other clients' funds but also their own funds; but such arrangements would involve a degree of negotiation and such loans are no longer accepted practice (Case 761/89).

It should be noted that rule 8 of the Solicitors (Scotland) Accounts Rules 1992 makes various provisions regarding bridging loans, including a provision that any contract or arrangement for bridging does not impose personal liability for repayment of any overdraft facilities on the solicitor concerned.

In another case in 1987 the Tribunal had to consider a Complaint where it found Professional Misconduct established in relation to two situations involving the same solicitor. In the first situation the circumstances were somewhat unusual in that a Mr A, notwithstanding the intimation of a claim against him by the Court Department of the Respondent's firm, instructed the Respondent in June 1984 in connection with a house purchase and sale; and after proceedings had been raised by the Court Department he again instructed the Respondent in July 1985 in regard to the sale of his house. In August 1985 the Respondent's partner C instructed an Inhibition on Mr A. At this point the Respondent was still unaware that the Inhibition had been served when he had a brief conversation with his partner C but the Tribunal took the view that the nature of the conversation should have been sufficient to alert the Respondent and in any event the Tribunal considered that the whole circumstances soon became apparent to the Respondent when his client, Mr A, consulted him shortly afterwards and Mr A asked the Respondent whether he could continue at act. The Tribunal in its Note said:

> The Respondent's understanding was that there was no conflict between any of *his* clients in that only Mr [A] was his client and that he had only one duty namely to receive the proceeds of sale of Mr [A's] house and make it over to him. Because the Inhibition was not effected until after the missives had been concluded, the Respondent was of the opinion that the Inhibition should have no effect on the sale and he considered that he could still continue to act for Mr [A], independent of his Court Department, and conclude the transaction.

> It was then that one had the extraordinary situation of Mr [C] instructing arrestments on his own firm; and the Respondent anticipating further diligence and arranging for the purchaser's Solicitors (who were also Mr [A's] own Solicitors in the defence of the action) to effect the settlement of the transaction, and the Respondent advising Mr [A] to open another bank account to avoid the effect of any arrestment. As it happened, [Partner C] was successful in arresting Mr [A's] funds in a bank account with [. . . . .] Bank and also in stopping the movement of Mr [A's] furniture and effects. The Respondent did not dispute that he was trying to avoid diligence when he arranged for the purchaser's solicitors to carry out the settlement but he explained that he did not regard Mr [A's] creditors [X], as his client and that he had no duty towards them.

> The arrestment of Mr [A's] furniture and effects undoubtedly caused considerable inconvenience, resulting in an approach to the Respondent by letter on 22nd September. This was followed by the Respondent examining the [X] file within his office, speaking to his partner [D] (who had overall responsibility for the action) and then responding to Mr [A] on 10th October. The Respondent explained in his evidence that he had finished the sale and that at this point he was not acting for Mr [A]. Indeed in the letter of 10th October the Respondent observed with reference to the litigation that there was no way in which he could take instructions to assist Mr [A]. Nevertheless the Respondent went on in that letter to discuss the

case and comment on the likely outcome. The Respondent added in evidence that he merely made a suggestion which might have been given by the Solicitors acting for Mr [A] in the Court action to try to avoid needless litigation. There was no suggestion that the Respondent was not doing his best to help Mr [A]; but the observations in the letter of 10th October undoubtedly constituted advice, and advice of some considerable significance as it followed on the Respondent's examination of the relevant file and the conversation with Mr [D] (although the latter was not disclosed in the letter of 10th October).

In the second situation the same Respondent had acted for Mr B (who had been introduced to him by the Respondent's partner E, who was acting for Mr B in connection with his matrimonial affairs) in connection with the purchase of a flat from Y who were established clients of the Respondent's firm, and other members of the Respondent's firm dealt with this transaction on behalf of Y. When Mr B obtained access to the flat he made a complaint about the size of the rooms in the flat and suggested a reduction of the price, and the transaction settled on the basis of a retention. Later Mr B wrote to the Respondent about a leak in the roof and the Tribunal in its Note further said:

> The circumstances relating to Mr [B's] transaction were more straightforward in that throughout the transaction, the Respondent was aware of the respective interests of Mr [B] and the other client [Y]. At the relevant time, they were both established clients. The Respondent claimed that he took no part in the negotiations but he acknowledged that it was he who insisted on the penalty clause being inserted in Mr [B's] offer. It was apparent that the Respondent's firm had some superficial concern regarding the differing interests of their respective clients in that during the exchange of missives, the Respondent was in communication with Mr [B] and signed the offer and a subsequent letter on his behalf, whereas [Y] were in communication with an assistant Mr [F], with Mr [F's] letter being signed by another partner Mr [G].

> The Tribunal was not called upon to express any opinion regarding such procedure, but it is significant that the missives were of some complexity and it must be questionable whether such procedures were in the best interests of the respective clients. Thereafter the Respondent left both sides of the transaction with his assistant Mr [F]. However he failed to convey to the Respondent Mr [B's] concern and it was only in September 1982 after Mr [B] had taken entry that the Respondent became aware of Mr [B's] dissatisfaction regarding the size of the rooms in the flat which he had purchased. At this point it ought to have been apparent from Mr [B's] previous correspondence with Mr [F] that Mr [B] felt strongly about the matter and that it was not a problem which was capable of being immediately resolved. The Respondent's understanding was that in strict law Mr [B] only had the choice of resiling from the bargain or accepting the flat as it stood and that the former was not a practical possibility as Mr [B] was anxious to retain occupation of the flat. The Respondent conferred with his then senior partner Mr [H] and consulted with two separate firms of valuers and he offered Mr [B] a 'second opinion' of his partner [E] to ascertain wether Mr [B] had a proper claim for damages against [Y]. It is not without significance that in her reply, [partner E] raised the question of conflict of interest but regrettably the Respondent went on to advise Mr [B] and convey Mr [B's] figure of [£ ...] to [Y]. The Respondent claimed under cross-examination that at this stage he was not advising [Y] but this observation has to be regarded in the context that the Respondent had already been acting for [Y] in this transaction and it is significant that he informed Mr [Z] of [Y]

that if Mr [B's] figure were not to be accepted then he would have to withdraw from acting for [Y].

The Respondent similarly explained that he did not regard himself as acting for [Y] at the time when he advised Mr [B] on the matter of repairs in July of the following year.

In his address to the Tribunal, Counsel for the Respondent suggested that there only had been some doubt in the practice of 'double acting' until the enactment of the 1986 Practice Rules. This is not accepted. These Practice Rules merely restrict the circumstances in which a solicitor may act for two parties to a conveyancing transaction, but declare that any exceptions within the Rules are still subject to the overall prohibition in the event of a conflict of interest. Also Counsel pointed to the absence at the relevant time of any Rule relating to 'conflict of interest' and he sought to distinguish the joint and several liability under the law of partnership with the personal relationship between a solicitor and his client, submitting that the Respondent only acted for Mr [A], with the firm's Court Department acting for [X]; and that the Respondent's only professional duty was therefore to look after the interests of Mr [A] and to avoid the effect of possible arrestments. Counsel did not dispute that the Respondent had advised Mr [A] after his meeting with [his partner D] but he claimed that this had merely been 'friendly advice' and that it did not extend to professional misconduct. In relation to Mr [B], Counsel submitted that the Respondent had correctly advised him to the effect that his only option was either to accept the position or to resile. Counsel questioned how the Respondent could be faulted merely because his advice was unpopular; and that on the same principle, it could not be wrong for the Respondent to advise his client in such circumstances to offer a compromise figure.

The Tribunal does not accept Counsel's challenge based on the absence of a Practice Rule. The general principle is well established that a solicitor must not represent two clients where a conflict of interest has arisen or is indeed likely to arise. The matter is so fundamental that at the relative time, it had never been necessary to have the principle set down in any Practice Rule or other form of regulation and the Fiscal merely referred to the authority of Begg on Law Agent[s] (second edition, 1883) and the more recent publication by R.M. and Janice Webster, Professional Ethics and Practice for Scottish Solicitors (second edition, 1984) as illustrating the principle. There may indeed be occasions when it is not immediately apparent whether a conflict of interest exists and in these circumstances it may be necessary to ask the following questions (1) whether the conflict of interest concerns two separate clients of the particular solicitor, (2) is the solicitor continuing to act and advise at least one of the clients and (3) does the representation and advice have a bearing on the subject matter of the particular conflict or dispute. The first question requires the definition of a 'client'. The Fiscal relied on the dictum of Lord Gifford in *Clelland* v *Morrison* 1878 6R 156 at 169 that 'employment of a firm is employment of all the partners of the firm'. The circumstances of that case may bear little relevance to the present matter but that dictum has been adopted by this Tribunal as reflecting the accepted principle that the clients of one partner in a firm are clients of the firm and that clients of the firm are clients of each and every partner in that firm. Partners have a community of interest and this is reflected in the joint and several liability of partners. It is accepted that in some of the larger firms or in firms where there is more than one place of business, the *de facto* relationship between individual clients and other partners may be non-existent but nevertheless there remains a communal interest among the partners as a whole in relation to each and every client of the firm. This interest is not illusory, and accordingly the Tribunal cannot accept the submissions that [X] was not one of the Respondent's clients and that he did not have a responsibility towards that Company. Similarly [Y] and Mr [B] were both clients of the Respondent throughout the relevant period.

There was clearly a conflict of interest between Mr [A] and [X] in that during the whole of [1985], the Sheriff Court action was current; and at the relevant time, the Respondent was acting for Mr [A]. The diligence which was effected was merely upon the dependence of the action but it is recognised that such diligence can have a material bearing on the outcome of proceedings. As a partner in his firm, the Respondent must accept responsibility for the diligence which was taken against Mr [A] particularly after be became aware of the representation of [X] within his firm. The Respondent also advised Mr [A] with a view to defeating the effect of possible arrestment in the knowledge that his partner was likely to take such action, and thereby to the prejudice of his clients [X].

The content of the Respondent's letter to Mr [A] of 10th October 1985 contained material advice. It is accepted that the Respondent acted with the best motives in seeking out the file and discussing the matter with [his partner D], but in advising Mr [A] in the letter of 10th October, the Respondent was undoubtedly acting in a conflict situation. The Tribunal was informed that Mr [A] was ultimately successful in resisting the claim of [X] and therefore on that occasion the advice was not, in retrospect, prejudicial to [X] but in the opinion of the Tribunal this is not a relevant consideration. It is essential that at all times a client can look to his solicitor for advice and obtain advice which is not only independent and impartial but can be seen to be independent and impartial in that the solicitor is not representing the interests of any other connected party. The Respondent was not in that position in relation to Mr [A], certainly after the existence of the Court action became known to the Respondent on 13th August 1985. The gravity of the Respondent's actings is reflected by Mr [A's] conclusion regarding the whole matter. There was evidence that Mr [A] was more than satisfied with the Respondent's services in selling his house; and his dissatisfaction arose from the belief that there had been collusion between the Respondent and his Court Department. That view was wholly mistaken but it arose from an understandable conclusion of the facts as were then available to Mr [A]. Such circumstances were undoubtedly very disturbing to Mr [A] and damaging to the reputation of Solicitors. It should have been apparent to the Respondent that a clear conflict of interest had arisen when [partner C] spoke to him on 13th August and at that point the Respondent ought to have ensured that Mr [A] was then represented by an independent solicitor; and in any event the Respondent should have ceased acting for Mr [A] as from that date. The Respondent's decision to continue acting for Mr [A] after 13th August was serious and reprehensible and in the opinion of the Tribunal each of the three charges in relation to Mr [A] based on conflict of interest has been established. The Tribunal leaves open the question whether in the circumstances the firm, should also have ceased acting for [X]. Counsel submitted in relation to Mr [B] that in conveying Mr [B's] insistence on a reduction of [£ . . .] and stating that in the event of court proceedings, he would not be able to act for [Y], the Respondent was aware that a conflict of interest could arise but that until there were court proceedings there was insufficient conflict such as might preclude the Respondent from acting for both Mr [B] and [Y]. Counsel also observed with reference to Gloag on Contract (second edition, p 614) and *Hayes v Robinson* 1984 SLT 300 that the Respondent had given Mr [B] the correct advice in that his alternative was to resile from the bargain or accept the property as it stood, and that Mr [B] had no right to a reduction in the purchase price. Counsel submitted that the Respondent gave Mr [B] the correct advice in relation to the roof repairs. Further, in consulting with [his partner E], the Respondent was taking the opinion of someone already known to Mr [B] in that earlier in the year, Mr [B] had already consulted [the Respondent's partner E] regarding his matrimonial affairs.

The Tribunal does not accept that a dispute has to reach the stage of Court proceedings before a conflict of interest can arise. In day-to-day practice, there are many disputes which are capable of extra-judicial settlement. Such disputes may be of critical importance to the particular client and it is essential in such circumstances that each client is independently advised. If the same solicitor acts for both parties in such a matter, neither party has the benefit of independent advice in that whilst the solicitor may make a correct statement of law and properly apply the legal principles to the particular circumstances, each client is deprived of his right to be independently advised. This is clearly illustrated in the dispute between Mr [B] and [Y] in that although in strict law Mr [B] had to make a choice between two alternatives there was an equitable compromise open to each party, and it is significant that it was this compromise which was settled upon. The Respondent claimed that in conveying Mr [B's] position he was strictly not advising [Y] but [Y] remained his clients and clients of his firm and they were entitled to look to the Respondent for independent advice, which in the circumstances the Respondent would have been unable to provide.

The Tribunal is accordingly satisfied that there was indeed a conflict of interest between [B] and [Y] from July 1982 when the discrepancy in the room measurements became apparent to Mr [B] and that this conflict became known to the Respondent personally when Mr [B] consulted him in September 1982. As with Mr [A], it was the Respondent's duty in September 1982 to cease acting for at least one of the parties and it was culpable for the Respondent to continue acting, thereafter to advise Mr [B] on the law and then to become involved in the negotiations between his clients. For the same reasons, the Respondent was at fault in advising Mr [B] regarding the possible claim against [Y] in relation to roof repairs. As with Mr [A], the Tribunal is of the opinion that the Respondent committed a serious error of judgement in continuing to act for Mr [B] and [Y] after the conflict of interest had arisen. Eventually Mr [B] consulted other solicitors but until that stage, Mr [B] was deprived of independent advice on two important matters affecting his dwellinghouse and the Tribunal is satisfied that the Respondent's conduct in persisting in his representation of Mr [B] and [Y] was in itself serious and reprehensible justifying separate findings of professional misconduct. . . .

This Tribunal has always taken a serious view where it is established that a solicitor has acted in a conflict of interest situation. In regard to Mr [A], it was apparent that the Respondent's loyalties lay solely with that client, but there was a relationship through the partnership with [X] and it is significant that it was this connection which gave rise to Mr [A's] dissatisfaction. The Respondent had a more substantive relationship with both [Y] and Mr [B] and at the relevant time it was still open for the Respondent to act for both parties. However that privilege was available on the strict understanding that the solicitor would cease acting in the event of a conflict of interest arising. The Respondent was clearly aware of the principle in that he arranged for one of his partners to sign the counterpart of the missives, and later [his partner E] drew the possibility of conflict to the Respondent's attention; but he blindly carried on acting for both Mr [B] and [Y] and indeed Mr [A] long after the conflict situation had become acute. There was never any suggestion that the Respondent's continued actings were for any other motive than to continue the service for the particular client, but nevertheless in continuing to act, the Respondent showed a reckless disregard for his responsibilities towards each of the clients of his firm. The gravity of the Respondent's conduct is reflected in the amount of the fine (Case 689/86).

In a case where a solicitor (the Respondent) had acted for a client (A) in regard to a number of matters and knew that A had been in financial difficulties for some time, the Respondent's partner (B) was instructed by a Bank to call up a loan and personal guarantees by A and his wife on 19th October 1983. B told the Respondent of his instructions from the Bank and the Respondent told B that he had difficulty in recovering fees from A and that this had effectively terminated his acting for A. The Respondent confirmed that B could consider himself free to proceed against A, his wife and their company. The Bank later instructed B, as a matter of urgency, to register the personal guarantees and raise proceedings against A and his wife so that an Inhibition might be registered. B did not have any further discussions with the Respondent on the matter subsequent to the conversation on 19th October. B arranged for a Writ to be prepared by one of his assistants and the Writ and service copies were inadvertently signed by the Respondent. The Respondent was found guilty of Professional Misconduct in that:

> Having been made aware on 19th October 1983 that his firm had been instructed to act in the recovery from [A] of a sum in excess of £50,000, and having special knowledge of the financial circumstances of [A], he should have appreciated the conflict of interest and he should have arranged for his firm to decline any further instructions from [the Bank] in this matter.

The Tribunal said:

> In this case [A] never consulted the Respondent in regard to the action at the instance of [the Bank] but the Fiscal submitted that the special knowledge which the Respondent had regarding [A's] financial circumstances was such as to create a conflict of interest.

> Counsel for the Respondent submitted that if there had been a conflict situation, it had only arisen at the time when the Respondent signed the Writ, and that this arose through inadvertence. He further argued that conflict of interest supporting a charge of professional misconduct could only arise by looking at each case separately and ascertaining whether any party had suffered injury. He submitted that the Complaint contained no averment of damage or disclosure, breach of confidence, advantage or disadvantage and that if there had been any potential risk to [A], it had been arrested in December when the Respondent withdrew from acting.

> The critical point of time was the Respondent's conversation with his partner on 19th October 1983. It is apparent from the previous correspondence from [A] which was produced, that he was personally aware of [A's] financial difficulties and he still had instructions to appear for [A] at a proof [in another case] which had been set down for 6th January 1984. He was therefore closely involved with [A], and his partner made him aware that proceedings might be raised by [the Bank] against [A] personally in view of the guarantee. This Tribunal is not prepared to state that it is always improper for a Solicitor to act for one client in circumstances which may be contrary to the interests of another client; but in the opinion of this Tribunal, the Respondent's knowledge of [A's] financial circumstances was such

that it was improper for the Respondent to permit his firm to act in proceedings against [A]. It is apparent from the Respondent's letter of 21st October 1983 and his subsequent correspondence with [A] that he would have continued acting for him if his outstanding fees had been paid. Taking into account the Respondent's special knowledge of [A's] financial circumstances, the Respondent committed a serious error of judgement when on 19th October 1983 he agreed to his partner taking steps on behalf of [the Bank] against [A] even although he was only a guarantor to his company. In the opinion of this Tribunal, a reasonable Solicitor ought to have recognised the conflict of interest at that time and it was the Respondent's duty to ensure that [the Bank] were thereafter separately represented. This charge in the Complaint did not aver particular prejudice toward [A] and indeed it would appear that there may not have been a valid defence to the Action. Nevertheless in proceeding to take decree against [A], the Respondent's firm would be involved in advising [the Bank] of the steps to be taken to enforce payment; and the Respondent's knowledge of [A's] financial position could have materially affected such advice. From 19th October 1983, the Respondent knowingly entered into a conflict of interest situation and in the opinion of this Tribunal, such action amounted to professional misconduct.

The established rule where a conflict of interest arises is that the Solicitor should cease acting for one or other or both of the clients involved; and the charge before the Tribunal implied that the Respondent had the choice either to cease acting for [A] or alternatively to arrange for his firm to withdraw acting for [the Bank]. In the opinion of the Tribunal, the Respondent did not have such a choice on this occasion in that his special knowledge of [A's] affairs precluded his firm from properly acting for [the Bank] in this matter; and the only reasonable choice which the Respondent had was whether to remain as Solicitor for [A] (Case 649/84).

A solicitor (the Respondent) was found guilty of Professional Misconduct in circumstances where a conflict of interest was likely to arise and later arose. The solicitor had acted for both the seller and the purchaser of heritable property in terms of missives and a subsequent Agreement, which was to replace the missives, and which was not in the interests of the purchaser, without ensuring that the purchaser was separately advised and informed of the fact that the seller did not have a recorded title to settle the transaction in terms of the missives; and thereafter failing to ensure that the seller was represented in his subsequent Court action by a solicitor, other than a solicitor in the firm of which the Respondent was a partner, in the knowledge that he had witnessed the Agreement which was the subject of the litigation and would be a likely witness in such proceedings. In the Note to the Tribunal's Decision the Tribunal said:

In the event of a conflict of interest arising between two clients, it is the Solicitor's duty to cease acting for at least one of the clients. Whether a Solicitor having ceased to act for one client can properly continue acting for the remaining client after a conflict situation has arisen, depends entirely on the particular circumstances. In this case, the purchaser consulted another Solicitor who then raised an action against the seller for repayment of the £X [which he had paid to the seller]. The basis of the action concerned the precise terms of the Minute of Agreement and the surrounding circumstances. At the relevant time, the Respondent had been Solicitor to the seller and he would have had a special knowledge of the seller's affairs as a consequence of that relationship. It was acknowledged that the

Respondent would be a likely witness in the proceedings between the purchaser and the seller, and the Respondent's particular knowledge of the seller's affairs would be of material relevance in these proceedings. It is observed in Cordery on Solicitors, 7th edition, page 70, that:

> A solicitor who has been retained by a client is under an absolute duty not to disclose any information of a confidential nature which has come to his knowledge by virtue of the retainer, and to exercise the utmost good faith towards his client not only for so long as the retainer lasts but even after the termination of the retainer, in respect of any information acquired during the course of the retainer.

> In circumstances where there are proceedings between the Solicitor's former clients and the Solicitor has a material knowledge of the affairs of one of those clients, it is not open to him to continue to accept instructions from the other client. In the circumstances of this case, it was the Respondent's duty to cease acting for the seller as soon as the proceedings commenced. In fact it was the Respondent's Partner who was acting in the court action for the seller, but the position was the same; for it has been judicially observed that a client of a Solicitor is the client of all the partners of his firm and accordingly the Respondent ought to have ensured that his firm as a whole ceased acting for the seller when the action was raised (Case 600/85).

The Tribunal has said in finding a charge of Professional Misconduct established:

> It is not infrequent practice, particularly in remote areas, for the same firm of Solicitors to act for both parties in a conveyancing transaction but in such circumstances there is a heavy onus on the solicitor or solicitors concerned to ensure that there is no prejudice to either party in the transaction. In these circumstances if the possibility of a conflict arises between the purchaser and seller then the Solicitor or Solicitors concerned must cease acting for at least one of the parties; and it matters not that the purchaser and seller have been represented by different partners in the same firm (Case 565/82).

A solicitor acted for both the seller and the purchasers of a property in which the missives provided for 'entry and actual occupation' being given by a certain date. As a result of a pre-existing tenancy agreement in respect of part of the property the seller could not give actual occupation at entry. The Tribunal in its Decision said:

> There was accordingly a clear and unequivocal conflict of interest between the two sets of clients and this ought to have been apparent to the Respondent at the meeting on 15th June.

> It is well established that where a conflict of interest arises between two clients of a Solicitor, it is that Solicitor's duty forthwith to cease acting for at least one of the clients and advise that client to be separately represented.

> The Respondent in his evidence acknowledged that there was a clear conflict but he believed that [the Purchasers] were going elsewhere for advice when they left his office on 15th June and that it was therefore not necessary for him to advise them to take separate legal advice; and he further believed that by the time they had returned they had fully appraised themselves of the situation and had accepted the position.

The Respondent did not expressly state to [the Purchasers] at the meeting on 15th June that they should consult another Solicitor. In such circumstances and irrespective of his understanding of their intention, the Respondent should have written to [the Purchasers] with that advice and the Respondent was culpably at fault in failing to give such advice to [the Purchasers] in clear and explicit terms.

When [one of the Purchasers] again communicated with the Respondent's office on or about 19th June [. . .] the conversation was with the Respondent's unqualified assistant [A]. The Respondent failed to enquire whether [the Purchasers] had in fact taken independent advice and he failed to verify precisely their attitude in regard to the Missives of Let with a view to ascertaining whether the conflict had been resolved. The Respondent relied on [the] statement [of one of the Purchasers] as related to him by [A]. In effect the Respondent continued or at least resumed acting for [the Purchasers] in a situation where a conflict of interest had arisen and he culpably failed to take adequate steps to ensure that the conflict had been resolved. [The Purchasers] should have had independent legal advice regarding their remedies against [the Seller] arising from her failure or inability to implement her contractual obligation under the Missives of Sale. By proceeding to record the Disposition in the Register of Sasines, the Respondent materially prejudiced the rights of [the Purchasers] to pursue these remedies against [the Seller] and in the opinion of the Tribunal the Respondent was culpably at fault in proceeding with the transaction to the extent of recording the Disposition in favour of [the Purchasers] as the effect of such recording superseded the provisions contained in the Missives.

While it is open for a Solicitor in Scotland to act for both the purchaser and the seller in a conveyancing transaction, it is well established that the Solicitor must ensure that the interests of each party are wholly respected at all times and it is on this basis that the Solicitor must direct at least one of the parties to seek separate legal advice in the event of a conflict of interest arising. The Respondent regrettably failed to respect those established principles and persisted in acting for [the Purchasers] in circumstances which could have caused material prejudice to them. It is in these circumstances that the Tribunal finds the Respondent guilty of professional misconduct in respect of the foregoing (Case 552/82).

A solicitor (the Respondent) was charged with Professional Misconduct in that:

(*a*) having been instructed by Mr [A] to represent Mr [B] and Mr [C], he failed to take specific and direct instructions from Mr [C] before purporting to begin to represent him which was the only justification for taking possession of the papers in the hands of Mr [C] and reading them or making to read them, in a situation where the Respondent represented or intended to represent Mr [B] in a matter where there might be a conflict of interest, and

(*b*) he persisted in looking at the papers belonging to Mr [C], while Mr [C] was protesting that he did not wish the Respondent to see the papers nor to represent him, and that he already had an agent acting for him, putting Mr [C], into a state of fear for his safety because of the actings of the Respondent.

In the course of the hearing it was accepted by the Fiscal for the Complainers that Mr [A] had also instructed the Respondent to act for Mr [C]. In finding that Professional Misconduct was not proved, the Tribunal in its Decision said *inter alia*:

The Fiscal for the Complainers pointed out that there was no suggestion that there was any element of dishonesty in the actings of the Respondent when he spoke to Mr [C] on 17th April. The Fiscal submitted that where a solicitor is not instructed direct, he has a particular duty to ascertain his position before proceeding to act, particularly if there is a possible conflict of interest and he referred to paragraphs 2.06 and 2.07 of the Websters' 'Professional Ethics and Practice for Scottish Solicitors', 2nd edition, 1984. The Fiscal observed that the pressure on the Respondent was of his own making and that the whole episode could have been avoided if after lunch the Respondent had gone to see Mr [C] in the cells. The Fiscal submitted that the Respondent culpably failed to clear his position before beginning to read Mr [C's] papers and further that he persisted in this action after Mr [C] protested. The Fiscal accepted that events had occurred very quickly but he submitted that there were several serious consequences from the Respondent's actions, particularly that Mr [C] became upset immediately before his Judicial Examination, that the Respondent as agent for Mr [B] became aware of the voluntary statement, and that the outcome of the particular incident was that Mr [C] was granted bail in circumstances where it would ordinarily have been refused.

Counsel for the Respondent emphasised that the Respondent had indeed been instructed to act for Mr [C] and that Mr [C] had initially failed to respond when the Respondent began to read his copy of the Petition. Counsel submitted that the Respondent's actings required to be examined in the context of the particular Court situation and that the possibility of a conflict would not have become apparent until the solicitor had spoken to both of his apparent clients.

The Tribunal upholds the Fiscal's submission that where a solicitor receives instructions indirectly or from a third party, he has a particular duty to communicate with the apparent client and satisfy himself regarding the client's instructions before proceeding to act. However, without in any way diminishing the importance of the foregoing principle, the Tribunal recognises that in the particular circumstances of Court proceedings, a solicitor may be under considerable pressure to satisfy himself regarding the circumstances of a case before appearing in Court. Even although the Respondent might have acted differently and seen Mr [C] before he proceeded to Court, there remained the fact that the Petition was only served on Mr [C] less than a quarter of an hour before he was due to appear in Court. Mr [C] then had to be taken to the Court room from the cells. The Petition, with statement annexed, extended to two pages of closely typed charges and a further four pages of statement and this would have taken the Respondent some time to read even cursorily. The Respondent undoubtedly committed an error of judgment in not confirming to his absolute satisfaction that he had Mr [C's] instructions before taking possession and reading his copy of the Petition but having regard to the initial instructions and the whole circumstances, the Tribunal is of the opinion that on this occasion, the Respondent's failure to establish at first hand his relationship with Mr [C] was not reckless or culpable to the extent that would justify a finding of professional misconduct (Case 701/87).

See also cases referred to under the heading 'Impartial Advice', para 8.01.

9.02 SOLICITORS (SCOTLAND) PRACTICE RULES 1986
Professional Misconduct was established in Case 835/92 where a solicitor failed to comply with rule 5 of the Solicitors (Scotland) Practice Rules 1986 in that he acted for both sellers and purchasers in the sale of heritable property in circumstances where none of the exceptions set out in that rule applied. There had been no suggestion that the solicitor was unaware of the rule or that he was

misled by any party. His excuse was that he had misinterpreted the rule. The Tribunal did not accept that his misunderstanding in relation to the application of the rule was a circumstance which might constitute a reasonable excuse and cause the Tribunal to withhold a finding of Professional Misconduct. In coming to this decision, the Tribunal was fortified by the opinion of the Court in *Council of the Law Society of Scotland* v *J* 1991 SLT 662 in which the Court observed at p 665:

> It is well known that the Council goes to considerable lengths to publicise its decisions in regard to the making of such rules by circulation to its members and in the *Journal of the Law Society of Scotland* before they come into force. Each solicitor must be taken therefore to have seen and read the rules and to be aware of their existence unless an explanation is forthcoming as to why, in his case, this should not be so.

In that case the solicitor made a conscious decision to act for both the purchaser and the seller but he claimed that he had overlooked the precise provisions of rule 5. In the present case, the Respondent similarly made a positive decision to act for both parties to the transaction but claimed that in applying the rule, he had misconstrued its terms. The Tribunal also observed:

> Before the 1986 Practice Rules came into effect, it had been open to a solicitor to act for both the purchaser and seller in relation to heritable property provided that there was no conflict of interest; but a solicitor was obliged to cease acting for one of the parties in the event of such a conflict arising. Regrettably circumstances arose from time to time from which it was apparent that certain solicitors had difficulty in recognising a conflict of interest situation and the Practice Rules were introduced in order to limit the circumstances in which a solicitor might act for both parties and unwittingly continue acting where a conflict of interest arose. It is significant that the 1986 Rules did not qualify the principle in relation to 'conflict' in that Rule 3 specifically states that 'a solicitor shall not act for two or more parties whose interests conflict'. Rule 5 is stated to be without prejudice to that generality and for the first time negated in general terms the solicitor's notional freedom to act for more than one party in relation to the transfer of heritable property. The various exceptions to Rule 5 are clearly set out, and now, if a solicitor has the opportunity to act for both parties, it is for the solicitor to satisfy himself that the circumstances of the parties or the transaction indeed come within a particular exception. Clearly it is only the solicitor himself who will have all the information upon which a decision can be made and if the solicitor is in doubt, it is a straightforward matter for him to arrange for one of the parties to be separately advised. The interpretation of exception (*d*) is assisted by having a definition of 'established client' set out in Rule 2. The solicitor for the Respondent criticised this definition but in the opinion of the Tribunal, the definition is clear and ordinarily a solicitor should not have difficulty in determining whether a particular party is an established client (Case 835/92).

In relation to a breach of rule 5 of the 1986 Practice Rules in that the solicitor acted for a builder and a purchaser, the Tribunal, referring to the matter of conflict of interest, observed:

> [T]he council of the Law Society in promulgating the Rule, took the matter out of the judgment of the particular solicitor as in the circumstances covered by the Rule

there was clearly a high risk of conflict of interest and of consequent prejudice to one or other of the parties as a result of the solicitor not being in a position to give each party independent advice (Case 754/91).

In considering a case of conflict of interest relating to a solicitor acting in connection with clients accused of criminal offences, the Tribunal stated:

The direction that a solicitor should not act in a conflict of interest situation is clearly set out in the 1986 Practice Rules and more recently in paragraph 3 of the Code of Conduct published by the Council of the Law Society of Scotland; but the principle is of long standing having been clearly stated in *Begg* and the authorities referred to therein.

Put at its simplest, a solicitor cannot serve two masters whose interests conflict, and the most obvious case is that a solicitor cannot act for opposing parties in any dispute. That example refers to a situation where there are *active* interests to be pursued, but there are many circumstances where the wider interests of a client require to be protected. A client is entitled to a relationship of mutual trust with his solicitor and within that relationship, the client should have the understanding that he can freely give confidential information to his solicitor on the basis that the information will not be disclosed to any third party, except in relation to that client's business. It is part of the trust that the solicitor will not divulge that information to unconnected third parties or allow it to influence him when advising other clients, and accordingly the mere knowledge of a client's affairs may constitute an 'interest' which will require a solicitor to decline instructions from another client. The principle even extends to the interests of a former client where the knowledge of that person's affairs was acquired at a time when that party was a client, and it is this knowledge which sometimes precludes the solicitor from acting for either party after a dispute has arisen between them.

It is the same element of trust that enables a client to expect that the solicitor will maintain an undivided loyalty to that client and that as part of this relationship, the solicitor will not knowingly withhold any information which may be relevant to the interests of that client (Case 809/90).

The Tribunal found Professional Misconduct established in a case where a solicitor acted in conveyancing matters and had failed to give the written notice required under rule 5(2) of the Solicitors (Scotland) Practice Rules 1986. The Tribunal said:

The remaining charge directly concerned the 1986 Practice Rules. In the Answers, it was claimed that each of the clients were related or were established clients and that each client had been advised that if a dispute arose at least one of them would be required to consult an independent solicitor or solicitors; but it was conceded that no confirmation of this advice had been set in writing. It is accepted that on the particular occasions no conflict arose between the particular clients but this is a matter which in any event is separately covered under Rule 3 of these Practice Rules. The requirement of written confirmation is an essential provision of the Rules which gives protection not only to the client but also to the solicitor concerned and it allows the solicitor to demonstrate that the advice had indeed been given. It is now a privilege for a solicitor to act for more than one party in the exceptional circumstances set out in Rule 5 and the first Respondent was culpable in failing to have due regard for the whole provisions of this Rule (Case 738/88).

In a case which was decided by the Tribunal in 1993 where the solicitor had acted for both a developer and a purchaser in apparent contravention of rule 5(1) of the Solicitors (Scotland) Practice Rules 1986, it was claimed that the seller was not involved in any development in relation to the particular property but it was held by the Tribunal that it was the status of the developer which was critical for the purpose of interpreting the particular rule. The Tribunal also found the solicitor to have been in breach of rule 5(2) of the Solicitors (Scotland) Practice Rules 1986 in that although correspondence was produced in which it was apparent that the respective clients accepted that the solicitor was acting for both parties, nevertheless the solicitor failed to follow the precise directions set out in the rule, namely to write to each client confirming the advice which had been given in terms of that rule (Case 861/93).

10

RESPONSIBILITY TOWARDS FELLOW SOLICITORS

10.01 RELATIONS BETWEEN SOLICITORS

Solicitors shall not knowingly mislead colleagues or where they have given their word go back on it.

A solicitor must act with fellow solicitors in a manner consistent with persons having mutual trust and confidence in each other (Code of Conduct, para 9).

The Tribunal had to consider a case where a solicitor (the Respondent) acting for the purchasers of heritable subjects entered into missives with a firm of solicitors acting for the sellers. Subsequently it turned out that the sellers did not own part of the subjects which they occupied and a title to the area in question had to be obtained from a third party. The Respondent indicated that the third party required a consideration of £X for the outstanding area of ground and the solicitors for the sellers agreed that £X could be deducted from the price. The Respondent then approached the solicitors for the third party and was able to agree that the price of £X of the said area should be reduced to £Y but did not communicate this reduction of price to the solicitors for the sellers. In finding the Respondent guilty of Professional Misconduct the Tribunal said:

It is an essential feature of negotiations between solicitors that they are conducted in an atmosphere of mutual trust and a solicitor has a professional duty to respect that element of trust in all his dealings. It was entirely on the basis of the information conveyed by the Respondent to [the agents for the sellers] on [...] that their clients agreed to a reduction on the price to be paid at settlement. That information was given by the Respondent in the expectation that [the agents for the sellers] and their clients would rely on it. The Respondent in conveying such information had a duty to be frank and honest not only at the time, but throughout the period when the arrangement subsisted, because it was only at settlement that the arrangement was to crystallise. Accordingly the Respondent had a professional duty to inform [the agents for the sellers] in the event of any material change of circumstances which significantly affected the basis on which the arrangement had been made, and the Respondent was culpable in failing to disclose the variation in the sum to be paid to [the third party] and allowing the settlement to take place without further modification.

In the Respondent's Answers, it was submitted that the Respondent was acting at all times, as he was bound to do, in the best interests of his clients. It is not doubted that the outcome of the particular course of events was of significant financial advantage to his clients; but this is not the only consideration. It is essential that at all times a solicitor has regard for his professional relationship with his fellow solicitors. As mentioned above, there is a special relationship of trust between solicitors, and solicitors are entitled to expect and rely on a course of action whereby this relationship of trust is not breached. In the particular case, [the agents for the sellers] were entitled to rely on the representations of the Respondent in seeking their clients' agreement to the reduction of £X in the price. The Respondent was aware of the consequences of the reduction and notwithstanding the potential benefit to his own clients, he had an overriding professional duty to inform [the agents for the sellers] of the change of circumstances in so far as it affected his representations to them. The Respondent's failure to do this constituted a serious breach of trust and it is in these circumstances that the Tribunal has pronounced a finding of professional misconduct. The profession must never stoop to the lowest levels of the market place and their professional duties must never be supplanted without the best possible reasons. . . .

. . . The Tribunal takes a very serious view of the Respondent's course of action which had the effect of breaching the special relationship of mutual trust which subsists between solicitors and [is] rightly expected by the public. This breach resulted in his clients obtaining a financial benefit which was not otherwise open to them; and it is in these circumstances that a substantial fine has been imposed. . . . (Case 726/88).

A client (A) consulted a solicitor (the Respondent) with a view to raising finance and A volunteered that his house, which was in the joint names of himself and his wife (Mrs A), might provide the necessary security; the Respondent was thereafter instructed by a Bank to attend to the formalities of securing the loan. A Complaint against the solicitor was later brought before the Tribunal. In the first part of the Complaint, the Respondent was charged with Professional Misconduct in that

(a) [H]aving prepared a Standard Security on the instructions of only one of two proprietors of a dwellinghouse he permitted that person to remove the Standard Security from his office in order to obtain the signature of the other proprietor. He had received no instructions from the other proprietor whom he had not met in connection with the transaction.

(b) On the deed being returned to him with the purported signature of the other proprietor, he signed as witness to that signature and arranged for a second witness also to sign the deed. He had not in fact witnessed the signature nor had he received an acknowledgment of signature.

(c) He caused a partially false testing clause to be appended to the deed.

(d) By registering the deed in the General Register of Sasines, he committed [Mrs A] (for) whom he had no instructions in connection with the transaction] to the various sanctions set out in the Standard Security.

Evidence was led at the Tribunal both of A and Mrs A. A freely admitted that he had adhibited his wife's signature to the Standard Security outwith the Respondent's office. Counsel for the Respondent submitted that the forgery of the wife's signature had not been established but the Tribunal took the view that the authenticity of the signature bearing to be that of the wife was not an essential matter in relation to the charges in the Complaint and made no finding in relation to the signature.

The Tribunal in its Decision said *inter alia*:

The critical matter is what happened at the meetings on 16th and 17th July 1981. On the former date [A] called at the Respondent's office. Mr [B] may also have been present on that occasion. The likelihood is that [A] signed the Standard Security. He then removed the deed from the Respondent's office. Whilst the deed was outwith the Respondent's office, the signature ['X- A-'] was adhibited to the deed. On the following day [A] returned to the Respondent's office. Mr [B] may have been present on that occasion. Of particular importance is the question whether [A] was also accompanied by a woman on that date. The evidence was that [A] called at the Respondent's office on a number of occasions around this period in connection with the loan and there is the further evidence of the Respondent, corroborated by his cashier, that on one occasion [A] was accompanied by a woman. The Respondent appeared to be an honest and credible witness and frankly acknowledged when he was unable to recall the precise details of any particular event. If a woman had been present on 17th July 1981, it is accepted that the Respondent would have presumed such woman to have been [Mrs A] and that he would have asked her to acknowledge the other signature. In contrast, [A] denied that he was accompanied by any woman on 17th July; but this was the evidence of a man who admitted falsifying a signature. [A's] evidence was uncorroborated.

For a complaint to be established before this Tribunal, it has been judicially confirmed that it is necessary for the relevant facts to be established 'beyond all reasonable doubt'. In the present case, there is insufficient evidence to prove that the formalities of attestation were not properly carried out by the respondent and accordingly the Tribunal finds not established the charge that he neither witnessed nor received an acknowledgment of the signature ['X- A-'] and the same finding must follow in relation to the charge that (knowingly) he caused a partially false testing clause to be appended to the deed.

It was also averred that the Respondent was culpable in that he prepared a Standard Security on the instructions of only one of two proprietors and permitted that person to remove the Standard Security from his office in order to obtain the signature of the other proprietor. The proprietors were husband and wife. There was no evidence to suggest that the Respondent was in any way aware of the friction between [A and Mrs A] and in such circumstances, the Respondent assumed that [A] had his wife's authority and on this basis he permitted [A] to remove the deed in order that he might procure his wife's signature. In the opinion of the Tribunal the Respondent's actings fell short of the standard expected of a competent solicitor. [Mrs A] was as much the Respondent's client as was [A]. This was a Standard Security in respect of a loan being taken out for [A's] business purposes. The loan was being secured over their dwellinghouse, and the Respondent had a duty towards [Mrs A] to ensure that she understood the consequences of executing the deed. The Respondent failed to fulfil this duty, but bearing in mind the relationship of trust which normally exists between husband and wife and the absence of any indication of difficulty, the Tribunal finds that the Respondent's actings in this matter fall short of professional misconduct. In recording the deed in the General Register of Sasines, the Respondent was also charged with committing [Mrs A] to the various sanctions set out in the Standard Security but if the Respondent had no reason to doubt [Mrs A's] instructions, it would have been in order for him to proceed with the Security transaction, and in any event the recording of the deed was carried out by him in his capacity as solicitor for [the Bank].

The Second part of the Complaint contained a charge that the Respondent in his letter of 3rd February 1983 made a misleading statement to [agents for the Bank].

At that time the Respondent was aware that the authenticity of the signature ['X-A-'] was being questioned and that it would have a material bearing on [the Bank's] future actions. In such circumstances, the Respondent was under a very high duty to give a full and accurate reply. His response is preceded with the words 'we have checked back our file and notes covering this loan transaction' and he then goes on to say that the Standard Security was 'signed by both parties in this office on 17th July 1981 in the circumstances narrated in the testing clause'. That reply gives a clear impression that the deed was physically signed by two persons within his office on 17th July and that this information is set down on the basis of the information contained in his files and notes. In his evidence, the Respondent stated that he had no written record of the meetings with [A] in July 1981. Counsel for the Respondent sought to excuse the Respondent's statement with reference to the phrase 'it does appear that ...' but in the opinion of the Tribunal this last mentioned phrase requires to be taken in context. This was a serious enquiry by [the Bank's agents] affecting a fundamental aspect of the Standard Security. The Respondent was under a duty to provide [the Bank's agents] with a full and accurate reply. The terms of the Respondent's letter and in particular the reference to his 'files and notes' gave the impression that the deed had been executed in a particular manner. This information was critical in relation to the proceedings which would inevitably follow upon the calling up of the Standard Security and this Tribunal finds that the Respondent's statement was misleading and in the circumstances culpable to the extent of amounting to professional misconduct (Case 612/85).

10.02 CORRESPONDENCE WITH OTHER SOLICITORS

Not only may the Tribunal regard failure to reply to correspondence from a solicitor's own client to be Professional Misconduct but also failure to respond timeously to the solicitor representing 'the other side' in a conveyancing transaction may be regarded as Professional Misconduct (Case 842/93).

The Tribunal has said when finding a solicitor guilty of Professional Misconduct:

> In addition to the delay, a serious aspect in this Complaint was the Respondent's failure to communicate with Messrs [a firm of solicitors who were making inquiries on behalf of a former client of the Respondent] and the Law Society. In order to transact business, it is essential that solicitors respond promptly and fully to inquiries from other firms and there is the same obligation on a solicitor to reply promptly and adequately to any inquiries which he may receive from the Law Society of Scotland (Case 660/86).

In a case where a solicitor was charged with Professional Misconduct in that he failed to reply to correspondence from a solicitor acting on behalf of a client with a contrary interest to the interest of the client of the solicitor charged, the Tribunal said:

> It is observed in *The Guide to the Professional Conduct of Solicitors*, published by the Law Society in England, at paragraph 16.01 on page 124, that:
>
> > A solicitor must at all times maintain his personal integrity and observe the requirements of good manners and courtesy towards other members of the profession or their staff, no matter how bitter the feelings between clients. He

must not behave in a manner which is acrimonious or offensive or otherwise inconsistent with his position as a solicitor.

Nevertheless a solicitor who is in negotiation with a colleague in relation to the mutual interests of their respective clients, is entitled to a wide discretion in the manner and the frequency of his communications with such fellow solicitor consistent with professional courtesy; and this Tribunal would not ordinarily expect such a solicitor to maintain the same level of communication as is encumbent on a solicitor who is transacting non-contentious business (Case 806/90).

In Case 884/94 the Tribunal said:

It is ordinarily a solicitor's duty to reply to all correspondence relating to a client's affairs which calls for an answer and if exceptionally a solicitor is instructed not to reply to a line of correspondence, the solicitor should convey to the other party in writing that the correspondence is being terminated. In the absence of such intimation, the correspondent is entitled to expect a reply and it is with these considerations that the Tribunal finds that the Respondent inexcusably failed to reply to the correspondence addressed to him in this matter, and that the extent of the neglect warrants a finding of professional misconduct in respect of each head.

10.03 COMMUNICATION WITH CLIENT OF ANOTHER SOLICITOR

It is not permissible for a solicitor to communicate about any item of business with a person whom the solicitor knows to be represented by another solicitor. A solicitor in such circumstances must always communicate with the solicitor acting for that person and not go behind the solicitor's back (Code of Conduct, para 9).

In a case where, in the particular circumstances, Professional Misconduct was not established but it was determined that the solicitor had acted unprofessionally, the Tribunal said:

... Mr [A] and his Company had been clients of the Respondent before the incident which was the subject matter of the Complaint, and he had consulted Messrs [X & Y] and given them instructions both in regard to his personal affairs and to the affairs of his Company. There was no material conflict in the evidence of the witnesses in this matter and the principal question before the Tribunal was the propriety of the Respondent's telephone call to Mr [A]. It is a well-established principle that a Solicitor should not communicate with the client of another Solicitor particularly in pending proceedings without consent and approval of that Solicitor. However, that principle is open to exception and in Sir Thomas Lund's 'A Guide to the Professional Conduct and Etiquette of Solicitors' at page 79 there is reference to a case where the facts were not materially different from that of the Respondent and Mr [A] in that the Solicitor was sued by his former client and he subsequently wrote three letters direct to the client although he knew that the client was represented by another Solicitor. The English Disciplinary Committee held 'that for a Solicitor for a party to litigation to communicate directly with the other party, who was separately represented, is universally condemned as contrary to the etiquette of the profession and to good taste, but is not in itself professional misconduct'. It was noted that the Respondent had a business relationship with Mr [A] and that the subject of this business relationship was discussed in the course of a particular telephone conversation. However, the Respondent did extend the subject matter of the telephone conversation to the matters at issue between himself and Mr [A] and that immediately after his conversation with Mr [B] of Messrs [X & Y] and in these circumstances the Tribunal consider that the Respondent acted unprofessionally and improperly but that his actings fell short of 'professional misconduct' (Case 428/79).

In a case where a solicitor, who had been acting on behalf of Mrs B, the seller of property, delayed settling the transaction, and the seller consulted other solicitors Messrs A, the Tribunal said:

Messrs [A] wrote to the Respondent on 30th August in relation to the [. . .] transaction, stating that they had been consulted by Mrs [B] and that they 'understand that you are acting for her with regard to the above sale'. Messrs [A] asked for information and repeated this request in a reminder of 12th September. It is clearly understood by the profession it is only in particular and exceptional circumstances that a solicitor can communicate direct with the client of another solicitor in relation to a matter of mutual interest to the respective clients. It should have been apparent to the Respondent from Messrs [A's] letters of 30th August and 12th September 1985 that Mrs [B] had transferred her instructions to that firm; but if the Respondent had been in any doubt, the terms of Messrs [A's] letters should at least have required him first to communicate with Messrs [A] to ascertain the true position. The Respondent failed to do so but called directly on Mrs [B]. It is understandable that Messrs [A's] letters may have caused the Respondent to act precipitately in the matter but this must be regarded in the context of many months of prior delay. There were no exceptional circumstances which might have justified this visit and the Tribunal is satisfied that this act in itself amounted to professional misconduct (Case 660/86).

The Tribunal had to consider a case where a solicitor (the Respondent) was instructed by a client, Mrs A, in connection with a matrimonial dispute with her husband, Mr A, who had instructed his own solicitors. There were various communications between the solicitors for each party until the Respondent wrote direct to Mr A. The Tribunal in its Decision said:

The Complaint contained two specific charges:

(a) That he wrote direct to [Mr A], notwithstanding that [Mr A] had instructed Solicitors to act on his behalf, a fact of which the Respondent was fully aware, and

(b) That he wrote to [Mr A] in terms which were offensive and contrary to reasonable and proper professional practice.

There is a well-established general rule that a solicitor should not interview or otherwise communicate with the client of another solicitor, particularly in pending proceedings, without the consent and approval of that Solicitor. This general rule is, however, subject to a number of exceptions, such as when the other solicitor has himself failed to reply to communications; and it is acknowledged that there is also a greater tolerance when a copy of the particular letter has been sent at the same time to the other solicitors.

In this Complaint it was suggested that the particular letter was offensive and contrary to reasonable and proper professional practice in that the Respondent 'alleged that [Mr A's] conduct was unacceptable, that he was refusing to act in a reasonable manner, that he indulged in quite disgraceful conduct and that he was clearly guilty of a criminal breach of the peace'. It was also averred in the Complaint that the suggestion that [Mr A] should seek some form of psychiatric help was in itself offensive and scurrilous.

In the opinion of the Tribunal, such a letter should not have been addressed directly to [Mr A]. The terms of the letter were most unfortunate. The observations made and the suggestions were quite improper and fell below the standards expected of a reputable Solicitor (Case 510/81).

In the particular circumstances of this case the Tribunal found that Professional Misconduct was not established.

10.04 TOUTING

The Solicitors (Scotland) (Advertising and Promotion) Practice Rules 1991 repealed the Solicitors (Scotland) (Advertising) Practice Rules 1987, which said:

5. A solicitor shall not apply for or seek instructions for business in such a manner, or do or permit in the carrying on of his practice any such act or thing, as may reasonably be regarded as touting or as calculated to attract business unfairly.

These earlier rules defined 'touting' as:

[A] direct approach by or on behalf of a solicitor to a person, who is not an established client, with the intention of soliciting business from that person.

The 1991 Rules provide that subject to rules 5 and 8 (of the 1991 Rules), a solicitor shall be entitled to promote his services in any way he thinks fit. Rule 5 of the 1991 Rules provides that

A solicitor shall not make a direct or indirect approach whether verbal or written to any person whom he knows or ought reasonably to know to be the client of another solicitor with the intention to solicit business from that person.

Rule 8 of the 1991 Rules makes various provisions regarding any advertisement of or by a solicitor or promotional material issued by or on behalf of a solicitor or promotional activity by or on behalf of a solicitor.

In a case prior to the introduction of the 1991 Rules, the Tribunal said, regarding touting:

The Respondents have been found guilty of touting for business contrary to Rule 5 of the Solicitors (Scotland) (Advertising) Practice Rules 1987. The first Practice Rules prohibiting touting were made in 1964 but even before that date, there was a long-standing prohibition of touting and the rule against touting is common to most professions. It is of significance that although the 1964 Practice Rules were materially amended in 1985 and repealed by the 1987 Practice Rules, the prohibition against touting remained, and indeed the 1987 Rules now contain for the first time a definition of touting as reflecting what has always been understood to be the meaning of that word. It is the essence of the professional approach to acquiring business that it should come without being actively sought by the practitioner and it is wholly to the public advantage if success in the profession comes through merit rather than through other causes. By touting, a solicitor takes an unfair advantage of his brethren. Touting is also contrary to the public interest as any direct approach by a solicitor, however well intentioned, can have the effect of pressurising a prospective client who may be in a vulnerable position; and this can never be an acceptable method of attracting business. It is with these considerations that this Tribunal will always take a serious view of any finding of touting (Case 762/89).

See also Case 407/76, referred to at para 10.05, and Case 481/80 at para 7.02.

10.05 DUTY TO FORMER EMPLOYERS

The Tribunal found Professional Misconduct established where a solicitor who had been an assistant with a firm of solicitors and then left to establish a practice on his own account, removed a file and relevant papers relating to an action from his former employer's firm without the permission of that firm and without intimation to them and without any permission of or intimation to the client (Case 782/90).

In a Complaint brought by one solicitor (the Complainer) against another solicitor (the Respondent), where the Respondent had formerly worked as a qualified assistant for the Complainer, the Tribunal said:

> It has long been recognised that if a Solicitor invites a person who is known to be the client of another Solicitor to consult him in his professional capacity, this constitutes touting and such can result in a finding of professional misconduct. . . .

> . . . A Solicitor who ceases to be employed as a qualified assistant and commences business on his own account has a particular duty to ensure that he does not unfairly attract the clients of his former employer. However, it is significant that the Respondent was employed by the Complainer to have sole charge of the office [. . .] and it is possible that the Respondent had built up a close working relationship with each of the particular clients. There was no averment that the Complainer had personally been consulted by any of the clients after the Respondent had left the Complainer's firm. In the circumstances as averred by the Complainer, the Tribunal is not prepared to find that the Respondent's actings in relation to these clients could have amounted to professional misconduct.

> This Decision is based solely on the averments as made by the Complainer and it must be emphasised that this Decision may not be regarded as permitting a Solicitor to approach the clients of a firm [of] which he was previously an assistant. Indeed, as indicated above, there is a duty on a Solicitor on such an occasion to take the greatest care to ensure that there is not unfair attraction of business. . . .

> . . . It is unfortunate that a dispute between two Solicitors should become the subject of a Complaint before the Discipline Tribunal. In dismissing this Complaint, the Tribunal wish to make it clear that this Decision is not to be regarded as adjudication on any aspects of the dispute between the parties but merely a finding that the averments as stated in the Affidavit which accompanied the Complaint could not result in a finding of professional misconduct (Case 407/76).

11

PROFESSIONAL MISCONDUCT OUTWITH SOLICITOR'S PRACTICE

11.01 SOLICITOR'S CONDUCT ON ALL OCCASIONS

Solicitors' actions and personal behaviour must be consistent with the need for mutual trust and confidence among clients, the courts, the public and fellow lawyers (Code of Conduct, para 7).

In a case decided in 1975 the Tribunal when finding a solicitor guilty of Professional Misconduct in connection with various matters relating to the winding up of executry estates said:

> The particular work which was the subject matter of the Complaint was not work which necessarily requires to be done by a solicitor, although it is ordinarily undertaken by a solicitor. Nevertheless the Committee are satisfied that the professional standard to be maintained with regard to such work is the same whether or not the particular solicitor holds a practising certificate, and that it is not necessary to point to work which is restricted to solicitors in practice in order to establish professional misconduct (Case 360/74).

In a Decision of the Discipline Committee made in July 1959, the Committee said:

> ... It was contended on behalf of the Respondent that professional misconduct must necessarily be restricted to misconduct in relation to the Solicitor's professional practice, save as provided by paragraph (*b*) of section 5 of the Solicitors (Scotland) Act 1958. It was further maintained that the Respondent's actions were not related to a client and even if amounting to misconduct were not professional misconduct. In the view of the Committee the provisions of paragraph (*b*) do not limit the circumstances in which a Solicitor may be dealt with by the Committee under paragraph (*a*) but only the circumstances in which the statutory powers given to them may be exercised without enquiry. Nor are they prepared to accept that in no circumstances can personal misconduct amount to professional misconduct. However that may be, the Committee are satisfied that the incidents held to have been proved occurred during the course of the Respondent's professional actings. ... (Case 228/59).

NB. Paras (*a*) and (*b*) of section 5 of the Solicitors (Scotland) Act 1958 correspond approximately to the terms of section 53(1) (*a*) and (*b*) of the 1980 Act.

The Tribunal has said:

> ... [A] solicitor is expected to conduct himself in a manner consistent with his membership of an honourable profession and this responsibility is concisely set out

by Lord Donaldson in *United Bank of Kuwait Ltd* v *Hammoud and others* [1988] 3 All ER at p 430.

> I say nothing about the position of members of the Bar as being immaterial for present purposes, but the solicitors' role is much wider than this. They are, to use an old-fashioned expression, 'men of affairs'. The public would be wise to consult them, and does consult them, when faced with unusual problems which may or may not have hidden legal aspects and which do not clearly raise issues within the special expertise of some other profession. The great, and perhaps unique, value of the professional advice of solicitors is to be found in a combination of factors which those who consult them are entitled to expect, and usually get: total independence, total integrity, total confidentiality, total dedication to the interests of the client, competent legal advice and competent other more general advice based on a wide experience of people and their problems, both in a personal and in a business context. The need to maintain this enviable situation is, of course, the reason and justification for the unforgiving attitude adopted by the profession towards those of their number, and there will inevitably be few, who fall below the standards required by them.

In the opinion of this Tribunal, the solicitor is required to maintain the same standards of propriety in his private life and in relation to any commercial ventures as are expected of him in his professional practice; and it is on the basis of this principle that the Tribunal considers the actings and conduct of the Company [a Company of which the solicitor was the sole director] in the same light as if they had been the actings of the Respondent in the course of his professional practice (Case 768/89).

The Tribunal found a solicitor (the Respondent) guilty of Professional Misconduct following his conviction, after a trial in the Sheriff Court, of attempting to pervert the course of justice, the charge (as amended) being that:

> In the medical room, Divisional Police Headquarters [. . .] you [the Respondent], having supplied a blood sample in relation to section 6(1) of the Road Traffic Act 1972, did attempt to pervert the course of justice by seizing the police part of the blood specimen and running from the medical room towards the toilet with it with the intention of disposing of said sample in the WC and thereby perverting the course of justice and you [B] did attempt to pervert the course of justice by deliberately standing with your arms outstretched between police witnesses and you [the Respondent], in an attempt to enable said [the Respondent] to run off with the police specimen aforesaid.

The Respondent was fined £50 by the Court. In its Decision, the Tribunal said:

> It has been judicially observed that when a man joins the profession of the law, he becomes bound to observe certain standards of dignity and restraint; and these standards apply to him not only when he is actively engaged in the work of his profession. He cannot disregard the responsiblity to observe these standards as he can lay aside a wig or gown. The Respondent's conduct was not only in breach of the common law but represented a serious departure from the standards expected of the profession of Solicitors particularly as the occurrence was closely concerned with legal process. It was therefore proper for the Council of the Law Society to bring the Respondent's conviction to the attention of this Tribunal and without hesitation, this Tribunal finds that the event [. . .] giving rise to the conviction warrants a finding of professional misconduct (Case 591/84).

In a case where a solicitor was found guilty after trial of being in unlawful possession of drugs in contravention of section 1(1) of the Drugs (Prevention of Misuse) Act 1964 and fined £100, he was later found guilty of Professional Misconduct by the Tribunal. The Tribunal said:

[The solicitor for the Complainers], who appeared for the Council of the Law Society of Scotland, did not lead any evidence. He referred to *Cordery's Law relating to Solicitors*, 5th edition, at page 462 and *A Guide to the Professional Conduct and Etiquette of Solicitors* by Sir Thomas Lund at page 49 and submitted that the conviction of a solicitor for a criminal offence, whether in connection with his character as a solicitor or not, and whether involving money matters or not, *prima facie* makes him unfit to continue on the Roll. [The solicitor for the Complainers] acknowledged that the nature of the offence had to be taken into consideration, and gave examples from Sir Thomas Lund's *Guide* where convictions for breaking and entering, assault and acts of indecency have all been held to be professional misconduct. He argued that the Respondent's offence was not merely of a technical nature, but required criminal intent; and he pointed out the serious consequences to those who might ultimately have received the drugs. [The solicitor for the Complainers] placed considerable emphasis on the fact that the offence had been committed within the Respondent's office, and that whilst no client was present at the time, it was to that office that the public looked as the place where the Respondent carried on his professional duties; and he added that the Respondent's conviction had resulted in considerable adverse publicity to the profession. . . .

. . . [Counsel for the Respondent] submitted that there had not been professional misconduct on the part of the Respondent, and pointed out that he had only been convicted on one single charge, that this was merely of having unlawful possession of the drugs, that the drugs concerned did not come into the category of 'hard drugs' such as heroin, that the case had only been taken in the Sheriff Court under summary procedure, and that a less than maximum penalty had been imposed. [Counsel for the Respondent] also added that the alleged conduct had not struck at any solicitor/client relationship, that as a result of the conviction the Respondent had lost only two to three clients, and that events had not prejudiced his relations with other solicitors.

. . . A conviction of a solicitor for a criminal offence creates a presumption of professional misconduct, but consideration has to be given to the nature of the offence and the surrounding circumstances. The offence of which the Respondent was convicted merely related to unlawful 'possession' of drugs, and the relevant statute only came into effect within the last few years. However, there has been increasing public concern on the matter of drugs, and the problem only has to be looked at as a whole for the seriousness of any breach of the statutory provisions to become apparent. In the course of the Hearing, the Committee were referred to the account of the Respondent's trial which appeared in 'The Scotsman' newspaper, and they also heard the Respondent and his Solicitor, [Mr A], separately relate their account of the trial. The Respondent's account of events at the time when the drugs were discovered differed materially from the account given by the police witnesses at the trial, and it appears that the Sheriff preferred the evidence of the police witnesses. Standing the conviction, however, Counsel for the Respondent had no alternative but to concede unlawful possession of the drugs, and this obviated any question of the Committee having to adjudicate upon the evidence which was given at the trial. The most important fact which was confirmed by the evidence, was that the drugs were found in the office where the Respondent carries on his practice as a solicitor.

The Committee have taken into consideration all the submissions which were made on behalf of the Respondent. However, any offence involving drugs is of particular consequence to the whole community, and bearing in mind that the offence related to the possession of drugs by the Respondent in his professional office, the Committee are satisfied that the Respondent has been guilty of professional misconduct, and that he should be censured . . . (Case 289/67).

A solicitor who pled guilty to a charge of reset in the Sheriff Court and was fined £600 was later found guilty of Professional Misconduct (Case 544/82).

A solicitor pled guilty to charges on indictment at the Sheriff Court that:

(i) On 18th November 1982 in the house at [. . .], he had in his possession a firearm viz a Walther Automatic Pistol and a quantity of ammunition without holding a firearm certificate in force at said time or otherwise than as authorised by such certificate, contrary to the Firearms Act 1968, section 1(1); and
(ii) On the same date and place, he, not being a registered firearms dealer, did have in his possession, a shotgun which had a barrel which had been shortened to a length of less than 24 inches viz 12 inches without holding a firearm certificate authorising him to have it in his possession, contrary to the Firearms Act 1968, section 4(4).

Following a subsequent hearing before the Tribunal, the Tribunal said:

At the commencement of the hearing, Counsel for the Respondent challenged the relevancy of the Complaint and submitted that the alleged misconduct on the part of the Respondent was not 'professional' in character, and argued that such non-professional misconduct could only be dealt with by this Tribunal if it followed on a conviction and related to an act involving dishonesty or if the penalty was a term of imprisonment of not less than two years.

Counsel for the Respondent submitted that 'professional misconduct' implied conduct relating to a solicitor's professional practice and he pointed out that in England where a solicitor is convicted of an offence, the Disciplinary Committee can find the solicitor guilty of 'conduct unbefitting a solicitor' and that such behaviour is contrasted with 'professional misconduct'. It was further pointed out that in regard to convictions, the Disciplinary Committee in England was not confined to the limitations contained in section 53(1) (b) of the Solicitors (Scotland) Act 1980. The Tribunal was particularly referred to the decisions:

Re a Solicitor [1956] 3 All ER 516
Re a Solicitor [1960] 2 All ER 621

In reply, the Fiscal for the Complainers argued that professional misconduct had the widest meaning and that the distinction contained in subsections 53(1) (a) and 53(1) (b) was merely procedural to the extent that the latter subsection set out circumstances in which the gravity of the conduct is such as to empower the Tribunal to proceed direct to the matter of penalty. The Fiscal also questioned whether the circumstances were wholly unrelated to the Respondent's profession.

This Tribunal has always given a wide interpretation to the phrase 'professional misconduct'. Clearly it relates to a solicitor's actings in relation to his clients and other solicitors, and there are various statutory provisions relating to the solicitor's practice alone which may give rise to professional misconduct. However, in addition it is significant that a solicitor is a member of an honourable profession which is generally held by the public to be of good standing and absolute trust. The reputation of solicitors in the eyes of the public is an essential aspect of this standing; and this Tribunal is of the opinion that any action by a solicitor falling below the standards expected of him by his professional brethren must be open to a finding of professional misconduct even although the particular actings are entirely unrelated to that solicitor's practice, his clients or other members of the profession (Case 575/83).

The Tribunal had to consider a case which was submitted by the Law Society under the provisions of section 53(1) (b) of the Solicitors (Scotland) Act 1980 which provides that the Tribunal may make an order 'if a Solicitor has . . . been convicted by any Court of an act involving dishonesty . . .'.

The Respondent (aged 26 years), who was a law apprentice, was found guilty after trial of embezzling £306.75. The Tribunal said:

It had been averred by the Fiscal at the Trial that the Respondent had embezzled sums of £21 and £20 which he had received for his employers from a client and that he had embezzled further sums of £89.50, £93.75 and £82.50, which sums ought to have been used for the payment of Stamp Duty on three separate conveyances. The Respondent had pleaded Not Guilty but he was convicted after a trial extending over four days.

The Respondent insisted on his innocence at the hearing before the Tribunal but in view of the terms of section 53(1) of the Solicitors (Scotland) Act 1980, the Tribunal is precluded from looking behind the conviction. . . .

It is usual for a Solicitor in the course of his practice to handle sums of money for clients and the public rely absolutely on the integrity of Solicitors. Accordingly a conviction of embezzlement represents a serious departure from the highest standards expected of a Solicitor and there is ample precedent for striking a Solicitor off the Roll of Solicitors where he has been convicted of embezzling sums of clients' money.

In this case, it is significant that the Sheriff imposed a relatively modest fine. The Tribunal have also noted the Respondent's age, that he was in employment as an apprentice at the time when the offences occurred and that it was the funds of his employers which had been misappropriated; and in these particular circumstances, it is considered that it would [be] inappropriate to exclude the Respondent from ever practising as a Solicitor in the future. Nevertheless some time should pass before the Respondent might enter into practice and for this reason a period of suspension has been imposed. It will thereafter be within the discretion of the Council of the Law Society of Scotland, acting under the provisions of section 15 of the Solicitors (Scotland) Act 1980 to decide when it might be appropriate to issue a Practising Certificate to the Respondent (Case 489/80).

Other circumstances resulting in findings of Professional Misconduct:

A solicitor was found guilty in the Sheriff Court and fined £200 for attempting to pervert the course of justice in that he had falsely represented to police constables that he was the driver of a car at the time of a road accident when he was not (Case 782/90).

A solicitor issued a cheque for a substantial sum representing rent *inter alia* for his office premises which was not honoured (Case 782/90).

A solicitor had been convicted and admonished in the Sheriff Court on a charge of assault and breach of the peace (Case 673/86).

A solicitor was found guilty of repeated motoring offences. The Tribunal in this case said:

> It was averred in the Complaint in relation to the repeated motoring offences that the Respondent was guilty of criminal conduct which was seriously detrimental to and inconsistent with the good name and dignity of the profession. It was further stated that the Respondent's conduct was calculated to bring the profession into disrepute and was unbefitting and a gross departure from the standards to be expected of a Solicitor.

> In the English case, *Re a Solicitor* [1960] 2 All ER 621 at 622, Lord Parker refuted the suggestion that the mere conviction of any criminal offence is evidence of conduct unbefitting a Solicitor. The nature of the offence and the frequency were matters to be taken into consideration in determining whether there had been professional misconduct and in the event of misconduct being established, this Tribunal has a duty to enquire into the circumstances before determining the appropriate penalty. On the first occasion on which the Respondent was convicted he was found guilty of failing to produce a Certificate of Insurance within the prescribed period, but on the second and third occasions the Respondent was found guilty of using the particular vehicle without insurance inferring that he knew or ought to have known that the vehicle was not insured. In the event of an accident, failure to have third party insurance can have very serious consequences and the seriousness of this offence is demonstrated by the penalty of disqualification on each occasion. The events giving rise to the first conviction ought to have alerted the Respondent to the importance of ascertaining the insurance arrangements before driving any vehicle and this Tribunal cannot but regard as reprehensible the Respondent's successive failures to comply with the particular provisions of the Road Traffic Act.

> In his Answers, the Respondent explained his failure to produce the required documents for the reasons:

> (a) He was too heavily engaged in work for his clients during the five-day period allowed, and

> (b) He was disheartened by the fact that he was being stopped regularly by the Police and almost always for no apparent reason.

> He further explained in relation to the vehicle driven on the earlier occasions that he accepted the assurance of the former owner of the vehicle that it was properly insured, and that he accepted a similar statement by the owner of the vehicle which he was driving on [. . .] 1983. In the opinion of this Tribunal, these explanations do not in any way minimise the gravity of the Respondent's conduct in relation to these motoring offences (Case 636/84).

12

CONVEYANCING

12.01 DUTY OF DISCLOSURE OF WHOLE CIRCUMSTANCES

A bridging loan had been arranged with a Bank to settle a conveyancing transaction pending receipt of a Building Society loan and a solicitor (the Respondent) told his client that the Building Society loan was through, although this was false.

He then sent a draft cash account to his client purporting to show that there was an amount of £1,040.98 due as interest to the Bank on bridging facilities, and that there was an amount due to the Respondent's firm of £1,447.91 to settle the transaction. The client settled this balance and requested a Certificate of Interest in relation to the bridging loan. After some delay the Respondent prepared and sent the client a document purporting to be such a Certificate showing a sum of £761.98, being the interest charged on the account up to the 5th April 1979. Said Certificate purported to be executed on the 1st June 1979 by 'agents for X Bank . . .' although the Bank had not authorised the issue of the purported Certificate.

The Tribunal said:

> . . . Counsel for the Respondent did not dispute that he had misled [the client] and gave false information to him, and that this amounted to professional misconduct. The Tribunal noted the Respondent's explanation that he had been over-confident in regard to [the client's] loan and that even in April 1979 when he falsely said that the loan was through, he expected the situation was about to change. However, it is significant that up until August 1979, [the client] was never aware of the loan position. The Respondent deliberately deceived [the client] on 20th April 1979 and in these circumstances the Tribunal is satisfied that this part of the Complaint was wholly established.

> The Respondent explained that his conduct in issuing a Certificate of Interest on behalf of the [X] Bank without the authority of the Bank was also a consequence of the situation which he got himself into by falsely claiming that he had received the loan cheque from the Building Society. This explanation is not accepted by the Tribunal. His action in issuing a Certificate of Interest without authority was particularly reprehensible, for such a Certificate would ordinarily have been relied upon by the Inland Revenue and others and the unfortunate consequences of such a false document could have been considerable . . . (Case 436/80).

In Case 426b/79 the Tribunal found:

> (4) . . . [The Respondent] guilty of professional misconduct in that upon obtaining the [X] Bank bridging loans of £20,000 specifically to assist himself and a client with house purchases, he failed to inform the Bank that the principal dwell-

inghouse had been burned down and that he could not offer a title to the client, further that no part of the bridging facility was paid to the seller of the subjects but the whole of it was appropriated to [the Respondent's] private Bank Account and £16,500 was drawn therefrom and paid into his firm's office and client accounts.

The following facts were established:

(2) In May 1978, [the Respondent] completed Missives to purchase from [A] a property [.....], which consisted of a substantial dwellinghouse and separate cottage. In terms of the Missives, the price was stated to be £71,000 with entry on 1st August 1978. Mr [B] was a personal friend of [the Respondent]. At about this time [the Respondent] showed the property to Mr [B]. He suggested to Mr [B] that he might like to purchase the cottage but Mr [B] indicated that he was not then interested. On 19th May 1978, the main dwellinghouse was destroyed by fire. The cottage was not affected. [The Respondent] did not at any time make a payment toward the purchase price of the subjects. On 4th August 1978, [the Respondent] persuaded Mr [B] to sign an acceptance to an offer which [the Respondent] had prepared whereby Mr [B] would purchase the cottage at a price of £25,000. Mr [B] had no intention of occupying the premises and he had agreed to sign the Missives as an obligement to [the Respondent]. At the time when these Missives were concluded, a former employee of the seller was still residing in the cottage. The Missives which were concluded between [the Respondent] and Mr [B] did not provide for a specific date of entry and [the Respondent] did not discuss with Mr [B] the arrangements for payment of the purchase price or for providing the finance for the purchase.

(3) On or shortly before 29th September 1978 [the Respondent] telephoned the [X] Bank. He informed the Bank that [Y] Building Society was lending him £20,000, [an] Assurance Company £15,000 and that the balance of the price was to come from the net proceeds of sale [of] his existing house at [.....]. He asked the Bank to provide him with bridging facilities of £20,000 to assist him in the purchase of the whole subjects. [The Respondent] did not disclose to the Bank at this time that the dwellinghouse had been destroyed by fire. The Bank granted the facility but restricted the drawing to £5,000 until such time as [the Respondent] procured the signature of his partner, Mr [C]. On 29th September 1978, [the Respondent] drew a cheque for £5,000 on the bridging account and paid the cheque to his private account with the [Z] Bank. No part of the sum was paid to the seller of the subjects. On 29th September 1978, the Respondent also withdrew £5,000 from his private account and transferred this sum to his firm's client account. As at the commencement of the hearing of this Complaint, namely 20th November 1979, [the Respondent] had not repaid the said £5,000 or any interest thereon, to the [X] Bank.

(4) On or shortly before 16th October 1978 [the Respondent] made written application to the [X] Bank for bridging facilities of £15,000 to assist Mr [B] in the purchase of the cottage and in the written application, [the Respondent] stated that the [Y] Building Society were to be the lenders. At the time no formal application for a loan had been made to the [Y] Building Society by Mr [B] or on his behalf. The application form stated that [the Respondent] held an irrevocable instruction signed by Mr [B] to repay the Bank but no such instruction had been signed by Mr [B]. [The Respondent] did not disclose to the Bank that the cottage was then still occupied. The request for bridging facilities was granted and on 16th October 1978 [the Respondent] drew a cheque for £15,000 from the bridging account in his favour. This cheque was also paid into [the Respondent's] private account with the [Z] Bank. No part of the sum was paid to the seller of the whole subjects and at this

time [the Respondent] had himself not made any payment towards the price of these subjects [nor] did he hold a title to the same. On or about 16th October, [the Respondent] transferred two sums of £5,000 from his private account and paid these amounts respectively into his office and client account on the same day. On or about 24th November 1978, he withdrew a further £1,500 from his private account and paid this amount into his firm client account on that day. In February 1979, the missives between Mr [A] and [the Respondent] and between [the Respondent] and Mr [B], were rescinded. . . .

In its Decision the Tribunal said:

. . . In making his first application for a bridging loan, [the Respondent] failed to disclose to the Bank that the principal dwellinghouse had already been destroyed by fire. Furthermore he transferred the £5,000 from the bridging loan to his personal account and no part was paid over to the seller of the subjects. The service of providing bridging loans to Solicitors and their clients is the subject of well established practice and it is clearly understood within the profession that it is the duty of a Solicitor when making an application for a bridging loan to disclose all relevant circumstances to the Bank and thereafter, unless specific arrangements are made to the contrary, to use the monies towards the purchase of the property concerned. The Tribunal is satisfied that the [destruction] of the principal dwellinghouse was a matter which ought to have been made known to the Bank; and furthermore that [the Respondent] acted contrary to established practice when he applied the monies for his own personal use and did not make over any part of the same to the seller. The Tribunal wholly reject the suggestion that the Bank did not require the bridging monies to be paid over to the purchaser.

The Tribunal did not have the advantage of personally hearing the evidence of Mr [B] and no opinion is expressed on the genuineness of Mr [B's] intention to proceed with the purchase of the cottage.

Mr [B] himself did not make any loan application to a Building Society but it is accepted that [the Respondent] may have mentioned the matter to the [Y] Building Society. The Tribunal did not find [the Respondent] to be a credible witness and in particular the Tribunal did not accept [the Respondent's] evidence that he had Mr [B's] authority to arrange a bridging loan in his name or that he wrote to Mr [B] to confirm this arrangement.

The duties of a Solicitor in arranging a bridging loan have already been set out above and [the Respondent] failed to fulfil the duties incumbent on him when he arranged the loan in the name of Mr [B]. In particular he did not disclose to the Bank that the cottage was still subject to a tenancy and that as he himself had not paid [for] the property, he was unable to grant a title to Mr [B]. The Tribunal is satisfied that [the Respondent] ought to have conveyed this information to the Bank when applying for the bridging loan. Furthermore [the Respondent] retained the amount of the bridging loan and did not pay any part of the purchase price even to the seller of the whole subjects. It is also significant that when [the Respondent] subsequently submitted a form to the [X] Bank confirming the bridging loan he failed to delete the provision which stated that he held irrevocable instructions signed by his client to repay the Bank.

The Tribunal is satisfied that [the Respondent's] whole actings in relation to the bridging loans for the property at [. . . . .] amount to professional misconduct . . . (Case 426b/79).

See also Case 748/89, referred to at para 12.08.

12.02 PROBATIVE DEEDS

In a case where the Tribunal found that a solicitor had forged the signature of the grantor of a Disposition of heritable property and then framed a fictitious testing clause thereon, the Tribunal having found Professional Misconduct established said:

> The system of probative deeds is an essential part of our whole conveyancing system; and the public expects and relies upon the Profession of Solicitors to carry out the various procedures with the utmost of propriety. Forgery is always a serious matter and where as in this case it was committed to cover up the deficiencies of the solicitor's own conveyancing and might have resulted in a false deed appearing on the Public Registers, this can only be regarded as most grave conduct which was aggravated by the Respondent's foolish attempt to deceive his partner into believing that the deed was genuine (Case 829/92).

See also Case 709/88.

A solicitor was found guilty of Professional Misconduct when he altered a probative deed, after it had been executed by the parties, without authority from or notification to either party to the deed, and he added the authenticating initials of both parties to the deed in order to create the impression that the alteration had been approved by them. In that case the Tribunal observed:

> Clerical errors not infrequently arise in deeds and, for the sake of expediency, there is an accepted practice in very limited circumstances which may result in deeds being altered after signature. Where the effect of an alteration is wholly inconsequential it may even be acceptable for the alteration to be made without the express approval of the solicitors for the other parties but if the intended alterations are of any significance whatsoever, the solicitor has a duty to seek the approval of the agents acting for the other parties. Such practices demand the utmost of propriety from solicitors and under no circumstances should practitioners seek to make any alteration which has a significant effect in relation to the interests of the parties, without insisting that the alteration is authenticated by all the parties and then declared in the Testing Clause. Indeed there are occasions, and this particularly applies to Testamentary Deeds, where the only satisfactory solution is to have the deed re-extended and subscribed *de novo*.

> In this case, it was apparent that it had been the Respondent's practice to insert in matrimonial deeds the full clause of consent to registration for preservation and execution, and the omission of the words 'and execution' seems to have been a typing error or an error in drafting. It is significant to look at the deed separately in the form in which it was signed and at the later stage when it was eventually recorded and extracted. The omission of the words 'and execution' did not invalidate the deed. The agreement, as signed, contained all the provisions which had been agreed between the parties and it would have been enforceable by recourse to the Courts. However, the addition of the words 'and execution' had a material consequence in that an extract of the deed if recorded would in effect have had the same authority as a decree of the Court in whose Books the deed had been registered. This facility can undoubtedly accelerate the enforcement of any obligation contained in the deed with the claimant being able to proceed immediately to arrestment in execution without the notice which an obligant would ordinarily receive in the form of a Court Writ. A deed containing consent to registration for preservation and execution should not be lightly signed by an intending obligant and it is the solicitor's duty to explain the effect of this Clause if it is appropriate

that it should appear in any deed to be signed by his client. By adding the words 'and execution' after the agreement had been signed, the Respondent deprived [the agents for the other party to the deed] of the opportunity of explaining the effects of these words to their client. The Respondent should have been aware of this and it is in these circumstances that he could not have expected the implied consent of that firm to the alteration. The addition of the offending words was a material alteration having significant effects on the client of [the agents for the other party to the deed] and the only acceptable alternatives open to the Respondent upon the omission becoming apparent would have been to accept the deed as it stood or to return it to that firm and ascertain whether their client would have been prepared to authenticate the intended alteration.

The addition of the purported initials of each of the signatories did not in itself affect the apparent terms of the Agreement and the absence of any declaration [in] the Testing Clause was in contrast to the other alterations appearing in the second and third pages of the deed. In the absence of any declaration it might have been questionable whether the alteration was effective, even with the addition [of] the purported initials but that question is not a matter for this Tribunal. Nevertheless it is apparent that these 'initials' were added with the intention of conveying to third parties that the alteration had the approval of the signatories to the deed. The essence of a probative deed is that no further evidence is required of the obligations or rights which it purports to involve or confer. The onus of disproving the provisions of a probative deed rests on the party who disputes them and the method of proof is limited. It is in these circumstances that the Tribunal finds the Respondent's actings in altering the particular agreement to have been serious and reprehensible, warranting a finding of professional misconduct (Case 798/90).

A solicitor was charged with Professional Misconduct in that he procured the signature of persons who purported to act as witnesses to the signatures of parties to deeds whereas, in fact, they had neither seen the parties sign the deeds nor heard them acknowledge their signatures and thereafter he added a false date of execution. The Tribunal said:

The remaining charge related to the execution of the Feu Contract, the discount Security in favour of the Development Corporation and the Building Society Standard Security. When the Respondent separately sent these deeds to his clients for signature, he failed to give any instructions for witnesses nor did he enclose a signing schedule and it is understandable why the deeds were returned to him without have been witnessed. The effect of witnessing is to create a probative deed and in relation to such deeds the authenticity of the signatures is presumed; but for proper attestation the witnesses must see the parties sign or hear them acknowledge their signatures and must have credible information as to their identity. In the particular circumstances, the Respondent deliberately ignored the established formalities and by procuring the signatures of two members of his staff, he fraudulently abused the procedure; and in relation to the Standard Security he compounded his reckless conduct by backdating the deed (Case 774/89).

The Tribunal stated in a case in 1991:

The Register of Sasines is a public register and the cornerstone of conveyancing practice in Scotland. For a solicitor knowingly to use a fictitious name in a document [and to cause that document to be registered in the Register of Sasines] is to undermine the confidence which the public ought to have in the Register. Furthermore, for a solicitor to use a fictitious name for a client to give the impression that the transaction was at arms length, when it was truly by a client to himself, is further to undermine the confidence which the public ought to have in the legal profession and to bring the profession into disrepute.

Hence the solicitor, who knew that the purported granter and grantee of the Disposition who appeared on the face of the deed prepared and recorded by the solicitor, to be different persons were in fact one and the same person, was guilty of Professional Misconduct (Case 817/91).

In a case where a solicitor (the Respondent) was charged that he had acted without authority and instructions when he had recorded a Disposition in the Register of Sasines, he having previously ceased to act for the parties on whose behalf he had recorded the Disposition, the Tribunal, in the particular circumstances of the case, found that the degree of culpability would not in itself justify a finding of Professional Misconduct and said:

> The signing of a warrant of registration is an important step in the conclusion of any conveyancing transaction and such warrant should only be signed and a deed presented for recording where the Solicitor has continuing instructions from his clients (Case 611/85).

A solicitor (the Respondent) received instructions to act on behalf of Mr A in connection with the purchase of a house and from a Local Authority (the Council) to act on their behalf in connection with a loan which the client A was receiving to assist in the purchase. In its Findings the Tribunal noted:

> (4) The Respondent presented the Standard Security and Disposition for registration on [...]. The Disposition bore to be in favour of the Council instead of Mr [A]. Both writs were accordingly returned to the Respondent unrecorded because of the error [in] the Disposition. On [...] the Respondent represented the same Disposition, now bearing to be in favour of Mr [A], dated 31st January and 2nd February 1977 and the Standard security by Mr [A] in favour of the Council dated 31st January 1977 [in each case the date year should have been stated as '1978']. In the narrative clause of the Disposition Mr [A's] name was typed over an erasure and the names of Mr X (the seller) and Mr [A] were typed over a white substance which was used to obliterate the original typescript. Further, Mr [A's] name in the dispositive clause and in the warrant for registration were also typed over a similar substance, obliterating the previous typescript. The testing clause, which had originally been typed, was imperfectly obscured and was overwritten in the Respondent's manuscript. One signature below the testing clause was partly erased. No attempt had been made to authenticate any of these alterations. The Standard Security was in [normal] form. The Keeper refused to record the Disposition because of the unauthenticated alterations which had been made after execution.

> (5) By letter dated [...] the Keeper wrote to the Law Society of Scotland and complained that the Respondent had attempted to obtain registration of a writ which had been altered as aforesaid after its execution ...

In finding the Respondent guilty of Professional Misconduct the Tribunal, in respect of '. . . . . her conduct in presenting to the General Register of Sasines a deed containing extensive and unauthenticated alterations,' said:

12.02 PROBATIVE DEEDS

... Furthermore, there was gross incompetence on the part of the Respondent in regard to her completion and the ultimate recording of the particular Disposition. Initially the Disposition purported to be in favour of [...] Council but when it was returned, extensive alterations were made to the deed before it was then represented to the Register of Sasines. Originally the Respondent was charged with making the alterations without having them authenticated but in her Answers, the Respondent claimed that contrary to the usual practice, the deed had been extended by the Seller's Solicitor and that she had not made the alterations; and in respect of this the Complainers amended the relative charge. Nevertheless the Respondent signed the warrant of registration on the Disposition and presented it to the Register of Sasines for recording; and by so doing, the Respondent must be held responsible for the condition of the deed. Even although she herself did not effect the particular alterations the Tribunal is satisfied that the Respondent ought to have been aware that the alterations had not been authenticated, and her presentation of the deed in the particular condition demonstrated her gross lack of appreciation of the practical requirement of having a deed properly drawn and executed ... (Case 471/80).

12.03 EXECUTION OF INCOMPLETE DEED

Where a solicitor was found guilty of Professional Misconduct following on his failure to record timeously a Disposition in favour of the borrowers and a Standard Security in favour of a Building Society after cashing Building Society loan cheques, the Tribunal said:

The Respondent explained in mitigation that prior to settlement, he had procured his clients' signatures to a blank Standard Security form. There are occasions when it is acceptable to have a security deed signed with an incidental matter such as the commencement date for repayments left blank but it is wholly unacceptable for a Solicitor to procure his client's signature to a blank form of Standard Security, particularly at the time when a Building Society loan cheque is being cashed and accordingly the Tribunal do not accept this particular explanation (Case 626/85).

12.04 USE OF FICTITIOUS NAMES

A solicitor (the Respondent) was found guilty of Professional Misconduct in that *inter alia*:

(*a*) His actings were likely to bring the profession into disrepute in that he was carrying on property transactions truly for the benefit of himself, his wife and one other under an assumed name.
(*b*) His actings in using a fictitious name relative to a conveyancing transaction amounted to a deception of his professional colleagues.
(*c*) His actings in recording or permitting to be recorded deeds in which one of the parties was named fictitiously could undermine the confidence which the General Register of Sasines enjoys as the foundation of the Scottish Conveyancing System.
(*d*) In the event of the death of himself and his wife prior to the conclusion of any transaction, the other party could have been placed in a very damaging position in that there would have been no contracting party against whom he could take action for implement or reduction of the missives and in respect of each purchase, no named person to whom he could look for the purchase price and in respect of each sale, no named person to whom he could look for a title to the particular property.

The Tribunal said in its Decision:

... Counsel further explained that the Respondent was anxious to avoid disclosing his wife's interests either to his staff or to other members of the legal profession. He mistakenly believed that it was open to anyone in Scotland to use any name which he or she might choose. It was on this basis that the Respondent advised his wife to use a different fictitious name for each property which was purchased. The missives were concluded in that name, the Respondent carried on correspondence with other solicitors as if that was the name of his client and the name appeared as the disponee of each conveyance.

Although it has been judicially observed that 'any person may, without authority of the court, call himself what he pleases' and that a person 'has a perfect right to change his name, and no one can prevent him from adding to it or altering it', such does not justify or authorise the indiscriminate use of fictitious names. As Counsel acknowledged, quoting from the Encyclopaedia of the Laws of Scotland, Volume 10, page 138, 'the standard rule in Scotland is that the surname of an individual is the name by which he is at the time called and known, which he uses in his contacts and transactions with the public, and by means of which as a sufficient designation of him, his identity is rendered indisputable'. It is further observed in the same volume (at page 146) that 'a man's name is that by which he is generally known. How he may have acquired it does not matter. It is his name and he has a right to be called by it, if it is the name which he usually receives amongst his friends and acquaintances. In making changes of name it is obviously necessary that some formal step be taken so that the party's identity under the new name and the old name be conclusively established'. It is clear that none of the names used by the Respondent were the name by which his wife was generally known and Counsel for the Respondent properly acknowledged that they were 'fictitious names'.

It was accepted by the Respondent that the use of such fictitious names was conduct likely to bring the profession into disrepute and furthermore the use of such names amounted to a deception of other solicitors dealing with the Respondent in regard to these particular properties ... (Case 609/85).

12.05 CONDITIONS ATTACHED TO A CHEQUE

In a case where a solicitor had accepted and allowed to be cashed a cheque, being an advance from lenders to his clients, without implementing or being in a position to implement the whole conditions attached to the encashment of the cheque imposed by the lender's solicitors and, in particular, without providing to the lenders and their solicitors a new Disposition in favour of the borrower as had been agreed, the Tribunal said:

The settlement of a conveyancing transaction is an established formality which enables each solicitor to protect fully the interests of his client. It is becoming increasingly common for settlements to be effected in the course of correspondence, but the duty remains on each solicitor to respect the formality of the settlement and to carry out the same procedures as if the settlement was effected in the traditional manner.

Additionally there is an unequivocal duty on a solicitor to comply with any undertaking which he gives to a professional colleague and where a cheque is sent 'on the understanding' that the recipient solicitor will forward certain documents, the mere retention or encashment of that cheque in itself constitutes a professional undertaking; and it is the duty of the recipient solicitor to comply with such undertaking. ...

12.05 CONDITIONS ATTACHED TO A CHEQUE

Nothwithstanding the pressure from his clients, the Respondent should not have cashed the loan cheque until such time as he had been in a position to deliver not only the executed Standard Security and Assignation but also the fresh Disposition in favour of his clients. If *per incuriam* the cheque had been cashed in circumstances where any of these documents had not been available, then it would have been the Respondent's duty to return the loan monies to the lenders' solicitors, or if the funds had already been forwarded to his client, then to make restitution to the lenders out of his own personal funds. Even in these duties the Respondent culpably failed and the gravity of his actings was compounded by his additional failure to inform the lenders' solicitors of the circumstances which had arisen. The Respondent's actings constituted a gross breach of trust which strikes at the very special relationship between solicitors within the profession and although this Complaint related merely to a single transaction, it is appropriate that the Tribunal should take a very serious view of the Respondent's conduct. . . .

It is fundamental to the conveyancing system that a solicitor follows at all times the established procedures. On this occasion the Respondent demonstrated a serious breach of trust and it is in these circumstances, taken with the previous finding, that the Tribunal has resolved to impose not only a substantial fine but also to direct that the publicity to be given to this decision will include the name of the Respondent (Case 695/86).

Similarly, a solicitor acting for a seller of property was found guilty of Professional Misconduct where a firm of solicitors in delivering a cheque to the solicitor for the purchase price of a property in their covering letter imposed the express condition that if he cashed the cheque the solicitor would send by return an executed Disposition and various other specified documents and if he could not meet these conditions he was to return the cheque. On receipt of the letter the solicitor telephoned to say that he would comply with the conditions; he cashed the cheque and the purchaser took entry but the solicitor did not send the said documents to the purchaser's solicitors (Case 674/86).

12.06 STOPPAGE OF A CHEQUE

[T]he settlement of property transactions in Scotland is facilitated by the underlying trust between solicitors. A specific example of this is the payment of the price by a cheque drawn by the purchaser's solicitor on a joint stock bank in favour of the seller's solicitor. Were the purchaser's solicitor to instruct the bank to stop payment of the cheque such action could amount to professional misconduct (Code of Conduct, para 9).

A firm of solicitors received a cheque from their client, to settle the purchase price of a property, and banked the cheque to the credit of their client account; they later settled the transaction with a cheque drawn on their client account in exchange for which they received the titles to the property, the keys, executed Disposition and other usual documentation in terms of the missives. Two days later the solicitor (A) for the purchaser was informed that the purchaser's cheque had been returned 'refer to drawer'. Mr A telephoned the solicitor for the sellers to advise that the cheque which Mr A's firm had received from their client had not been met and that his firm were accordingly issuing instructions to their own bank to stop the cheque in favour of the sellers' solicitors; the sellers' solicitors did not consent to this course. The solicitors for the purchaser made attempts to restore the position to what it was prior to settlement including returning the keys, the titles, etc.

The Tribunal in finding the solicitors for the purchaser (the Respondents) not guilty of Professional Misconduct said:

> The Tribunal have carefully considered the circumstances in this particular case. Due consideration has also been given to the expert evidence which, as has been seen, was conflicting and inconclusive. In all the circumstances, it is the opinion of the Tribunal that the Respondents and Mr [A] in particular should not have stopped payment on their cheque. The Respondents in deciding to settle this transaction in advance of their client cheque being cleared, took a material risk. This was specifically conceded by Mr [A] in his evidence. The Respondents were in the best position to determine the strength of this cheque and it is the opinion of the Tribunal that the Respondents must bear the responsibility for the risk which was taken by them.
>
> The Tribunal were informed that the Respondents attempted to effect *restitutio in integrum* by returning the titles, the executed Disposition and the keys to the sellers' Solicitors. They also ascertained that the sellers' solicitors had apparently remitted a sum of [£ . . .] to the Local Authority in settlement of the current year's rates and they sent a cheque to the sellers' solicitors to reimburse them for this payment. However, it is significant that the sellers' solicitor had, previous to the settlement, given an assurance to his clients, the sellers, that it would not be necessary to await the clearance of the Respondents' cheque before releasing the keys; and in any event it is usual for a solicitor acting for a seller to indicate to his client that he will account for the proceeds of sale immediately upon settlement taking place. By stopping the cheque the Respondents put the sellers' solicitor in a difficult position and the effect of this action would undoubtedly have an adverse effect on the reputation of that solicitor and the profession in general. In addition the sellers themselves could have been relying on payment of the proceeds in order to honour other commitments; but in any event the mere return of the titles and keys leaves the sellers with no alternative but to seek another purchaser. Such would ordinarily give rise to additional expense and loss of interest and there is no certainty that the sellers would have obtained a similar price upon the resale. The Tribunal were informed that the Respondents' client eventually appeared and attempted to effect settlement at a later date and that the sellers declined to proceed with the transaction. However, the Tribunal are not concerned with such developments which might have taken place at a later date. The significant considerations are that the sellers' solicitor and the sellers were separately and materially inconvenienced by the Respondents' action in stopping payment on their cheque and in failing to issue a substitute cheque as soon as it was made known to the Respondents that the sellers and their solicitor did not acquiesce.
>
> The material question before the Tribunal is whether the Respondents' actions in stopping the cheque drawn on their client account at the settlement of this particular transaction and their subsequent failure to issue a substitute cheque when called upon to do so by the sellers' solicitor amounted to professional misconduct.
>
> Whilst the Tribunal are of the opinion that the Respondents acted improperly there is a not insignificant body of opinion within the profession which would support the actings of the Respondents.
>
> It is accepted that the Respondents considered their position carefully at each stage. At the time when Mr [A] made the decision to stop payment on the cheque,

there was no other partner with whom he could confer; but he took the earliest possible opportunity to speak with his other partners and he also conferred with the Secretariat of the Law Society of Scotland. The terms of the article contained in the May 1978 issue of the Journal of the Law Society of Scotland were carefully considered and although it is the view of the Tribunal that the Respondents misdirected themselves in interpreting this article, it is accepted that they acted in good faith in persisting with their decision not to fund the transaction personally.

It is the opinion of the Tribunal that in the particular circumstances, the Respondents' actings narrowly fell short of professional misconduct; but the Tribunal reserve their position in the future to make a finding of professional misconduct in the event of a cheque drawn by a Solicitor on his client account and handed over in settlement of a conveyancing transaction being subsequently stopped in circumstances arising only from the purchaser's conduct; and it is therefore appropriate that publicity should be given to this decision although such publicity will not include the names of the Respondents or their firm (Case 493/81).

12.07 FAILURE TO IMPLEMENT LETTER OF OBLIGATION

It is in the public interest and for the benefit of clients and the administration of justice that there be a corporate professional spirit based upon relationships of trust and co-operation between solicitors. For example, the settlement of property transactions in Scotland is facilitated by the underlying trust between solicitors (Code of Conduct, para 9).

The Tribunal has observed that a Letter of Obligation is a document common to every conveyancing transaction but it should never be granted lightly because, by the issue of such an undertaking, the solicitor commits his or her own personal funds as guarantee, and it is on this basis that the purchase price is handed over in full. In a particular case the solicitor had given a Letter of Obligation to deliver an executed discharge of a security which would only be available if the whole loan monies were repaid to a Building Society, which the solicitor had failed to pay out of the sale price, having omitted to ascertain the precise amount required to discharge the loan. Having failed in this regard the Tribunal stated that it became the solicitor's absolute duty to implement the obligation even although this meant advancing funds out of the solicitor's own resources. The Tribunal went on to find that the failure on the part of the solicitor to implement the Letter of Obligation amounted to Professional Misconduct (Cases 831/92; 807/90; 777/89; 778/89).

In a case where a solicitor, who knew that there was a valid Inhibition recorded by a creditor against his client (the seller of a property), granted a Letter of Obligation, at the settlement of the sale of the property, which contained an undertaking to discharge the Inhibition but then following on the settlement made no provision for the sum of £3,000 due to the inhibiting creditor when disposing of the free proceeds of the sale; the Tribunal found the solicitor guilty of Professional Misconduct in that *inter alia*:

(*a*) he failed to make provision for discharging the Inhibition before distributing the proceeds of sale; and (*b*) he failed to ensure that he would be in a position to implement his Letter of Obligation,

and observed that:

> In settling any conveyancing transaction, there is a duty on the solicitor to fulfil his professional obligations and these include the discharge of any outstanding incumbrance and the recording without delay of the appropriate conveyance and security deeds. Failure to fulfil such obligations results in the particular party being uninfeft or unsecured and this can have grave consequences.

> The Tribunal similarly takes a serious view of the failure of any practitioner to co-operate with his fellow solicitor in relation to any conveyancing transaction. It is essential for the smooth working of the conveyancing system that solicitors co-operate fully, and the Respondent's failures and in particular in not being in a position to implement his letter of obligation, were reprehensible. It is in these circumstances that the Tribunal had no hesitation in pronouncing a finding of professional misconduct in relation to each of the charges in connection with his actings for [Mr and Mrs A] (Case 707/87).

12.08 FAILURE TO RECORD DEEDS TIMEOUSLY

The Tribunal on a number of occasions has found solicitors guilty of Professional Misconduct as a result of their failure to record Dispositions and Standard Securities timeously following the settlement of a transaction; such failures put the purchaser/lender at risk and the Tribunal takes a serious view of such failures. In one such case (in which the solicitor was acting for a purchaser and a lender) the Tribunal, when making a finding of Professional Misconduct, stated:

> It is a prerequisite of any heritable security that the borrower has a title to the security subjects; and the security can only be perfected upon the security deed being recorded in the Property Register. Although it did not arise in this case the solicitor must also be satisfied that there is no adverse entry relating to the borrower in the Personal Register and (in the case of a corporate borrower) the Register of Charges.

> Regarding the title, the matter is usually straightforward where the borrower is already infeft in the property, but when the loan transaction coincides with acquisition of the property, the solicitor for the lender must be satisfied from a prior examination of the title deeds, an Interim Report on the Search and a draft of the conveyance that such deed will confer on the borrower a clear title and the executed conveyance will be delivered not later than the occasion when the loan transaction is settled. To complete the security, the solicitor for the borrower must also be in a position to ensure that the conveyance and the relative security deed can be recorded without delay. This presupposes that the security deed has already been executed (as was the case in this matter). However, the Respondent regrettably failed to ensure that an executed conveyance was to be available at about the time of the settlement of the loan transaction, and the fact that the Respondent believed that an onward sale of the property was imminent, was wholly irrelevant (Case 834/92).

The Tribunal has also found a solicitor guilty of Professional Misconduct where, while acting on behalf of a lender, he recorded the Discharge of a security without repaying the loan. The Tribunal stated that a solicitor had an implied professional duty to retain the executed Discharge and release it only at the stage when the loan monies were repaid, thereby ensuring that the lender continued to have a heritable security throughout the whole period the loan was outstanding (Case 832/92).

The Tribunal has recognised that for practical reasons a Certificate to the effect that a title 'is good and marketable' requires to be given by a solicitor some days before the loan transaction is settled and it is not uncommon, particularly when a property purchase coincides with the granting of a loan, that certain documents may still be in the course of preparation or awaiting signature and that the essential recording of particular title deeds will only be attended to after the settlement date. This is ordinarily covered by the solicitor for the lender taking possession of the Disposition in favour of the borrower and recording it along with the Standard Security immediately following the settlement of the loan. Accordingly it is accepted practice in such circumstances for the lender's solicitor to certify that the borrower has a good marketable title on the understanding that the foregoing procedure will be followed immediately the lender's loan cheque is encashed. The security deed and the supporting title deeds should not however be allowed to pass out of the hands of the solicitor acting on behalf of the lender into the hands of a person with a contrary interest in the transaction after the loan cheque has been cashed and the loan monies have been handed over. Furthermore, whether or not the borrower, or the solicitor for the borrower, is closely related to the solicitor for the lender, the duties remain the same (Case 818/91).

Where a solicitor is acting for a borrower and a lender, it is for the solicitor to satisfy himself that he is in a position to settle any Stamp Duty payable as soon as practicable after the settlement either from his own resources or the funds of his client; and if a solicitor is unwilling or unable personally to finance the Stamp Duty, his only alternative may be to delay the settlement if the client's own funds are not forthcoming (Case 773/89).

In a case where a solicitor acting on behalf of purchasers and lenders had settled transactions without the precaution of having sufficient clients' money to cover the Stamp Duty and then failed to record the deeds timeously because the clients had failed to pay the Stamp Duty, the Tribunal found Professional Misconduct proved in that the solicitor had to accept the consequences of his failure to have money available to meet the Stamp Duty at settlement, because the lenders had been put at risk by the failure to record the purchasers' titles and the lenders' securities (Case 773/89).

In another case the Tribunal said:

> In each of the five conveyancing transactions, the Respondent had been instructed by both the purchasing client and the respective Building Society which was making an advance on the security of the particular property being purchased by each client. In such transactions, it is the established procedure for the solicitor, prior to the expected settlement date, to apply to the Building Society for the loan

cheque. Some Building Societies stipulate, but in any event it is an implied condition and established practice, that the solicitor will only intromit with the loan monies when he is in a position to receive and record his client's title and to record a valid Standard Security in favour of the Building Society; and if there is any delay in these procedures after the loan cheque has been cashed, it is the solicitor's duty forthwith to return the loan monies to the Building Society. If *per incuriam* the solicitor has already intromitted with the loan monies and he is no longer in a position to complete his client's title and record a valid standard security, the solicitor has an unequivocal duty to remit such of his own monies as represent the amount of the loan.

It is accepted that when a solicitor presents a Building Society loan cheque to his own Bank, it may take some days for the funds to be cleared, and it is accordingly permissible for the solicitor to present the loan cheque to his Bank a reasonable period prior to the expected settlement date so that the solicitor can hold cleared funds when he intromits with the loan monies. In terms of the Accounts Rules, the amount of a loan cheque requires to be regarded as client's money from the time when the cheque is presented and the appropriate amount must be credited to the solicitor's client account at that time (Case 733/88).

A solicitor was found guilty of Professional Misconduct where he failed to report to a Building Society that there was an outstanding Inhibition against the borrower and he thereafter proceeded to settle the loan transaction without express authority of the Building Society or having a writ recorded in the Register of Inhibitions and Adjudications evidencing the discharge of the Inhibition (Case 711/87).

In a case where a solicitor was found guilty of Professional Misconduct in that, while acting for the seller of a property and a heritable creditor holding a Standard Security over the property, he acted contrary to the condition on which a Discharge of the Standard Security had been sent to him, by recording the Discharge before the loan monies had been repaid to the creditor, the Tribunal said:

Where a solicitor acts for both the seller and the heritable creditor in a transaction involving a sale and repayment of a loan, the solicitor has an obligation to safeguard the respective interests of each party in the same way as if he were acting for only one of them; and if the solicitor finds that this involves him in a conflict situation then it is well established that he must forthwith cease acting [for] at least one of the parties. However, if the solicitor continues to act for both parties, he must not, without the express consent of the lender, permit the signed Discharge of the Standard Security to be delivered or recorded without the solicitor having in his possession and being in a position to remit to the lender the whole balance of the loan monies and all other monies secured by the Standard Security. In addition, as soon as the discharge is delivered or recorded, the solicitor must remit all such monies to the lender without delay as the lender no longer has the protection of the Standard Security. In this transaction, the Respondent regrettably allowed the Discharge to be recorded and failed to account immediately to [the lenders] for the whole balance due to them; and he aggravated his failure by ignoring a condition in a cover[ing] letter which accompanied the signed Discharge to the effect that the same was to be regarded as undelivered until such time as the Respondent was in a position to repay the loan. The Respondent's actions were wholly contrary to established conveyancing practice and this Tribunal also takes a serious view of his continuing failure to reply to the solicitors for [the lenders] and to account for the balance of the loan monies, which delay resulted in [the borrowers] being liable for additional interest (Case 713/87).

In a case in 1989, the Tribunal, in relation to a solicitor acting for a purchaser of heritable property and a Building Society, said:

> In relation to loans over domestic property the majority of Building Societies ordinarily instruct the solicitor who is already acting for the borrower and the acceptability of this practice is confirmed in rule 5(1) (*f*) of the Solicitors (Scotland) Practice Rules 1986.

> Most of the Building Societies have their own established procedures and particular forms of instruction for solicitors. Many of these arrangements are common to all the Societies and are well known to solicitors who are experienced in domestic conveyancing. In particular, it is well known to solicitors that Building Societies will not ordinarily lend more than 95% of the valuation figure or the actual purchase price of a property, whichever is the lower.

> In the circumstances of this Complaint, an estate agent had advertised the particular property with the attraction that a Building Society loan of up to 100% was readily available. The Tribunal was informed that the estate agent negotiated the price with the purchasers and arranged the loan with the Building Society before the Respondent was instructed to submit an offer. These instructions provided for a nominal price of £23,000 and a discount of £2,000, resulting in an actual price of £21,000. The Respondent followed these instructions in submitting an offer and the offer formed the basis of the missives which were concluded between the parties. In itself, there was nothing improper in providing for a discounted purchase price but the Respondent should have been on notice to disclose the true purchase price when this information was required of him. No satisfactory explanation was given for the Respondent committing himself in the missives to insert the larger figure of £23,000 in the subsequent Disposition.

> In retrospect, it is apparent that there was an arrangement whereby the purchasers would obtain an inflated loan calculated on 95% of the nominal price. Counsel for the Respondent reminded the Tribunal that the property had been valued for security purposes at £23,000 but in the opinion of the Tribunal, that statement does not reflect the whole situation. In this transaction, there had been a freely negotiated price agreed at £21,000. The actual price reflected the true value of the property at the relevant time; and the effect of calculating a loan on the inflated figure of £23,000 resulted in the Building Society granting a loan in excess of the market value of the property. It is in these circumstances understandably that a Building Society will not normally lend more than 95% of the valuation or the actual purchase price, *whichever is the less.*

> There was no suggestion that the Respondent was involved in formulating the arrangement for securing an increased loan; but as the Respondent was acting for both the purchasers and the Building Society, he had a professional duty to act with the utmost propriety towards each client.

> A solicitor must not withhold any relevant information from his client. ... The Respondent ought to have known that the actual purchase price could have had a bearing on the amount of the loan and in such circumstances he had a duty to point out the true purchase price as soon as he was instructed by the Building Society. As it happened, the Building Society's Form of Instructions clearly showed the purchase price as £23,000 and the printed instructions required the solicitor to report

any discrepancy between the details of offer and the actual purchase. Regrettably this discrepancy was not pointed out by the Respondent in his Report on Title which also constituted the request to remit the loan monies and the Respondent culpably encashed the loan cheque when he ought to have been aware that an excessive loan was being made on the basis of incorrect information.

... On the other hand it appeared that in drafting the Disposition in favour of his clients, the Respondent had set down the nominal price as a consideration and it is this figure which would have appeared on Record. It is of the utmost importance that deeds recorded in the Register of Sasines reflect the true consideration for a property and although this was not the subject of [a] separate charge, the Tribunal takes this opportunity of expressing its strong disapproval of the Respondent's actings in this regard ...

[T]his Complaint illustrates an important matter of principle; and if solicitors are to retain the trust of Building Societies they must continue to act diligently and with the utmost propriety (Case 748/89).

In a Complaint dealt with in 1980 the Tribunal in finding Professional Misconduct established said:

The Respondent was charged with the professional duty of acting for the [A] Assurance Group in connection with a personal loan for £2,500 to be secured by a second Standard Security over his house and the Assignation of various [A] Policies. The loan cheque was cashed by the Respondent on or about 13th March 1973. The loan was partially repaid on or about 10th January 1978 and the Respondent settled the balance of the loan and the outstanding interest on or about October 1979. Prior to cashing the loan cheque, it was the Respondent's duty to execute a Standard Security in favour of [A]. He failed to do this and indeed no Standard Security was ever executed during the currency of the loan. The Respondent claimed that his omission was an oversight, but this explanation is not accepted by the Tribunal. It is significant that in May and November 1974, [A] wrote to the Respondent seeking the Security Deeds and the Solicitors [X Y], whom they subsequently instructed also wrote to the Respondent in September 1976 and on four subsequent occasions. As a consequence of the Respondent's failure, [A] never had a recorded Security. In addition the Respondent failed to execute an Assignation of the Life Policy until 21st June 1974 and he did not forward such loan papers as he had until about 22nd June 1977. The Respondent had an implied duty to complete all security documents and forward them to the lenders immediately after the settlement of the transaction and the Respondent abused his position of trust in neglecting these duties over a considerable period. The Respondent pointed out that [A] had some protection in that the policies had been issued by their own company and that in any event the surrender value of the policies was nominal; but the Tribunal do not accept that these aspects limited the Respondent's duty in any way.

The seriousness of the Respondent's conduct was compounded by the fact that over a considerable period he did not pay either the interest on the loan or the premiums on the Life Policies.

In his letter of acceptance of the loan, the Respondent stated to [A] that he was in a position to offer a satisfactory title. At this time there was already a second security over the property in favour of the [B]. The Respondent produced to the Tribunal a Discharge of this Security bearing to be executed three days prior to the date on which the loan cheque was cashed, but he was unable to produce any receipt or other evidence to establish that the [B] loan had been repaid or that the Discharge had been delivered at this time. In any event it was the Respondent's duty to record this Discharge at the time when he accepted the loan from [A] but regrettably the Discharge was not recorded until more than three years later. The Respondent claimed that his delay in recording the Discharge did not prejudice [A] in that [B] would have been personally barred from enforcing their security, but the Tribunal does not accept that this explanation in any way lessened the Respondent's duty to clear the Record.

The Respondent further aggravated the situation when he executed a further Standard Security in favour of [a Bank] in December 1975 as he then rendered it impossible to comply with the conditions upon which he had accepted the [A] loan. The Respondent explained that he had personally not acted in regard to the Security given to the [. . .] Bank, and that it was in connection with a guarantee for finance to a commercial company in which he was interested The Respondent added that he disclosed the existence of the [A] loan to the [. . .] Bank but in the absence of any security in favour of [A], such disclosure was of no significance . . . (Case 467/80).

(Note that the provisions of rule 10 of the Solicitors (Scotland) Accounts Rules 1992 now prevent a solicitor acting for a lender to the solicitor or connected persons.)

13

COURT AND TRIBUNAL PROCEEDINGS

13.01 EXECUTION OF SERVICE

In Case 203/61 the Discipline Committee in finding Professional Misconduct established said:

> The gravamen of this complaint is that the Respondent signed executions of service on summonses although he knew or should have known that he had not signed the citations on the relevant service copy summonses, and that notwithstanding the clear and explicit warning which he had received from Sheriff [A], Sheriff Substitute of [. . .], he failed to take adequate steps to prevent the continuance of these malpractices. One of the Respondent's staff, a young girl of 18, admitted that she had in the absence of the Respondent signed his name to citations on service copy summonses to enable the summonses to go out timeously and the Respondent stated that another member of his staff had made a similar admission to him. . . .

13.02 EVIDENCE ON OATH

Professional Misconduct was established in relation to a solicitor who gave evidence on oath at a hearing on an Open Commission that was incorrect and amounted to a careless misstatement (Case 782/90).

13.03 PREPARATION FOR TRIAL

A solicitor was found guilty of Professional Misconduct in respect of his failure to precognosce witnesses, to arrange a consultation with Counsel prior to Mr X's trial, to represent Mr X at the Pleading Diet and timeously lodge a Special Defence, to cite the necessary witnesses for the defence, properly to instruct Counsel with the necessary papers to enable him to conduct the trial, and at any time to attend Mr X's trial or arrange for another solicitor to attend on his behalf. In its Decision the Tribunal said:

> In his representation of [X] the Respondent failed to fulfil virtually the whole range of duties which were incumbent on him as a Solicitor, and the Tribunal are satisfied that the compound of the Respondent's failures from the initial enquiries through to the trial constitute a particularly serious case of professional misconduct (Case 367/75(b)).

13.04 APPEARANCE IN COURT

A solicitor was found guilty of Professional Misconduct in respect of his 'gross' failure in his professional duty to take reasonable steps to ensure his timeous attendance or to make other satisfactory arrangements for the representation of his clients at three separate Courts, viz:

In connection with a deferred diet at [X] Sheriff Court on 3rd September 1982.
In connection with a trial diet at [Y] Sheriff Court on 29th April 1983.
In connection with a trial diet at [Y] District Court on 29th April 1983.

In relation to the Respondent's failure to appear at [X] Sheriff Court for an earlier trial diet at 11 am on 18th August 1982, the Tribunal said:

The question for the Tribunal was whether the Respondent, in allowing less than two hours from [Y] to [X], had failed to make adequate provision for the journey and thereby shown gross disregard of his duty to the Court and the Jury.

The Tribunal is inclined to prefer the evidence of the Sheriff Clerk Depute and the Procurator Fiscal who had made the journey on many occasions at various times of the year, particularly as the Procurator Fiscal accurately recorded the times of each of his journeys. However, driving is a subjective matter and the Tribunal is therefore hesitant to find that the travelling time claimed by the Respondent was not possible. Nevertheless it ought to be stated that in attempting to travel a journey over difficult roads in the holiday season, the Respondent was taking an increased risk of failing to reach the Court in time, and a prudent Solicitor ought to have allowed considerably longer for the journey.

The Tribunal also heard the evidence of the Respondent, corroborated by [A], that their car had been held up for about an hour between [...] and [...]. These circumstances were not the subject of challenge by the Complainers, and on the basis of the decision in *McKinnon v Douglas* 1982 SLT(N) 375, it would be inappropriate for the Tribunal to make any findings based merely on the Respondent's lateness where there was such an excuse. . . .

In relation to his failure to appear at the deferred diet in [X], the Respondent's client was represented by a local solicitor. The Tribunal said:

The question before the Tribunal was whether, even accepting the foregoing explanation, the Respondent had made satisfactory arrangements for the representation of [the client] at [X] on Friday, 3rd September 1982. It is not uncommon for a Solicitor to find that he has a conflicting engagement when a case is continued for sentence and it is acceptable practice in such circumstances for the Solicitor to arrange for another Solicitor to take his place. On occasions, the second Solicitor may even be instructed on the same day as the continued diet and this is acceptable provided the Solicitor is adequately instructed and there is sufficient time for the second Solicitor to consider the papers and to meet with the client.

In this case, [the client] had already been found not guilty on the more serious charges, but [the local solicitor] still had insufficient time to consider the Social Inquiry Report and to discuss the same with [the client]; and as a result the Court was inconvenienced by having to adjourn the Diet until such time as [the local solicitor] had met with [the client].

The Respondent had prior notice of the conflicting duties in [X] and [Y] on 3rd September 1982 and he ought to have taken early steps to ensure that another Solicitor was properly instructed for one of the Courts. Even accepting the Respondent's explanation in full, it was inexcusable for the Respondent to leave the matter until the immediately preceding evening and the Respondent must accept responsibility for the inconvenience to the Sheriff at [X]. In the opinion of the Tribunal, the Respondent's culpability in the matter amounted to professional misconduct . . .

In relation to the trials due to take place in the Sheriff Court and District Court at [Y], both on 29th April 1983, the Tribunal noted that the Respondent had known since 6th January 1983 that he had at least one trial in each Court on 29th April and said:

> . . . In the opinion of the Tribunal, the Respondent took a grave risk in retaining instructions to represent clients in trials in the Sheriff Court and the District Court up to the close of business on the preceding day and that the Respondent must accept responsibility for the consequences which resulted (Case 636/84).

In a Petition to the Court against a finding of Professional Misconduct by the Solicitors' Discipline Committee in 1960 the Lord President (with whom the other judges concurred) said:

> In the present case the circumstances briefly are that when the incident in question took place one of the Sheriff Substitutes in Glasgow was dealing in his official capacity with a series of bail applications. In accordance with normal if not universal practice in Scotland these applications were being heard in a private room since they arose in cases which might ultimately be tried before a jury and were not mere summary cases. The petitioner, who is a solicitor practising in the Sheriff Court in Glasgow came into the private room in which the Sheriff Substitute was sitting. The Sheriff Substitute informed him that he was in course of hearing a bail application. The petitioner replied that he was aware of that. The Sheriff Substitute then stated that applications for bail were heard in private, to which the petitioner replied that he was in the room about his business of solicitor, that he had a bail application to present later, that he was a solicitor and that he had no intention of leaving the room. The Sheriff Substitute, after informing the petitioner that his case would be dealt with later, instructed the petitioner to leave the room on at least two occasions. He refused to do so. He offered physical resistance and used abusive language when police officers proceeded to remove him from the room on the instructions of the Sheriff Substitute. The contention put to us this morning was that however one might describe this conduct on the petitioner's part it did not constitute professional misconduct and the conviction should therefore be quashed.

> The argument was based upon a series of observations regarding what amounts to professional misconduct to be found in earlier cases. Three cases in Scotland were referred to: *The Solicitors' Discipline Committee* v *B* 1942 SC 293; *The X Insurance Company* v *A and B* 1936 SC 225 and *The S.S.C. Society* v *Clark* 13 R 1170. These cases do not purport to give an exhaustive definition of what will constitute professional misconduct, but they do indicate that to constitute professional misconduct the misconduct must be connected with the solicitor's professional duties. The matter is put in more direct terms by Darling J in the case of *In re A Solicitor* [1912] 1 KB 302 at page 311. The learned Judge in this passage applies to professional misconduct on the part of a solicitor the definition already attributed by the Court in an earlier case to the words 'infamous conduct in a professional respect' in regard to a medical man. He says,

> > I do not think I need attempt to add anything to the definition which was given in *Allinson* v *General Council of Medical Education and Registration*. In that case Lopes LJ said: 'The Master of the Rolls has adopted a definition which, with his

assistance and that of my brother Davey, I prepared. I will read it again. "If it is shewn that a medical man, in the pursuit of his profession, has done something with regard to it which would be reasonably regarded as disgraceful or dishonourable by his professional brethren of good repute and competency," then it is open to the General Medical Council to say that he has been guilty of "infamous conduct in a professional respect." '

The decision in this case was approved in the House of Lords by Lord Maugham in *Myers* v *Elman* [1940] AC 282 at page 288.

The contention in the present case is that the petitioner was not actually conducting a case at the time when the incident out of which these proceedings arose took place. He was in the room as a member of the public might have been and it was not therefore in his capacity as a professional man that he was there. For he was not conducting a case for a client, but was a mere observer. Any misconduct there may have been was therefore not professional misconduct.

But, my Lords, when a man joins the profession of the law he becomes bound to observe certain standards of dignity and honesty and restraint and not to behave like a wild animal. It is quite erroneous to assume that the standards of the profession only apply to him while he is actively engaged in a case or while he is earning a fee. He cannot discard the responsibility to observe these standards as he can lay aside a wig or gown. These standards operate and apply to him while he is performing his professional duties or is doing something in connection with his professional duties either in relation to his client, his opponent or the Court. In particular when a professional man in connection with his professional duties is in the presence of the Sheriff sitting in his official capacity, these standards in my view clearly apply. If the Sheriff in that situation issues an order or an instruction to the solicitor it is his professional duty to carry that order out. If the Sheriff's order or instruction is a wrong one there are other means than defiance for getting that order or instruction reviewed but the failure to carry out or the attempt to defy the Sheriff's order or instruction is in my view a clear breach of the solicitor's professional duty and constitutes professional misconduct. Indeed it is upon the recognition of this obvious fact by the profession as a whole that the due administration of justice in any civilised country depends.

In the present case the Sheriff Substitute was acting at the time in his official capacity in the course of hearing bail applications. The petitioner was in the presence of the Sheriff Substitute on his own admission engaged in his business of Solicitor. That was why he insisted on his claim to remain in the room. He was not there merely as a member of the public. Indeed he was there about to conduct a case of his own before the same Sheriff Substitute. The Sheriff Substitute issued an order which he flagrantly and unhesitatingly disobeyed and he had ultimately to be removed forcibly from the room by the police. A finding of professional misconduct in these circumstances appears to me to be the only possible finding that the Committee could have made and I should have been astonished if they had made any other ... (*A Petitioner*), Court of Session, unreported, 8.1.60).

13.05 MISLEADING THE TRIBUNAL
A solicitor was charged with Professional Misconduct in that:

He gave assurances to the Discipline Tribunal, the tenor of which was such as to convey to the Tribunal the impression that there were no other problems of substance in relation to the professional conduct of the Respondent, and no other matters likely to cause concern, which assurances were without substance and were known by the Respondent to be so.

In this particular case the Tribunal found that the line of questioning put to the Respondent at the original hearing of the Tribunal was open to an ambiguity and they did not find the charge proven but there is little doubt that had the facts as set out in the charge in the Complaint been proven the Tribunal would have found that Professional Misconduct was established in such circumstances i.e. if the solicitor had deliberately misled the Tribunal regarding a material matter (Case 819/91).

14

TRUST AND EXECUTRIES

14.01 EXAMPLES OF PROFESSIONAL MISCONDUCT

In a case where solicitors were found guilty of Professional Misconduct in respect of their unconscionable delay in the administration and winding up of an executry estate, the Tribunal said:

> In the Answers, however, there was a denial that the first Respondent received instructions to act in the winding up of [A's] estate. The circumstances were unusual. The papers had been passed to the first Respondent by a relative of the deceased's late husband: accordingly she had no interest in the estate on intestacy. The next of kin [B] was apparently incapax and without a *Curator bonis*; and accordingly it was submitted that there was therefore no one to give formal instructions to the first Respondent.
>
> However, in the opinion of the Tribunal, the basis on which a solicitor is instructed to wind up an executry estate differs from other business in that strictly there is never any party in a position to give formal instructions until an executor has been appointed. Nevertheless from a practical aspect the Solicitor's duties commence when he accepts responsibility for the deceased's estate. This may be when papers or keys or other property are delivered to him or otherwise when he undertakes to investigate the estate or trace the beneficiaries. It may be some time before the solicitor has identified the next of kin or completed his investigations into the estate, but during this period the solicitor has an ongoing professional responsibility notwithstanding that it is prior to the formal appointment of the executor. In this case, the first Respondent apparently settled the deceased's funeral account. He accepted responsibility for settling certain outlays on the deceased's property and made enquiries regarding the status of [B] the next of kin. In such circumstances, the first Respondent *de facto* accepted instructions even although the parties who first communicated with this Respondent were not in themselves related to the deceased. The Tribunal did not consider it relevant that the deceased had not personally been a client of the Respondents' firm during her lifetime (Case 685/86).

In a case in 1988 the Tribunal, in finding a solicitor guilty of Professional Misconduct in relation to his administration of an executry estate, observed:

> In this case, the Respondent diligently proceeded to have the deceased's eldest son appointed executor dative and the delay only commenced when the executor failed to sign and return the Bond of Caution. However, notwithstanding the appointment of an executor, a solicitor acting in an estate has a much wider duty than merely to implement the executor's instructions. The Solicitor also has an implied duty to the other beneficiaries, particularly in this case where he had already communicated with some of them; and when it became apparent that the executor was unwilling to respond and was thereby inhibiting further progress, the Respondent ought to have written the other beneficiaries and advised them on the basis of

the circumstances then prevailing; and on the death of the executor, the solicitor should have taken steps to procure the appointment of a substitute executor. Regrettably the Respondent failed to communicate with any of the beneficiaries, even when he became aware that the executor had died (Case 720/88).

In another case where a solicitor was found guilty of Professional Misconduct in connection with his winding up of an executry, the Tribunal said:

> In his capacity as solicitor and attorney for the executrix, the Respondent had a duty to administer the estate in the interests of all the beneficiaries and to conclude the winding up as soon as practicable. It was apparent that there were exceptional difficulties in that the employees wished to acquire the business but had insufficient funds to complete a purchase and that in these circumstances it was impracticable to sell the business to a third party. However, in addition, a solicitor has a duty to keep all the beneficiaries in an estate reasonably informed of progress and this was especially so when there was a matter of exceptional difficulty which might take considerable time to resolve. In such circumstances, the Respondent ought to have communicated with each of the beneficiaries from time to time in order to seek their continuing approval for his course of action and in failing to do this, he must accept a degree of culpability for the delay of six years between 1978 and 1984 even although this delay was otherwise justifiable and resulted in the ultimate benefit of the estate (Case 749/89).

In a Complaint where a solicitor was found guilty of Professional Misconduct following his failure to communicate with a beneficiary on an executry estate and to give her a truthful explanation of the problems which had been encountered, the Tribunal said:

> It is an essential duty on the part of a solicitor to keep his clients informed; and in relation to an executry, this duty extends toward the beneficiaries on the estate (Case 661/86).

In finding a solicitor guilty of Professional Misconduct on various charges relating to the winding up of an executry estate, the Tribunal said:

> A solicitor acting in the winding up of an Executry or a Trust Estate is under a duty to provide a beneficiary with an up-to-date report on progress when called upon to do so . . . (Case 543/82).

The Tribunal, in finding a charge of Professional Misconduct established, has said:

> It was submitted by the Respondent that his duty lay towards the Executors on the Estate but in the opinion of this Tribunal, a solicitor in accepting instructions to wind up an Estate, also has a duty to the beneficiaries to wind up the Estate as soon as practicable (Case 588/89).

A solicitor was found guilty of Professional Misconduct in respect of his unconscionable delay in dealing with the winding up of a deceased's estate and in producing executry accounts and in continuing to act in the winding up of the estate after a conflict had arisen. In the course of its Decision, the Tribunal said:

> . . . There were substantial liabilities on the estate, including a claim for arrears of

aliment from the deceased's first wife, and there were tax complexities resulting from his overseas work. As at the date of the hearing, the winding up of the estate had still not been concluded, but the Respondent did not seek to rely on the various difficulties as an excuse for all the delay.

[The deceased's] second wife had consulted the Respondent shortly before his death and it was this fact that caused the solicitor nominated [as executor along with the widow] in the Will to resign in favour of the Respondent and his [partner]. For some time, there was doubt regarding the solvency of the estate. The Respondent might have petitioned the court for the appointment of a Judicial Factor, but he proceeded to be confirmed as executor, along with his [partner] and the deceased's widow and entered on the administration of the estate; and in these circumstances he accepted responsibility for its winding up. By mid [. . .], when the tax matters were cleared up, the Respondent ought to have been well advanced in the administration of the estate and his delay between that time and handing over the papers to other agents in [. . .], was inexcusable.

The other charge related to the Respondent's failure to act on a mandate signed by the widow and sent to him in [. . .]. The widow was, of course, only one of the three executors and the Respondent with his [partner] were both executors and the solicitors acting on the estate. In such circumstances, it was the Respondent's duty carefully to distinguish between his position as executor and as solicitor. The intimation of the mandate constituted a formal demand that the Respondent should hand over the administration of the estate to another firm of solicitors. This was a matter for the Respondent (and [his partner]) to consider in their separate capacity as executors. As a solicitor engaged in the winding up of the estate, he had a financial interest to continue with the administration and this interest directly conflicted with the wishes of the widow who sought to have the administration transferred to another firm.

In the circumstances of this conflict, the Respondent (and [his partner]) should not have used their position as being a majority of the executors to retain control of the administration.

Whether the Respondent should have continued as executor, was an entirely different matter. Although the Respondent and [his partner] had indeed been assumed as executors when the administration of the estate was passed over to their firm, they would have been under no obligation, legal or professional, to resign office in the event of the administration passing to another firm. In his Answers, the Respondent stated that he and [his partner] were of the opinion that they had a duty to creditors to continue to act as executors, and in the circumstances, it would have been open to them to have so continued even after the administration had been handed over, notwithstanding what they might have believed to have been the wishes of the widow. If however the Respondent had any doubt regarding the suitability of the firm nominated by the widow, he could have even then petitioned the Court for the appointment of a Judicial Factor; but continuing with the administration of the estate was not an option which was properly open to him after the wishes of the only outside executor had been made known (Case 604/85).

In a case where two solicitors who were formerly partners were found guilty of Professional Misconduct *inter alia* on the grounds of unconscionable delay in winding up an executry, the Tribunal said:

The first Respondent must however take the greater responsibility for this distressing case . . . . He is seventy-five years of age and he stated that he had retired on.

[. . .] Nevertheless it is particularly significant that the first Respondent was the sole executor. In such an estate, where all the residuary beneficiaries were [institutions], he ought to have ensured that there was reasonable progress. . . . (Case 625/85).

In a case where the Tribunal found a solicitor guilty of Professional Misconduct on various grounds including:

(1) unconscionable delay in the carrying out his professional duties to prosecute his clients' business to finality, (2) his unconscionable delay in supplying appropriate information, documentation and accounting to the beneficiaries in the said estates or their agents, in gross disregard of their interests, notwithstanding repeated applications, (3) his unconscionable delay in carrying out the reasonable instructions of the said beneficiaries, in gross disregard of their interests, notwithstanding repeated applications . . .

the Tribunal said in its Decision:

The circumstances of this Complaint related to a minority holding of [. . .] shares in a family company known as [X]. The Respondent acted for the Company and [A], the principal shareholder; and at the time he was also a director of the Company along with [A]. The minority holding had been registered in the name of Mrs [B—the mother of A]. Mrs [B] died in [. . .]. In terms of her Will, the Respondent and [A] were appointed Trustees and the minority shareholding was left to be divided amongst the deceased's [. . .] daughters. The Respondent was instructed to act as solicitor in winding up the estate.

On [. . .], the Solicitor acting for the [. . .] daughters intimated to the Respondent that the daughters wished to have the shares transferred to them.

In his evidence to the Tribunal, the Respondent explained that he had actively helped Mrs [B's] late husband when he had established the Company and he was of the opinion that the minority shareholding should not be transferred to the [. . .] daughters. He conveyed this opinion to [A] and also to the Solicitor acting for the [. . .] daughters but the daughters insisted on having the shares transferred.

In such circumstances, it was the Respondent's duty as Solicitor for the Trustee[s] to comply with the daughters' wishes and prepare transfers to be submitted to the Company for registration, and then place the transfers before the Board of Directors and take instructions upon whether the transfers were to be approved. The Respondent found himself in a difficult position but this was wholly because of the conflicting interest of himself as Trustee on Mrs [B's] estate and as Director of the Company and in acting for both parties. He had a duty as the Solicitor on Mrs [B's] estate to comply with the wishes of the daughters as beneficiaries and if he considered that he was unable to fulfil their wishes because of his conflicting interest then he should have ceased acting for one of the parties . . . (Case 465/80).

See also case 470/80, referred to at para 7.05.

15

UNDERTAKINGS

15.01 RECKLESS ISSUING OF UNDERTAKINGS

A Complaint was brought against a solicitor alleging Professional Misconduct in respect that he had issued over a period of months a series of letters undertaking to pay substantial sums of money within specified periods, none of which undertakings were ever implemented. Some of these undertakings were stated in terms to be 'for and on behalf of' a named client but others were not specifically made 'for and on behalf of' a named client. After issuing certain of the undertakings which had not been timeously implemented, and before he issued further undertakings, it came to his notice that a forged undertaking had been issued, apparently on his notepaper, which falsely purported to have been granted by him.

In addressing the Tribunal, the Fiscal pointed to the varying forms of the respective undertakings and he submitted, on the basis of the decision in *Dryburgh* v *A. & A. S. Gordon* 1896 24R 1, that a solicitor incurred personal liability where the solicitor made an unqualified undertaking to a third party even although it was apparent from the terms of the undertaking that the undertaking was issued in relation to the affairs of a particular client. The charge of Professional Misconduct in relation to the undertakings issued by the Respondent was set out under four separate heads but, in addressing the Tribunal, the Fiscal confined his submissions to the undertakings which were given by the Respondent in September and October 1992 in that, by that time, it was apparent that payment had not been made in accordance with the earlier undertakings and there should have been sufficient doubt in the mind of the Respondent about the implementation of future undertakings.

The Agent for the Respondent sought to distinguish the case of *Dryburgh* and referred to the unreported Court of Session decision, *S* v *B*, 25th February 1981, and maintained that, as a general rule, any statement made by a solicitor in good faith should not give rise to criticism and he contrasted this position with the case of *United Bank of Kuwait* v *Hammoud* [1988] 3 All ER 418, where the solicitor had exceeded his authority in issuing the particular undertaking and he submitted that a solicitor's first duty is to his client and that he has no obligation to a third party other than to do no wrong as by way of a delict or crime or misconduct. He added that it was not part of a solicitor's duty to sit in judgment on his client. In the particular matter there was sufficient external business information to indicate that funds would be forthcoming and there was no reckless conduct on the part of the Respondent.

In the course of its Decision the Tribunal said:

> By early September, a number of earlier undertakings were outstanding and by this time the Respondent had established that a forged undertaking for a very substantial sum of money had been issued on what appeared to be his headed notepaper by someone connected with his client. The Respondent had by that time been pressed for the obligations in these undertakings to be implemented and he seemed very willing to accept whatever explanations were proferred to him as to why the money was not forthcoming as promised. At this stage it would have been abundantly apparent to a competent and responsible solicitor that there was a very considerable element of doubt as to whether his client and his client's company were in a position to comply with any future undertakings within the strict time limits set out in these documents and in these circumstances, a competent and responsible solicitor should have had regard to the reasonable expectations of any third party in receipt of these undertakings, particularly as the latter undertakings were not qualified by the words 'on behalf of' . . . .

> Having regard to the record of the earlier undertakings and the circumstances surrounding the forged undertaking dated [. . .] the Respondent acted in a reckless and irresponsible way in issuing these further documents and the Tribunal is satisfied that the Respondent's actings in relation to the issue of these further undertakings amounted to professional misconduct (Case 852/93).

15.02 FAILURE TO IMPLEMENT UNDERTAKINGS

In finding a charge of Professional Misconduct established the Tribunal, in a Decision in 1980, said:

> In this Complaint, the Respondent was charged with professional misconduct in that
>
> (1)   he failed to honour the express or implied professional undertaking . . . to the effect that, in exchange for the keys of said shop, the consideration of [£. . .] was being or would be placed by him on deposit receipt pending settlement of the transaction, and that notwithstanding the fact that the keys were delivered to him on the basis of that undertaking;
>
> (2)   he delivered the said keys to his client notwithstanding the fact that his client had failed to put him in funds to enable him to honour said undertaking;
>
> (3)   he failed to inform the [sellers' solicitors] that the sum mentioned above had not in fact been placed on deposit receipt and allowed them to proceed, in the mistaken belief that said sum had been so deposited, to renounce their clients' interest in the subjects in favour of his client. . . .

> It was admitted that the Respondent acted for [X] in the particular transaction, and that an undertaking was given by a member of his staff to the effect that a sum of [£. . .] would be consigned on deposit receipt. The undertaking was verbal and was confirmed in writing by the letter from the Respondent's firm dated 1st September 1976. In this letter it was not specified that the deposit receipt was to be in the joint names of the parties' solicitors, but Counsel for the Respondent very properly conceded that this was the only reasonable inference from the arrangement in the particular circumstances.

> . . . It was particularly significant that the undertaking was given at the time when the keys to the property were handed over and the Tribunal accept the evidence of

[the seller's solicitor] that the undertaking was a material consideration in regard to the arrangements for this settlement. . . .

. . . . It was suggested that there may not have been any duty on the Respondent to the extent that he himself did not give the undertaking, and further it was claimed that he did not sign the confirming letter as he was on holiday at the time. Nevertheless it is significant that the Respondent was personally attending to the transaction and dealing with it shortly before the undertaking was given, and particularly in these circumstances, the Respondent had a duty to look into the transaction on his return and ascertain what had occurred during his absence.

In 'A Guide to the Professional Conduct of Solicitors', 1974 edition at page 67, it is stated

> that a solicitor is responsible as a matter of professional conduct for carrying out an undertaking given by a member of his staff, whether admitted or unadmitted.

The Tribunal wholly concurs in this view and the Tribunal is of the opinion that the Respondent was under the same obligation to comply with the particular undertaking as if it had been given [by] himself; and even if the Respondent had been on holiday for a fortnight at the time when the undertaking was given as claimed in his Answers, he ought to have sufficiently enquired into the history of the transaction to ascertain the circumstances of the undertaking and ensured that the undertaking had been properly complied with.

It was suggested in the Answers that the Respondent's client perhaps declined to make the funds available for consignation. A Solicitor should ordinarily avoid giving an undertaking which he is not personally in a position to fulfil but in the event of such obligation being given he cannot rely on the failure of his client to co-operate as an excuse. In such circumstances, it is open to the solicitor to explain his position to the party to whom the undertaking was given but that if such party insists on compliance with the undertaking then the Solicitor must make the funds available, if necessary from his own monies, in order that the undertaking is fulfilled.

In the opinion of the Tribunal, the Respondent culpably failed to honour the particular undertaking (Case 463/80).

In finding a solicitor guilty of Professional Misconduct in that in the knowledge that X were major creditors of his client, and notwithstanding his having given to A, the Managing Director of X, and X, by letters dated (three dates), professional undertakings to keep them fully advised of developments in relation to the sale of the client's property and business, (*a*) he culpably failed to honour said undertakings and, in particular, he culpably failed to inform them of the receipt of the offer dated . . . of the receipt of the further qualified acceptance dated . . . and the dispatch of the further qualified acceptance dated . . . and (*b*) in the letter dated . . . he culpably provided X with misleading information, the Tribunal said:

> The first of the two remaining charges was that the Respondent failed to honour the undertakings contained in his letters dated 11th September 1984 and 11th February and 1st March 1985. In considering whether the Respondent's words amounted to 'professional undertakings' the Fiscal referred to the definition set out in 'The Professional Conduct of Solicitors', published by the (English) Law Society (1986), at para 15.01:

15.02 FAILURE TO IMPLEMENT UNDERTAKINGS

An undertaking is any unequivocal declaration of intention addressed to someone who reasonably places reliance on it and made by:

(a) a solicitor in the course of his practice, whether personally or by a member of his staff; or

(b) a solicitor as 'solicitor', but not in the course of his practice; whereby the solicitor (or in the case of a member of his staff, his employer) becomes personally bound.

The Fiscal also referred to the following paragraphs, and the observations contained in the earlier publication by the Law Society, 'A Guide to the Professional Conduct of Solicitors' (1974) at pp 67 and 68. Counsel for the Respondent submitted that 'undertaking' was a very special word and that a 'professional undertaking' required to contain a strict undertaking, and as an example he referred to the formal Letter of Obligation granted by solicitors upon the sale of heritable property. Counsel also pointed out that in the course of his evidence, Mr [A] was never asked whether he had placed reliance on the expressions contained in the Respondent's said letters. In the opinion of the Tribunal there requires to be clear words of intention before a 'professional undertaking' can be inferred, but the undertaking does not require to have the degree of formality as appears in a Letter of Obligation. Indeed it is significant that 'The Professional Conduct of Solicitors' observes that a professional undertaking may be given orally or in writing and that an oral undertaking can have the same effect as a written undertaking. There is no doubt that an unequivocal declaration of intention 'addressed to someone who reasonably places reliance on it' will constitute a professional undertaking, but it is not accepted that this is an exclusive definition. Clearly there requires to be an ongoing relationship between the grantor and the grantee and provided that the grantor intended that the obligation was to be relied upon it may not be necessary to establish actual reliance in order to establish an undertaking.

In this case the Respondent expressed his intention on three separate occasions and although there was no direct evidence of Mr [A's] reliance on the Respondent's letter, it is significant that the letters were written at a time when the Respondent's client was under considerable financial pressure and the letters were no doubt written in the expectation that Mr [A] and his Company would refrain from having recourse to Court proceedings: and the Tribunal is satisfied that the Respondent's three letters indeed contained professional undertakings (Case 700/87).

In a case where a solicitor had been charged with persisting in his client's claim for the return of allegedly stolen goods notwithstanding the solicitor's 'undertaking' to the Procurator Fiscal that he would not be pursuing the matter further following the Procurator Fiscal marking the case papers against the client 'no proceedings', the Tribunal said:

It is a regular aspect of the practice of Solicitors in both Court and Chamber practice to give undertakings to fellow Solicitors. It is preferable for such undertakings to be in writing but from time to time undertakings are given verbally and there is the same absolute duty on a Solicitor to comply with even a verbal undertaking. Because of the critical consequences of such an undertaking, it is essential that the terms of any undertaking are clearly understood by each party and that there is a consensus between them (Case 536/82).

In the exceptional circumstances of this case, Professional Misconduct was not established.

16

MANAGEMENT OF PRACTICE

16.01 CONTROL OF WORKLOAD

Solicitors shall accept instructions only where the matter can be carried out with due expedition and solicitors shall maintain appropriate systems in order to ensure that the matter is dealt with effectively.

Where a solicitor considers, for example, that the service to a client would be inadequate, owing to pressure of work or the like so that the matter would not be dealt with within a reasonable period of time, it would be improper for the solicitor to accept instructions and agree to act (Code of Conduct, para 5(c)).

Where a solicitor (the Respondent) had been found guilty of Professional Misconduct based *inter alia* on 'delay', it was said on his behalf in mitigation that the amalgamation of his firm with another firm, followed by alterations to his office premises and changes of office equipment and staff, gave rise to material difficulties. The Tribunal referring to these submissions said, however:

These are significant mitigating circumstances but the Tribunal was unable to accept these explanations as an answer to the Complaint.

The Respondent also added in mitigation that during the relevant period, he had been under considerable pressure of work and that he had been working extended hours for seven days in each week.

The Tribunal have taken the whole circumstances of this Complaint into account in determining that the Respondent should be censured and bear a substantial fine.

The Tribunal regarded with concern the fact that the Respondent had found it necessary to work a seven day week and observed that this pointed to the Respondent being unable to control and cope with the work load of his practice (Case 645/84).

In another case the Tribunal's Note contained the following passage:

The Tribunal has carefully considered these submissions in relation to the whole circumstances of this Complaint. It is noted that the material events occurred over a relatively short period and coincided with the Respondent's medical condition. Nevertheless it is of significance that the particular matters related to the transfer of clients' monies to his own account. The Solicitors (Scotland) Accounts Rules contain clear and unequivocal directions to ensure that clients' monies are fully protected and it is apparent that the Respondent persisted in disregarding these Rules to a material extent. The Tribunal noted with concern that the shortage on the Respondent's client account continued to increase and the gravity of the position is demonstrated in this particular case where there is an insolvency situation. It is accepted that during the relevant period, the Respondent was suffering a medical condition which may have materially affected his capacity and his powers of judgment. Nevertheless there was no obligation on the Respondent to remain in practice on his own account; and in electing to continue in a condition where his capacity was apparently limited, he allowed himself to enter into a position where he put clients' funds at risk. Notwithstanding the Respondent's medical history, his conduct was wholly unbecoming that of a solicitor.

To maintain the good name of the profession of solicitors in Scotland, it is essential that the profession demonstrates its disapproval in the strongest possible terms of any action which endangers clients' funds. In continuing to practice, the Respondent recklessly disregarded his responsibilities; and it is with these considerations that an order has been made for the name of the Respondent to be struck off the Roll of Solicitors in Scotland (Case 856/93).

16.02 EFFECT OF ILL HEALTH

In a case where a solicitor was convicted of Professional Misconduct where *inter alia* he had been neglecting the affairs of his clients and failing to reply to correspondence and the explanation was advanced on his behalf that he had been suffering from a medical condition giving rise to excessive tiredness, which could relate to a post viral-syndrome, the Tribunal nevertheless stated:

> It is a cardinal principle that a solicitor should only accept and continue with such practice as he can reasonably undertake. Notwithstanding the Respondent's apparent disability, he continued to have the same professional responsibility which is incumbent on all solicitors: that is to carry out the work entrusted to him with diligence and to respond to all reasonable enquiries in relation to his practice. If the Respondent felt that he was becoming unable to maintain his practice, he had a professional duty to arrange for his clients' affairs to be passed to other solicitors, either by transferring his whole business or passing on the files of individual clients with which he was no longer able to cope (Case 735/88).

In a case where it appeared from medical reports submitted to the Tribunal that a solicitor's state of health had a material effect on his capacity to carry on his practice, the Tribunal nevertheless took the view that during his indisposition the solicitor had been subject to repeated reminders and requests to which he continually failed to respond, and these communications ought to have caused the solicitor to reconsider his position as he always had the alternative of either bringing in an assistant to relieve the pressure on him or alternatively passing the respective clients outwith the firm (Case 853/93).

In a case where the Tribunal was told that a solicitor, who admitted charges of Professional Misconduct, had been under considerable personal and business pressures at the time of the offences, the Tribunal said:

> The Tribunal have carefully taken into consideration all the circumstances of this Complaint. It is appreciated that at the relevant time, the Respondent was under considerable stress but nevertheless a solicitor has a personal responsibility to conduct his practice in a responsible manner. The Respondent must accept the consequences of allowing himself to work under exception[al] pressure. The public are entitled to expect that solicitors will carry out the work entrusted to them in a diligent and professional manner and pressure of work can never be accepted as an excuse for delay. It is particularly regrettable that in his case the Respondent's

failure was compounded by a series of misleading statements to his client in order to cover up the neglect and delay in attending to that client's affairs. The Respondent's actings were inexcusable. The Respondent abused the position of trust which solicitors enjoy and materially damaged the reputation of the profession in the eyes of the public. It was particularly disturbing that the Respondent persisted in his deception where court officials were involved in carrying out a search for a non-existent action and it was only when the client ultimately satisfied herself regarding the true position that the Respondent admitted the extent of his deception (Case 696/87).

See also Case 857/93, reported at para 16.01.

16.03 SUPERVISION OF ASSISTANTS

Where a solicitor has failed to carry out a client's instructions, to carry out a piece of business and to respond to telephone calls from the client inquiring about the matter, it will not suffice to exculpate the solicitor that the business was passed to an experienced qualified assistant, because the solicitor nevertheless has a duty to supervise the assistant (Case 832/92).

In finding two solicitors (the Respondents) guilty of a charge of Professional Misconduct, the Tribunal said:

> In the course of the hearing, it became apparent that neither of the Respondents had any personal knowledge of the action by [A] against [B] and indeed the matter first came to the attention of each of the Respondents when the Complaint was received at their office in August 1969. It was accepted that in the particular circumstances [Y, an enrolled solicitor who had been suspended and was employed by the Respondents to take charge of the chamber procedure and civil cases of the Respondents' practice,] was acting in the capacity of a clerk to the Respondents' firm and that he was acting on behalf of the Respondents when he saw Mr [B] and his son, and subsequently attended to the Defence of the action which was raised against [B].

> In such circumstances, the Committee consider that it is relevant to look at Mr [Y's] position in the firm and the extent of the supervision exercised by the Respondents over him in order to ascertain, for the purposes of professional misconduct, whether the Respondents were responsible for Mr [Y's] actings; and on this point, the Committee found particular guidance from the case of *Re A Solicitor's Clerk* [1956] 2 All ER 242 at 244 referred to in Cordery's 'The Law Relating to Solicitors', 6th edition at page 477, and more generally in Bennion's 'Professional Ethics' at pages 100 and 101.

> Mr [Y] was employed to conduct the whole of the Respondents' civil practice without supervision and he only conferred with the individual Respondents in matters of particular importance or when one of the Respondents had been personally consulted in a particular case. He regularly opened and distributed the firm mail without supervision and it was his practice to sign all the letters which he had dictated with the firm name, adding only the abbreviation 'p' and his initials [X.Y.]. The Respondents were aware of the foregoing and approved of the same. The circumstances were such that affairs could be conducted by Mr [Y] within the firm in such a manner as the Respondents might not be aware of the circumstances, and this was particularly so as the Respondents did not even require Mr [Y] to make any general report on the work under his charge. The file covering the particular case of [B] was kept in a cabinet in an open part of the office, and the

only personal connection with the action was when the Second Respondent signed the Defences. There would also have been a debit entry in the firm cash ledger relative to the court dues, but the foregoing would not have been such that the Respondents would have taken any particular note of the case.

It was argued by [the agent for the Respondents] that the position in England differed in that the employment of managing clerks was much more developed but the Committee are not prepared to accept that there is any material difference between the two countries in the consideration of this aspect of professional misconduct.

Considering the Complaint as a whole, the Committee are satisfied that the Respondents failed to supervise adequately the actings of Mr [Y], and that in the circumstances they are responsible for his conduct. The facts submitted in support of each of the three charges were materially established and the Committee are in no doubt that the content of each of these charges is such as to justify a finding of professional misconduct against the Respondents . . . (Case 297/69).

In Case 596/85 (which was the subject of appeal and reported as *MacColl* v *The Council of the Law Society of Scotland* 1987 SLT 524), the Tribunal found a solicitor guilty of Professional Misconduct in respect that he charged his client, for whom he held a Power of Attorney, grossly excessive fees, made improper use of his client's funds and was in breach of rule 6(*c*) and rule 6(*d*) of the Solicitors (Scotland) Accounts Rules 1981. The Tribunal said:

A solicitor is not expected to carry out personally all work which he is instructed to undertake, but if he decides to delegate any work, there remains a duty of supervision and the solicitor must accept personal responsibility for any improper actions which result from a failure of supervision.

Later in the same case the Tribunal added:

The Feenotes were prepared by [Mr A—the Respondent's Office Manager] and it would appear that the Respondent may not have been aware of the particular charges or their amount. For the reasons already stated, this Tribunal does not accept this to be a relevant defence. The Respondent, as the principal of his firm, had a duty to supervise all aspects of his practice, including such fees as are rendered and transferred; and in this case he had a further duty in that he was [his client's] Attorney. If, in such circumstances, the Respondent was not aware of the particular fees and transfers, then he must accept the same responsibility as if he had issued the Feenotes and authorised the transfers personally.

At the Appeal, Counsel for the solicitor submitted *inter alia* that it appeared from its Note that the Tribunal accepted the Petitioner (the solicitor) had not been aware of the fees debited and of withdrawals made from the client account to meet them and that these things had been done by his unqualified office manager, Mr [A], without his knowledge. Upon that assumption the Tribunal was not entitled to find the Petitioner guilty of Professional Misconduct.

In upholding the Tribunal's Decision in the finding of Professional Misconduct established, the Court said *inter alia* at p 527:

Reading the decision as a whole—the Findings, the Interlocutor and the Note—it is far from clear that the Tribunal accepted that the petitioner was ignorant of the things which were done in relation to the particular client's affairs. They do not so find. This is not at all surprising since in his answers to the Complaint the petitioner admitted that he had been responsible for the debits and withdrawals complained of subject only to the explanation that Mr [A] had 'prepared' the fees. In his evidence before the Tribunal he repeated this explanation and went on to say merely that he had not been aware 'of the particular charges or their amount'. Be all that as it may, however, the Tribunal's view clearly appears to have been that even if the petitioner had been entirely ignorant of all that had allegedly been done by Mr [A] alone, he was still guilty of professional misconduct. The question is whether in expressing that view the Tribunal misdirected themselves in any material respect. We are of opinion that they did not. As we read their Findings and their Note they were well aware of the test which should be applied—the 'Sharp' test—in deciding whether a solicitor against whom a complaint is made ought to be found guilty of professional misconduct. In particular we are not persuaded that in considering the whole circumstances they proceeded upon the basis that if an employee commits acts which, if the solicitor himself had committed them, would constitute professional misconduct, the solicitor's ignorance of the commission of these acts could not be regarded, in any circumstances, as a relevant defence to the charge against him. Upon a fair reading of the decision as a whole that is not what the Tribunal did. In our opinion, in dealing with the matter on the assumption that the petitioner remained in a state of total ignorance until the inspection revealed what had been going on, they considered the whole circumstances and made the finding which they did upon the view that the petitioner, who had undoubtedly the duty to supervise the work done by members of his staff, particularly in relation to the affairs of a client in a special position such as this one, either knew what was done, or clearly ought to have known what was being done if he had carried out his duty of supervision in accordance with the standards to be expected of any competent and reputable solicitor. There was, we think, ample material before them on which they were entitled to form that view. The picture which emerges clearly from the decision as a whole is that if the petitioner really did not know what had been done he had no possible excuse for his remarkable ignorance. On the alternative basis the failure of supervision was serious, reprehensible and inexcusable.

In a case where a solicitor (the Respondent) had been charged *inter alia* with Professional Misconduct arising from delay in dealing with correspondence, the Tribunal said:

The Respondent sought to explain the circumstances and the associated failure to reply to correspondence by pointing out that the transactions had been passed to his qualified assistant [A] and that there had been a practice in the office whereby incoming mail was opened and distributed by the staff with the result that he was not aware of the seriousness of the matter. These explanations are not accepted. [A] was until October 1982, still in his post-qualifying year and the Respondent had an ongoing responsibility to read such incoming letters as were passed to him and generally to supervise the transaction (Case 646/84).

In another case the Tribunal said:

At the time when the Respondent employed [the assistant], he knew that he had previously been employed by a legal firm in Glasgow and a [local] authority. [The assistant] also had an LLB degree; but although this degree is frequently taken by those seeking admission as solicitors, the degree in itself does not necessarily contain all the elements necessary to gain admission as a solicitor and the holder of the degree may not have had the training which is a prerequisite for qualifying as a solicitor. . . .

It was accepted by the Fiscal that [the assistant] personally attended to each of the four transactions. Until [the assistant] left the Respondent's employment in [. . .], much of the relevant correspondence bears [the assistant's] reference, some of the letters were indeed signed by him in his own name and a number of incoming letters were addressed personally to [the assistant]. In his Answers, the Respondent claimed that [the assistant] deliberately intercepted letters and that certain letters might have been signed by [the assistant] outwith the Respondent's knowledge and permission. . . .

In any event, [the assistant's] conduct in relation to the missives of his own house and the discovery of shortcomings in [the assistant's] workmanship ought to have put the Respondent on his guard and from this time he should have taken positive steps to monitor [the assistant's] work. Instead the Respondent's lack of personal supervision permitted a situation which resulted in [the assistant] intercepting letters which would otherwise have alerted the Respondent to the various delays. . . .

As previously indicated, it is always open to a solicitor to employ an unqualified assistant for procedural work within his practice; but it is essential that the solicitor maintains a high level of supervision to ensure that the standard of work is not less than that which is expected of a qualified solicitor. It is customary for a solicitor or at least one or more partners in a larger firm to attend at the opening of incoming mail and similarly for the solicitor to adhibit the firm signature to outgoing mail. Such practice ensures that there is close supervision of written communications with clients and other agents. Having regard to the particular circumstances, it is apparent that the Respondent ignored several clear warnings regarding the progress of [the assistant's] work . . . (Case 736/88).

The Tribunal found Inadequate Professional Services established in a case where there was a failure to advise a client adequately prior to making an offer to purchase heritable property on behalf of the client. In the particular case the client had apparently 'only limited knowledge' relating to the purchase and sale of house property in Scotland and the solicitor left it to a relatively inexperienced assistant to explain the whole procedure to the client. It appeared that prior to entering into missives to purchase a property no advice was given as to the necessity of securing bridging finance should the client not have sold and obtained the price of his existing house prior to the date of entry of the property he was purchasing (Case 835/92).

See also Case 751/89, reported at para 7.03. On the subject of responsibility for an undertaking given by an assistant, see also Case 463/80, reported at para 15.02.

16.04 BLANK HEADED PAPER AND THIRD PARTIES
The Tribunal has said:

It should be added that the Tribunal particularly deplore the actions of the Respondent in making available a blank sheet of his firm's headed notepaper to a third party [a newspaper] even in circumstances where the content of a proposed letter had been agreed. Because of the nature of the business carried on by

Solicitors, serious consequences might arise from a third party making improper use of a Solicitor's notepaper. In this case, it is accepted that [the solicitor] had approved of the terms of the draft [letter] and in fact signed the letter which was typed by the newspaper; but in other circumstances, this Tribunal would seriously consider holding that a solicitor had contributed to any improper acts which might arise as a direct result of a sheet of headed notepaper being passed into the hands of another party (Case 629/85).

16.05 ACCOUNT FOR WORK INSTRUCTED FOR CLIENT

In a case where a solicitor instructed a translation agency to translate a document from a foreign language into English, the solicitor was found guilty of Professional Misconduct when he failed to settle the account for the work, despite a number of reminders. The Tribunal took the view that where in the course of his practice a solicitor gives instructions for professional services to be carried out on behalf of a client, there is an understanding that the solicitor will be personally responsible for the charges arising from these services (Case 828/92).

In another case a solicitor was found guilty of Professional Misconduct for failing to settle the professional charges of a firm of surveyors whom he had instructed in the course of his practice. The Tribunal said:

> When a Solicitor in the course of his practice instructs an Advocate or fellow Solicitor or a member of some other profession to carry out work on behalf of his client, that Solicitor should, unless special arrangements have previously been made, be prepared to accept personal responsibility for such fees as may arise, and it is on this principle that the Respondent accepted his culpability for his failure to settle the outstanding balance due to [the surveyors] (Case 646/84).

16.06 SETTLEMENT OF FEES TO WITNESSES/COUNSEL

A solicitor was found guilty of Professional Misconduct in respect of his failure to settle timeously the fee due to a witness whom he had cited to attend and had given evidence in a Court case. In its Decision the Tribunal said:

> The charges set out in this Complaint were (a) that the Respondent was guilty of unconscionable delay in settling a Chartered Surveyor's Account and (b) that he failed without reasonable cause to reply to correspondence addressed to him by the Complainers.

> Regarding the first charge, the Respondent did not dispute that Mr [A] was required to attend a Proof in the Court of Session on 16th January 1976 or that his account was not settled until on or about 18th May 1978. The legal position is that when a Solicitor cites a witness to attend Court he is personally responsible for his fee and such fee ought to be settled without delay. In this case the Respondent's client was an assisted person but section 2(6) (a) of the Legal Aid (Scotland) Act 1967 provides in effect that in such circumstances a Solicitor has the same responsibility as if his client was not in receipt of Legal Aid. The policy of the Legal Aid Central Committee is to sanction advances to Solicitors in reimbursement of outlays of this kind in cases where a litigation is still in progress but not after decree is granted. Thereafter, no payments are sanctioned until the account is completed and lodged.

The Complainers did not attempt to state what would be a reasonable time for the payment of a witness's account in the particular circumstances, and the Tribunal felt it unnecessary to lay down a ruling on this subject. However, it is beyond doubt that a period of over two years is grossly excessive, particularly bearing in mind the repeated reminders which came from both Mr [A] and the Law Society of Scotland.

The amount involved was just over £100 and, as stated above, it is the Solicitor's personal duty to settle such an account, irrespective of whether or not he has been put in funds by his client. It was suggested by the Respondent in his Answers that Mr [A] knew that his client was Legal Aided and that Mr [A] was, therefore, obliged to wait until settlement was effected by the Legal Aid Fund, but the Respondent did not attempt to argue this point before the Tribunal.

. . . In particular the Respondent showed clearly that he was aware in 1976 that he had insufficient funds to settle this witness's professional account and instead of reducing his workload and establishing a proper cash flow, he deliberately persisted in a manner of work which left him short of working capital and thereby unable to settle an account which it was his professional duty to clear. In this situation, the Tribunal is clear that the delay which is the subject of the Complaint was, in the whole circumstances of the case, inexcusable and certainly amounted to professional misconduct (Case 420/78).

In Case 877/93 the Tribunal said:

In particular the Respondent admitted that he had failed to provide a satisfactory explanation for the non-payment of Counsel's fees. There is a long-established practice that a solicitor has a professional responsibility in regard to the settlement of Counsel's fees in relation to work which he has instructed and the extent of this responsibility is set out in Schemes agreed in 1977 and 1987 between the Faculty of Advocates and the Law Society of Scotland. The Respondent had repeatedly failed to give an explanation for not settling the particular fees and the Tribunal is satisfied that such failure amounts to professional misconduct.

16.07 CLOSING PRACTICE DOWN
The Tribunal has observed that:

In the event of a solicitor closing down the premises from where he has carried on practice, he has a duty to intimate the change to all interested parties, and this includes the Law Society of Scotland, as the Council of the Law Society is the Registrar of Solicitors in Scotland and the Law Society has a statutory duty to represent the interests of the public in relation to the profession of Solicitors in Scotland. Normally the solicitor will also intimate the change to each of his clients (Case 768/89).

16.08 INQUIRIES FROM THE LAW SOCIETY
The Law Society has a statutory duty to inquire into allegations of Professional Misconduct and Inadequate Professional Services made to it concerning solicitors and in order that the Law Society can adequately deal with such allegations it is essential that solicitors respond promptly, accurately and fully to inquiries made of them by the Law Society. In a case where a solicitor had repeatedly failed to respond to the letters from the Law Society inquiring as to various allegations by clients, the Tribunal said:

> The statutory objects of the Law Society of Scotland include the promotion of the interests of the solicitors' profession in Scotland and the interests of the public in relation to that profession; and it is in pursuance of these objects that the Law Society makes enquiries of a solicitor in the event of any letter of complaint being received from a member of the public. . . .

> . . . The Respondent's conduct not only inconvenienced the Law Society and caused them to write additional letters but put the Law Society in the position that they were unable to provide each of the complainers with an explanation. Such a situation is damaging to the reputation of the profession of solicitors in Scotland and it is therefore appropriate that the Respondent should bear a substantial fine (Case 776/89).

Misleading, or attempting to mislead, the Law Society when replying to an inquiry has been held to be Professional Misconduct (Cases 843/93 and 851/93).

In one case the Tribunal said:

> Each matter was the subject of complaint to the Law Society of Scotland. In terms of section 1 of the Solicitors (Scotland) Act 1980 the Objects of the Law Society include the promotion of the interests of the public in relation to the Solicitors' profession in Scotland and it is in accordance with this function that the Law Society makes enquiries into any complaint which may be received. It is a solicitor's duty to reply promptly, fully and accurately to any such enquiry. It is particularly regrettable that in relation to each matter, the Respondent failed to provide the Law Society with an accurate report. Such failure not only inconveniences the Law Society in the performance of their statutory duty but can also give rise to considerable embarrassment and has an adverse effect on the reputation of the profession. It is in these circumstances that the Tribunal will always take a serious view when misleading information has been given to the Law Society (Case 697/87).

In a case where a solicitor (the Respondent) had been involved in a conflict of interest situation and where his partner, unknown to the Respondent, had been instructed to issue a Writ against the Respondent's client, and the Respondent had inadvertently signed the Initial Writ and service copy Writ against his client, which had been prepared by his partner's assistant, the Respondent was charged with Professional Misconduct in that *inter alia* he had supplied the Law Society with erroneous information about the signing of the Writ. In the Note to its Decision the Tribunal said:

> The final charge concerned the false statement made by the Respondent to the Law Society in his letter of 5th June 1984 when he claimed that the Initial Writ had been signed by his partner [B]. This Tribunal accepted the evidence of the Respondent that he remained unaware that he had signed the particular Writ until a copy of the same was made available and produced to the Complainers in August 1984; and that in answering the Complainers' first letter of 23rd May 1984, the Respondent had mistakenly assumed that his partner had signed the Writ because his name appeared on the backing of the copy in his firm's file. The Law Society of Scotland has a statutory duty to investigate all complaints directed to it by members of the public and others, and Solicitors have a corresponding obligation to provide the Law Society with full and accurate information in order that such matters can be properly dealt with. Upon receiving the letter of 23rd May 1984,

the Respondent had a duty to make such enquiries as might have been necessary to provide the Law Society with an accurate reply. He failed to do so, nor did he qualify his reply in any way as might infer that this answer was based only on his understanding and belief at the time. In the circumstances, the Complainers were entitled to rely on the complete accuracy of the Respondent's reply of 5th June 1984 and in the opinion of this Tribunal, the Respondent's failure to ensure a full and accurate reply was in itself professional misconduct (Case 649/84).

16.09 OBTEMPERING A SECTION 39 NOTICE

Following on a complaint made to the Council of the Law Society of undue delay on the part of a solicitor, the Council may serve a Notice in writing on the solicitor requiring him to give an explanation of the delay.

In a case where the Council served a Notice under section 39 of the 1980 Act on a solicitor requiring him to give an explanation (within twenty-one days) of undue delay in replying to a complaint of a client and failing to implement a mandate and the solicitor failed to comply with the Notice, the Tribunal found Professional Misconduct established (Case 670/86).

16.10 PREVIOUS WARNINGS BY LAW SOCIETY

In bringing a Complaint against a solicitor, the Law Society (the Complainers) referred to circumstances in 1986 giving rise to previous breaches of the Accounts Rules. An inspection on 6th July 1988 disclosed significant shortages on the Respondent's client account and it was averred by the Complainers that 'this failure, in light of previous warnings given ... amounts, in the whole circumstances, to professional misconduct'. The Tribunal in finding Professional Misconduct established said:

> The Respondent did not give any explanation for the shortages ascertained at the inspection on 6th July 1988. However, he claimed that there had been no 'previous warnings' and that although there had been correspondence with the Complainers following on the inspection on 23rd October 1986, there had been no 'letter of warning' and that in so far as there had been prior shortages in 1986 there had been no indication that these shortages in themselves reflected any discredit.

> In the opinion of the Tribunal, the charge as stated does not require the Complainers to establish that the Respondent had been given a formal warning. It is an essential principle that a solicitor in practice should at all times distinguish clients' money from other monies held by him and this principle is clearly set out in Rule 4(1) (a) of the Accounts Rules [the 1986 Rules]. The profession is regularly reminded of the importance of complying with this provision and the Tribunal would not accept that a prior warning is a necessary prerequisite before there can be a finding of professional misconduct in respect of any shortage. The outcome of the two inspections in 1986 ought to have alerted the Respondent to the importance of ensuring compliance with the Accounts Rules. The second inspection disclosed shortages in four separate months during that year. The Respondent was given the opportunity to comment on these circumstances and there was no evidence to suggest that the shortage was caused by some event which was outwith his control. The discovery of these shortages in 1986 should in itself have directed the

Respondent towards adopting measures to prevent any repetition of the same (Case 746/89).

See also para 2.02.

16.11 PRACTISING CERTIFICATE/INDEMNITY INSURANCE

Carrying on business (e.g. making an offer to lease heritable property on behalf of a client) without a current Practising Certificate is contrary to section 23(1) of the 1980 Act and has been found to be Professional Misconduct. That section contains a qualification to the extent that the solicitor might prove that he acted without receiving or without expectation of any fee, gain or reward directly or indirectly but the *onus* in establishing such exception, is clearly on the solicitor (Cases 713/87; 843/93 and 857/93).

The established procedure whereby a solicitor is required to obtain a Practising Certificate before he can practise or hold himself out to be a solicitor is of long standing and the provisions are clearly set out in the Solicitors (Scotland) Act 1980. These provisions are for the protection of both other members of the profession and the public. The issuing of a Practising Certificate enables the Law Society to maintain a complete record which is open to public inspection containing the names of all solicitors who are so entitled to practise (Case 843/93).

In Case 740/88 the Tribunal said:

Section 53(5) of the Solicitors (Scotland) Act 1980 provides that:

Where the Tribunal have exercised the power . . . to censure, or impose a fine on a solicitor, or both to censure and impose a fine, the Tribunal may order that the solicitor's practising certificate shall be subject to such terms and conditions as the Tribunal may direct; and the Council shall give effect to any such order of the Tribunal.

At the conclusion of a previous Complaint heard on 4th November 1987, the Tribunal censured the Respondent and fined him in the sum of [£ . . .] and in terms of the foregoing subsection the Tribunal directed that for a period of ten years with effect from 1st March 1988, any Practising Certificate held or issued to the Respondent would be subject to such restriction as to limit him to acting as a partner or a qualified assistant to such solicitor or firm as might be approved by the Council of the Law Society of Scotland. The Respondent failed to make any application to the Council of the Law Society for such approval with the result that as from 1st March 1988, the Respondent no longer had an effective Practising Certificate.

Section 23(1) of the Solicitors (Scotland) Act 1980 provides that:

Any person who practises as a solicitor or in any way holds himself out as entitled by law to practise as a solicitor without having in force a practising certificate shall be guilty of an offence under this Act unless he proves that he acted without receiving or without expectation of any fee, gain or reward, directly or indirectly.

And subsection (2) of the said section adds that 'failure on the part of a solicitor in practice to have in force a practising certificate may be treated as professional misconduct'.

Section 65 and section 4 together define an 'unqualified person' as including a solicitor who does not have a Practising Certificate and section 31(1) of the same Act provides that:

> Any unqualified person ... who either by himself or together with others, wilfully and falsely—
> (a) pretends to be a solicitor or notary public; or
> (b) takes or uses any name, title, addition or description implying that he is duly qualified to act as a solicitor or a notary public or recognised by law as so qualified;
> shall be guilty of an offence.

The Respondent continued to carry on a business from 1st March 1988 but in his Answers he claimed that he was in practice as a Secretary, Factor, Property Agent, Cashier and Income Tax Adviser. He added that in the absence of any guidance from the Secretary of the Law Society, he had to use his own judgment in restricting his business to work which was strictly non-legal and he claimed that this had been the case.

The Complainers led the evidence of several present and former members of their staff, and the Respondent gave evidence on his own behalf. In reply to questions from members of the Tribunal, the Respondent frankly admitted that he had practised as a solicitor in relation to the conveyancing transactions for Mrs [A] but he claimed that as from 1st March 1988, he had not otherwise practised or held himself out as a practising solicitor.

With the exception of the conveyancing transactions which have already been mentioned, the work carried on by the Respondent after 1st March 1988 appears to have been confined to the administration of executry estates and the receiving of income and the settling of accounts for elderly clients. Such work is not the exclusive jurisdiction of a solicitor but it is work which is frequently carried out by a solicitor in practice; and it is particularly significant in the case of the Respondent that these excutry estates were previously administered by the Respondent in [the] course of his practice as a solicitor and that it was in the course of his previous practice as a solicitor that he attended to the affairs of these elderly clients.

It is with these considerations that the Tribunal finds that the Respondent continued to carry on practising as a solicitor from 1st March 1988, contrary to the provisions of sections 23(1) and 31(1) of the Solicitors (Scotland) Act 1980.

The Complaint also contained a separate charge that the Respondent conveyed 'to the legal profession and the public alike that he was a Solicitor in private practice and by failing to demarcate clearly between the capacities in which he did act before and after 1st March 1988'. The Respondent's answer to this was that he was only carrying on the work of factor. Other than the transactions mentioned above, there was no suggestion that the Respondent was performing any of the duties which are within the exclusive jurisdiction of the solicitors' profession and it is therefore a matter of looking at the whole circumstances surrounding his business in order to ascertain whether he was in fact holding himself out as a solicitor entitled to practise. It is particularly significant that the Respondent had the same notice outside his office displaying the sign ['... & ... W.S.'] and that this notice was visible to the public in the street. It is accepted that there were few, if any, members of the public who may have been attracted by the sign to call at the Respondent's office but the significant fact is that the sign was in itself a public demonstration that the Respondent was in business at that address. The Respondent observed that the notice did not contain the word 'solicitor' but it is within the knowledge of the Tribunal that, especially in Edinburgh, the letters 'W.S.' are synonymous in the public eyes with the profession of solicitor and that indeed many solicitors in Edinburgh confine their designation to that of 'W.S.' The impression conveyed by the sign is reinforced by the use of the same designation on the Respondent's notepaper. It is particularly significant that prior to 1st March 1988, the Respondent was in active practice, carrying on business as a solicitor under the name of ['... & ... W.S.'] and there was no change in the sign or his notepaper, nor was there any intimation to clients, to his Bank or to the brokers attending to Professional Indemnity Insurance that there had been a change in his status with effect from 1st March 1988. The impression that the Respondent was still carrying on the same practice as a solicitor was reinforced by the statements which he made to [two officers of the Council]. It is in these circumstances that the Tribunal finds that between 1st March and 12th August 1988 the Respondent continued to hold himself out as a solicitor entitled to practise.

Subsection 23(2) provides that failure on the part of a solicitor in practice to have in force a Practising Certificate *may* be treated as professional misconduct.

In the previous decision, the Tribunal observed that:

> The Respondent did not indicate any immediate intention of retiring. However, having regard to the Respondent's persistent failure to comply with the requirements of the Accounts Rules and the Respondent's age, the Tribunal is of the opinion that it would be inappropriate to permit the Respondent to continue in practice indefinitely on his own account, and that early steps should be taken to assume a suitable partner or to amalgamate his practice. It is for this reason that an appropriate order has been made under section 53(5) of the Solicitors (Scotland) Act 1980 with the qualification that the order will not take effect for a period of three clear months.

The Respondent accordingly had ample time to amalgamate or wind down his practice. The Tribunal therefore repels the excuse put forward by the Respondent that he continued to deal with Mrs [A's] transactions in order not to put her to the trouble and expense of a hand over. It was the Respondent's decision not to seek an amalgamation of his practice and the duty was therefore on him to ensure that the transaction was passed on to other solicitors and that his client was kept free of any additional expense. The Tribunal also rejects the excuse put forward by the Respondent that he was entitled to wait until he was suitably advised by the Law Society Secretariat.

When a sole practitioner ceases to practise as a solicitor for whatever reason, he has a professional duty to inform his clients of his retirement and the arrangements which he is making for the disposal of his practice, and he has also a duty to inform those parties who have been dealing with him in his professional capacity of his retirement.

It was apparent to the Tribunal that the Respondent deliberately chose not to make any arrangements for the winding up or transfer of his practice and that he recklessly misguided himself into adopting a course of action which was in direct conflict with the order of the Tribunal. Professional misconduct has accordingly been established.

Professional Misconduct was held to have been established where a solicitor tendered a cheque for renewal of his Practising Certificate when he knew, or ought to have known, that there were insufficient funds in his bank account to meet the cheque, and also where the same solicitor tendered on two occasions cheques for payment of his professional indemnity insurance when he knew, or ought to have known, that there were insufficient funds in his bank account to meet the cheques (Case 682/86).

> Indemnity insurance is a prerequisite for the issue of a Practising Certificate and the Tribunal noted that the Respondent's cash-flow problems prevented her from paying the insurance premium and that latterly that period coincided with health problems. It is a solicitor's duty that there are sufficient funds available to finance a practice and the only acceptable alternative is for the solicitor immediately to withdraw from practice. In continuing to practise without indemnity insurance, the Respondent exposed herself to possible claims from clients which she would have been unable to meet from her own resources. This could have had very serious consequences and in these circumstances the Tribunal finds that this further failure on the part of the Respondent also amounts to professional misconduct (Case 864/93).

In a case where the prosecution resulted from an enquiry made to the Law Society by a member of the public the Tribunal observed that:

> it is a prerequisite of a Practising Certificate to cover general practice that the solicitor has Professional Indemnity Insurance under the Master Cover and subscribes to the Guarantee Fund, also that he contributes towards the overall costs of maintaining the administration of the profession through his subscription to the Law Society of Scotland. By failing to take out a Practising Certificate, the Respondent avoided his various obligations under these heads (Cases 733/88; 782/90 and 843/93).

Furthermore Professional Misconduct was found to be established, notwithstanding that there was no apparent prejudice to the client involved, although the Tribunal observed that the absence of Professional Indemnity Insurance could itself have had serious consequences (Cases 843/93 and 857/93).

16.12 COMPLIANCE CERTIFICATE
Failure to lodge compliance certificates required by the Solicitors (Scotland) (Conduct of Investment Business) Practice Rules 1989 has been found to constitute Professional Misconduct (Cases 807/90 and 826/92).

17

DUTIES AS NOTARY

17.01 DUTIES AS NOTARY

The Tribunal has said:

> Solicitors who become Notaries Public are in a privileged position. The formality of swearing before a Notary Public confers a higher standing on documents. Third parties are entitled to rely on them. Historically the employment of Notaries arose because of an increasing incidence of forgeries in private writings. It was, and is, crucial to the administration of justice that the public should have faith in deeds authenticated by Notaries.

> A solicitor acting as a Notary Public must therefore take reasonable steps to satisfy [himself] as to the true identity of the person taking the oath and signing the document and of the signatory's understanding of the document. The public and profession are entitled to the protection that documents, signed on oath before a Notary Public, have a status greater than ordinary documents, by virtue of the notarisation (Case 817/91).

In another case the Tribunal stated:

> The execution of deeds before a notary is a long-standing practice, giving such documents a measure of authenticity and it was significant that in the Matrimonial Homes (Family Protection) (Scotland) Act 1981, the statute specifically introduced the affidavit procedure to protect the occupation rights of one spouse in relation to the other. It is an essential feature of a notarial execution that the notary is present and personally attests to the genuineness of the deponent's signature. ... [I]t is important for the profession of solicitors to be aware that in exercising the functions of a notary, a solicitor must at all times respect all the formalities, however inconvenient or time-consuming that this may be ... (Case 842/93).

In one case where the solicitor had added his signature as Notary to an Affidavit when the deponent had signed in a different town outwith his presence and he had completed the particulars so as to indicate it had been signed in his presence, there was a finding of Professional Misconduct, notwithstanding that there was no doubt as to the authenticity of the deponent's signature (Case 842/93).

In a case where a solicitor acted as a Notary Public to a document which he himself had signed in a fictitious name, knowing that the document was a forgery, Professional Misconduct was established (Case 823/92).

The Tribunal found Professional Misconduct established in a case where in a conveyancing transaction, a solicitor acting as a Notary Public had notarised an Affidavit under the Matrimonial Homes (Family Protection) (Scotland) Act 1981 when, to the knowledge of the solicitor, the granter of the Affidavit used a fictitious name and that notwithstanding that the Affidavit was factually correct to the extent that the party swearing had been unmarried and there was no non-entitled spouse and that the property was not a matrimonial home as defined by the Act, because in the view of the Tribunal, the Affidavit was fatally flawed when it was sworn in the fictitious name, notwithstanding the truth of the remainder of the statements (Case 817/91).

However, in a case where a solicitor had misdirected himself on the statutory interpretation of a 'matrimonial home', the Tribunal had to consider whether the solicitor's course of action amounted to Professional Misconduct. The Tribunal said it would be slow to find that a solicitor who had misdirected himself on a question of law and had acted on the basis of that misdirection had been guilty of conduct falling within the definition of Professional Misconduct and having regard to the whole circumstances of the particular case found that the failure of the solicitor to follow the generally accepted interpretation of the Act was not of such gravity as might require a finding of Professional Misconduct (Case 804/90).

In a case in which a solicitor was found guilty of Professional Misconduct in that:

(i) he presented an Affidavit to his client for signature and signed as a Notary Public to the swearing of his client of said Affidavit, which Affidavit he knew was false in its terms in that there was a non-entitled spouse whose solicitor had been in correspondence with him, and

(ii) having been made aware by the Solicitors for his client's wife that she intended to claim her occupancy rights as a non-entitled spouse and having advised his client that the disclosure of this might delay settlement of the transaction, he deliberately proceeded to settlement without seeking from his client's wife a renunciation of her occupancy rights and her consent to the Disposition and deceived the solicitor for the purchaser by delivering to him at settlement said Affidavit which he knew was false in its terms,

the Tribunal said *inter alia*:

... The Tribunal regard the whole conduct of the Respondent to have been inexcusable and reprehensible, proceeding recklessly without due regard for the statutory rights of his client's wife or the possible consequences to the purchaser. Only one transaction was involved, and the Respondent had not previously been the subject of any proceedings before this Tribunal. It is also appreciated that any order of this Tribunal affecting the Respondent's right to practise would have serious financial consequences, affecting the Respondent's possible future with his present firm. Nevertheless the actings of the Respondent on this occasion have demonstrated to the Tribunal that at the relevant time, the Respondent was lacking in propriety and prepared to act in a reckless manner without due regard to the rightful interests of third parties. It is in these circumstances that the Tribunal is of the opinion that the Respondent should be suspended from practice for a material period. In the opinion of the Tribunal, the protection afforded to the public by this order should take effect at the earliest possible date and accordingly the Tribunal has also made a direction under the provision of section 53(6) of the Solicitors (Scotland) Act 1980 (Case 679/86).

Mr A consulted a firm of solicitors, X & Y, who instructed English solicitors, V & W, to make an application to the Divorce Registry of the High Court in London for the variation of an order for periodical payments to A's former wife. The English solicitors asked X & Y to prepare an accurate Affidavit containing certain details of A's means and sent X & Y a draft of the proposed Affidavit. X & Y wrote to A with the draft Affidavit and a copy of the English solicitors' letter and suggested that A should see the Respondent in order that the Affidavit might be completed and signed and returned to the English solicitors. The Tribunal said:

> This Complaint relates to the Respondent's actings as a Notary Public. The office of Notary Public is limited to enrolled Solicitors in Scotland and the duties of a Notary are associated with the ordinary work of a Solicitor to an extent that it is appropriate that any Complaint alleging improper actings as a Notary should come before this Tribunal. The Respondent did not seek to challenge this principle.

> The draft Affidavit which had been prepared by Messrs [V & W] set out the information regarding Mr [A's] financial and personal circumstances insofar as known to them and blanks were left in the draft with directions for completion of the document. Before calling on the Respondent, Mr [A] had inserted much of the required information in pencil; and in the course of the Respondent's meeting with Mr [A], a further paragraph was written into the draft by the Respondent on the basis of the information given to him by Mr [A]. The letters from [V & W] to [X & Y] and from [X & Y] to Mr [A] enclosing the draft affidavit had explained the urgency of having the Affidavit completed and returned as soon as possible, and this urgency was emphasised by Mr [A] when he called upon the Respondent. The Respondent acknowledged that he ought to have had the Affidavit extended before he administered the oath to Mr [A] and had the Affidavit signed, but the Respondent unfortunately did not resist the pressure on him and he administered the oath to Mr [A] on the basis of the draft document. At the Respondent's request, Mr [A] then signed two blank sheets of paper. Subsequently, and outwith Mr [A's] presence, the Respondent had the statement extended on the signed sheets of paper and the Respondent then added his notarial docquet. There was not produced to the Tribunal a copy of the document which was ultimately forwarded to [V & W] and lodged in the Divorce Registry; but it was not disputed that the content of the draft statement to which Mr [A] had sworn was the same as that which was lodged in the English Court, and the Tribunal accepted this.

> The established and proper practice for the swearing of an Affidavit is that the completed document should be before the Deponent and the Notary, the Deponent should then swear that the contents of the statement are true, and the Deponent and the Notary should immediately sign the document. The Tribunal are unable to accept that any variation of this established procedure is acceptable.

> In England and overseas, the use of Affidavit evidence has been widely used and since April 1978 this procedure has also come into general use in certain actions of divorce in Scotland. Such evidence is accepted and relied upon by the Courts as if it had been given personally and therefore there is an important duty on any Notary who is administering an oath in these circumstances to ensure that all the proper formalities are followed.

> In his submission to the Tribunal, [the Fiscal] referred to the case of *Stewart* v *Smith* 1680 M 15928. The circumstances in that case were that the two Notaries had subscribed a testamentary writing in blank on behalf of a person and sub-

sequently written up the document after the person's death. In that case the Court took a very serious view of the incident and not only deprived the Notaries of office but also imposed a penalty of a form which is now obsolete. That case differed from the present circumstances in that the deceased had been unable to give instructions at the time when the blank sheets were signed and that the Court accordingly found the document to be false but nevertheless the case demonstrates the seriousness where a Notary fails to follow the established procedure.

It is the duty of a Solicitor to uphold the highest standards of his profession and where a Solicitor acts as Notary, he has a further duty to the Court to ensure that his conduct is beyond reproach. The actings of the Respondent on this particular occasion fell below the required standard and in these circumstances, a finding of professional misconduct is appropriate ... (Case 410/78).

18

FEE CHARGING

18.01 PAYMENTS TO ACCOUNT OF FEES

The fees charged by solicitors shall be fair and reasonable in all the circumstances (Code of Conduct, para 6).

The Tribunal had to consider a case where it had been a practice within the firm to take payments to account of executry fees and in view of the lack of financial resources, a practice developed whereby a member of the cashroom staff would, on a weekly basis, assess the financial requirements of the firm and obtain the first Respondent's approval for the transfer from an executry of a payment to account of fees. The first Respondent routinely assented to such arrangement without regard to the amount of work done on the particular estate or the previous charges made against that estate. The first Respondent explained that upon each estate being wound up and the fees taxed, any overpayment of fees was refunded to the estate. The Tribunal in making a finding of Professional Misconduct against the first Respondent said:

> It is accepted that executry estates may take some considerable time to wind up and in such circumstances a solicitor may take a reasonable payment to account of fees. In doing so, it is essential that the solicitor should have regard to the value of the work already carried out and the amount of any interim fees already charged. Such a transfer will ordinarily be regarded as 'money properly required ... to account of the solicitor's professional account'. However, it is apparent from the four executries particularly referred to in the Complaint that the sums debited were in aggregate grossly in excess of the fees that could reasonably be charged against each estate and that the transfers were therefore not authorised under rule 6(*d*) [Accounts Rules 1986]. The first Respondent had agreed to the specific debiting of fees without regard either to the amount of work already carried out or to the interim fees already charged. That course of conduct was in itself reckless and constituted a serious breach of the Accounts Rules justifying a finding of professional misconduct.

In relation to the second Respondent (the junior partner of the first Respondent) his Counsel submitted that for Professional Misconduct to be established, it would be necessary to show that he had taken an active part in the procedure which resulted in the breaches of the Accounts Rules and that such had not been established.

The Tribunal found that in the particular circumstances, having regard to the *dicta* of the court in *Sharp* v *Council of the Law Society of Scotland* 1984 SC 129, the failure of the junior partner fell narrowly short of Professional Misconduct, stating that in its view it may not be necessary for active participation to be proved to establish Professional Misconduct.

By a particular date the junior partner was certainly aware of the practice being adopted by his senior partner and his unease had continued, notwithstanding an apparent assurance from the firm's accountant. He had, to his credit, taken certain steps but the Tribunal said it was unfortunate that he had not satisfied himself regarding the provisions of the Accounts Rules nor sought advice from the Secretariat of the Law Society, nor did he monitor the particular executry which gave him concern after speaking to his senior partner about the matter (Case 723/87).

In another case the Tribunal has observed that where business is of extended duration it is an acceptable practice for a solicitor to take a payment to account of his fees. However, the aggregate of such payments taken to account should not at any time exceed a reasonable estimate of the amount of fees chargeable for work to that date, and in taking a payment to account the solicitor should always have due regard to the provisions of the Accounts Rules which set out in what circumstances money can be drawn from a client account (Case 773/89).

> It is well settled overcharging fees to a client may amount to Professional Misconduct, particularly where this constitutes taking unfair advantage of the client (Case 596/85).

18.02 CLAIM FOR SERVICES NOT INCURRED

Professional Misconduct was established in circumstances where a solicitor had improperly charged a client for work which was not executed and for outlays which were not incurred in that he had charged for a 'visit to Edinburgh re Counsel's opinion and Edinburgh Agents' in circumstances where there had been no Counsel in the case and at no time was there a meeting between the solicitor and the Edinburgh Agents (Case 708/87).

18.03 INACCURATE CLAIMS FOR LEGAL AID FEES

Two solicitors who were in partnership were charged with Professional Misconduct in relation to fees charged in regard to Criminal Legal Aid. Each Complaint averred that on specific dates the Respondents claimed fees from the Legal Aid authorities for the attendance of the same solicitor for the same period of the day in respect of their respective clients and that these claims were contrary to the specific declaration in each claim form. In the particular circumstances the Tribunal found that the admitted errors and mistakes made by the Respondents fell narrowly short of Professional Misconduct, and said:

> The Fiscal for the Complainers conceded that the amount of fees concerned in regard to the inaccurate claims represented less than 1 per cent of the total fees received by the Respondents but contended that this margin of error was not excusable and should be sufficient to support a finding of professional misconduct. The Tribunal were not sympathetic to such argument, and it is considered that

each case should be considered on its own merits. The Tribunal was also not persuaded by the argument based on the fact that particular errors on the part of the Respondents did not give rise to an overpayment of fees.

The Form SCLA25 has been carefully prepared by the Legal Aid Committee and contains clear and precise instructions to the nominated Solicitor. In particular the nominated solicitor is directed—in completing the section dealing with Court attendances, to set down 'the actual times of day involved . . . as well as the number of hours engaged'. That instruction is clear and unequivocal and requires to be followed precisely and accurately by the nominated Solicitor on every occasion. It is appreciated that there are occasions when the pressure of Court attendances may be intense but the operation of the present scheme can only continue if Solicitors exercise the utmost care in the completion of the claim forms. The declarations to the effect that 'the person(s) concerned were not engaged in any other business at the same time and place . . .' and that 'the items charged in this account are accurate and represent a complete record of all the work done' are equally mandatory on nominated Solicitors and the Legal Aid authorities are entitled to expect that the Solicitor will respect and comply with these declarations and ensure as far as possible that the information set out is accurate in all respects. It matters not that some provision in the Table of Fees or concession on the part of the Criminal Taxation Department might result in duplication of payment for the same period of time. As has been shown by these Complaints, it is open to the Taxation Department to conduct an analysis and in these circumstances the Legal Aid Authorities are entitled to expect that the information contained in the claim forms is accurate in all respects (Case 533/82).

NB. This case is also referred to at para 3.04.

In another case where a solicitor was found guilty of Professional Misconduct in that he submitted to his Local Legal Aid Committee claims for fees contrary to a declaration which accompanied each claim, the Tribunal said:

The system for the payment of fees to Solicitors in Criminal Legal Aid proceedings is based on trust and in such circumstances, there is a heavy onus on the Solicitor to ensure that he is not associated with a claim reflecting a sum in excess of what he or his staff are entitled to for their services. The particular claim form contains the clear directions that

. . . the actual times of day involved must be given as well as the total number of hours engaged.

And above the claimant's signature there appears the words:

(*b*) the person(s) concerned were not engaged in any other business at the same time and place except as fully detailed and apportioned herein . . .

(*d*) the items charged in this account are accurate and represent a true and complete record of all the work done.

These declarations are clear and explicit and the Legal Aid Authorities are entitled to rely on a Solicitor respecting such assurances to the utmost. The last-mentioned phrases were [preceded] in some forms with the words 'I certify that . . .' and in other forms with the alternative 'having made the necessary enquiries I Certify that to the best of my knowledge and belief'. In the opinion of the Tribunal such differences in the wording is of little consequence. The catalogue of inaccuracies as set out in the Complaint as amended and as established by this Tribunal in circumstances where the Respondent would benefit financially, is sufficient in itself to support the charge of professional misconduct against the Respondent and the Tribunal find accordingly (Case 534/82).

18.04 SUBMITTING ACCOUNT TO TAXATION

Professional Misconduct was established where there was gross and persistent failure by a solicitor to submit for taxation business accounts to two clients who had consulted new agents and had requested that the solicitor's account be taxed (Case 708/87).

19

ACCOUNTING RULES

19.01 COMPLIANCE WITH ACCOUNTS RULES

[S]olicitors must observe the Accounts Rules which govern the manner in which clients' funds may be held by solicitors and which are designed to ensure that clients' monies are safeguarded (Case of Conduct, para 7).

The Tribunal has said:

... [If] solicitors are to continue to enjoy the public trust in regard to their financial affairs, they must have careful regard to all the requirements and obligations incumbent on them as contained in the Accounts Rules (Case 665/86).

It is probably the case that the Tribunal has to consider complaints where solicitors are charged with alleged breaches of the Accounts Rules more than any other type of case.

Breaches of the Accounts Rules may result in a finding of Professional Misconduct even where no dishonesty is involved but the Tribunal will always take into account not only the breach or breaches concerned but also the surrounding facts and circumstances. (*Sharp* v *Council of the Law Society of Scotland* 1984 SC 129). What was found to be Professional Misconduct in one case may not necessarily result in a finding of Professional Misconduct in another case, but equally well what was not found to amount to Professional Misconduct in a particular set of circumstances may in other circumstances be found to constitute misconduct. It should be noted that the numbering of the Accounts Rules has altered over the years.

The following breaches have been found to constitute Professional Misconduct.

Misappropriation of fees for personal use without a fee note being properly debited to the ledgers of the clients concerned (Case 844/93).

Withdrawing monies from a Client Account in circumstances other than those set out in the Accounts Rules for the withdrawal of such money (Case 844/93).

Failure to keep properly written up books and accounts to show dealings with clients' money (Case 844/93).

Failure to write up the books properly may take a multitude of different forms but common instances which have come before the Tribunal have been:

Inadequate narrative in the entries.

Undated entries.

Inaccurate entries as to narrative, dates, amounts, etc.

Fictitious entries (Case 845/92).

Failure to invest funds in separate interest-bearing accounts in the name of the clients as required by the Rules. It will not suffice to say that the solicitor did not know that these sums were uninvested because the solicitor has a duty to take steps to ensure that the money is appropriately invested (Case 826/92).

Deliberately debiting excessive fees against clients; to the extent that they were patently excessive (Cases 723/87 and 786/90).

Failure to lodge an Accountant's Certificate within six months of the end of the appropriate accounting period (Case 807/90).

Failure to keep and preserve for at least 10 years the books and accounts to be kept by a solicitor in terms of the Accounts Rules (Case 757/89).

Failure to be able to produce an immediate printout of accounts held in a computer system notwithstanding that immediate visual access is available (Case 858/93).

The Tribunal has said:

> In holding funds for clients, a solicitor is in a privileged position of trust. In order fully to protect clients at all times, a solicitor must comply with the detailed provisions of the Solicitors (Scotland) Accounts Rules, which not only ensure that all monies belonging to clients are distinguished from the solicitor's own funds, but also require the solicitor to set down and maintain detailed records so that the solicitor and the Law Society can immediately satisfy themselves that the solicitor is always in a position to account for all funds held for clients (Case 710/87).

19.02 CLIENTS' FUNDS

A solicitor (the Respondent) held a Power of Attorney for a client, A, in favour of himself which authorised him *inter alia* 'to make, vary and dispose of investments'. The Respondent was found guilty of Professional Misconduct in respect of a breach of the Accounts Rules (rule 6 of the 1981 Accounts Rules) in that there had been (unknown to the Respondent) a transfer of the funds of client A to a client B by way of an unsecured loan without the consent of client A or the Respondent as Attorney for A. The Tribunal said *inter alia*:

> The remaining charge also concerned the Respondent's failure to comply with Rule 6 in relation to another loan of [A's] monies. On this occasion, the Respondent was unaware of the loan and therefore no question of authority under the Power of Attorney arises. The loan was entirely arranged by [the Respondent's cashier] and he effected the advance by using one of the blank Building Society withdrawal forms which the Respondent had signed and left with him. The Tribunal accepts that there may be occasions where a sole practitioner has to rely on a member of staff to effect financial transactions in his absence but in such circum-

stances, it is the Solicitor's duty to limit such transactions to those that are absolutely necessary and to take every precaution to ensure that such an arrangement is not open to abuse. However, in this case, the Respondent by leaving signed blank withdrawal forms, acted recklessly in that he failed to ensure the highest standard of security in relation to clients' funds which is to be expected of a Solicitor, and the Tribunal is of the opinion that there was professional misconduct on the part of the Respondent in respect of this matter (Case 633/85).

The Tribunal has said on another occasion that it takes a serious view of a breach of the Accounts rule which requires that money held by a solicitor for a client shall, in the circumstances set out in the rule, be placed in a separate interest-bearing account in the title of which the client's name is specified so that the solicitor can account to the client for interest on the money while held by the solicitor, because the effect of a breach of this rule is to deprive the particular client of interest (now rule 15 of the 1992 Accounts Rules). In the particular case being considered the contravention related to a number of clients. By way of explanation the solicitor pointed out that in relation to certain clients there were outstanding fees. The Tribunal said in relation to that submission:

> Nevertheless under the provisions of the Accounts Rules, monies held by a solicitor at the credit of his client ledger account continue to be 'client monies' until such time as fee notes are raised and debited to that particular client account, and accordingly the mere fact that a particular client may be liable to the solicitor for fees does not in itself excuse the solicitor from the requirements of Rule 11 [of the Solicitors (Scotland) Accounts Rules 1986] in relation to that particular client.

and it found Professional Misconduct established (Case 729/88).

The Tribunal is reluctant to place much weight on averments by a solicitor that breaches of the Accounts Rules are the result of failures on the part of staff if the solicitor fails to understand the office accounts system and to supervise adequately the staff employed.

The Tribunal has observed:

> [T]he management of clients' funds is an essential part of the administration of a solicitor's practice. Clients entrust funds to a solicitor in the expectation that such monies are in safe hands, held by a person of professional standing and backed by a Guarantee Fund to which all solicitors contribute. Solicitors in Scotland are privileged to enjoy this degree of trust, but with this trust carries the obligation to take the utmost care of clients' money. Honesty and propriety is only a small part of this duty. The essential feature of the solicitor's duty is that the solicitor is in a position to account to each and every client at all times and this requires the solicitor to maintain full and accurate records of all the intromissions of the solicitor's practice.

> In implementing this duty, the solicitor is assisted by the detailed provisions of the Accounts Rules which set out, in precise terms, the various obligations of a solicitor in Scotland in order to ensure not only that funds of each client are separately safeguarded but also to enable the solicitor, the solicitor's accountants and the accountants employed by the Law Society to satisfy themselves at any time that the clients' funds are securely held and accounted for. The method of account-

ing is entirely up to the individual solicitor but it is the solicitor's duty to understand and supervise whatever system is adopted and if the solicitor elects to have a mechanical accounting system or a computer, then the solicitor must ensure that the system of recording and recall is no less capable of being monitored than a manual system (Case 845/92).

In a case where all the partners of a firm were charged with Professional Misconduct, following on a very substantial shortage on the firm's client account coming to light as a result of a routine visit by the Law Society's Accountants, and where it was alleged by the partners that the shortfall had been caused by embezzlement by a member or members of their cashroom staff, and it was accepted by the Tribunal that the shortfall was not directly attributable to the action of any of the solicitors concerned, the partner, A, in charge of the cashroom admitted Professional Misconduct in that his level of supervision was inadequate. The Tribunal in its Note said *inter alia*:

> There was no suggestion that Mr [A the Cashroom partner] had recklessly disregarded his duties either as a partner in general or as the particular partner responsible for the cashroom within his firm and the Tribunal acknowledges that it was reasonable for Mr [A] and his partners to place a considerable degree of trust in long-standing and apparently experienced members of staff. From time to time, Mr [A] saw documents which purported to demonstrate that the books of the firm were regularly balanced. In addition [the firm's Accountants] regularly visited the firm and he had their assurance that the books of the firm were in order. There was also the tangible, although secondary, evidence of the annual Accountant's Certificate being delivered to the Law Society, implying that the books had been checked in accordance with the guidelines set out in the Accountant's Certificate Rules. Counsel very properly pointed out the special significance of such a Certificate as stated in section 37 of the 1980 Act.

> There is no doubt that, in many firms, such a combination of circumstances would be more than sufficient to ensure a satisfactory financial position. In this case however the firm had the misfortune to discover that there were grave shortcomings in relation to both the long-serving staff whom they employed and also the accountants who supervised their practice. There were no circumstances which might have caused the partners to question the quality of these services, but nevertheless there was a grave shortage in the client account and a consequent breach of the Accounts rules. It is significant that the penultimate paragraph of both the 1986 and 1989 Accounts Rules provided that 'each partner of a firm of solicitors shall be responsible for securing compliance by the firm with the provisions of these rules'. The Opinion of the Court in *Sharp* v *Council of the Law Society of Scotland* 1984 SC 129 at 134 directed the Tribunal in similar circumstances to have regard to the whole circumstances, including the part played by the individual solicitor in question, and at this stage it is appropriate to look at the extent of the admission by Mr [A] as set out in the Joint Minute. Mr [A] is identified as 'having accepted the duty of supervision of the Cash Room Operations within his firm (all with effect from 31st December 1986 until March 1991)'. This is coupled with an admission that his level of supervision was inadequate to a material degree, and there is then a reference to the form of transfer of funds and false and materially inaccurate bank reconciliations as set out in paragraph (4), *supra*, which resulted from the inadequate supervision. The Joint Minute also contains an admission that the inadequate level of supervision contributed to the situation which resulted in a fraud on the firm; and that as a consequence of the

inadequate supervision there was a breach of Rule 4(1) (*a*) of the Solicitors (Scotland) Accounts Rules [1986 and 1989] resulting from shortages on the firm's client account.

It is a significant aspect of a solicitor's practice that the solicitor handles clients' funds, and it is essential that every solicitor maintains adequate books of account to demonstrate not only to the solicitor himself but also to the Law Society that the clients' monies are held separately from the solicitor's own funds. The primary purpose of the Solicitors Accounts Rules is to lay a foundation for such safeguard.

The Accounts Rules accordingly provide an appropriate framework for a solicitor's accounts to be meaningful. It is essential that the solicitor, and in the case of a larger firm, the solicitor responsible for the cashroom, is familiar with his firm's accounting procedures to the extent that he himself can and indeed does from time to time physically check the balances and the bank reconciliation. The audit by an outside accountant can be a valuable additional protection but it can never be regarded as a substitute for the solicitor's own verification as it is the solicitor and his partners who are personally liable and professionally responsible for their clients' funds. Similarly the production of the Accountant's Certificate is tangible evidence that *ex facie* the solicitor is maintaining a fully written up set of books but unless the solicitor is himself familiar with his own books of account, he leaves himself open to circumstances which appear to have occurred in the present case, namely that the supervising accountant failed to recognise that the firm's books of account did not truly reflect the firm's financial position. It was very significant that the Law Society accountant identified an apparent shortfall within a few hours of commencing the inspection and it is therefore reasonable to expect that a diligent solicitor should have ascertained the situation at a much earlier stage, particularly as the solicitor should have been seeing the list of client balances and checking the bank reconciliation on a regular basis.

Part of Mr [A's] admission related to an exceptionally casual arrangement which occurred between the cash department and the firm's bank. Transfers from any designated account should strictly only be made on the basis of the written instructions of an authorised signatory. It is not known to the Tribunal whether the practice followed by the Respondent's firm was common to other firms at that time but it is significant that the practice left the firm open to improper withdrawal of monies from their client account; monies for which the partners were personally liable (Case 841/92).

In a case where the Fiscal for the Law Society suggested that a breach of the Solicitors Account Rules might fall into one of three categories:

1. The result of some deliberate or wilful act involving an element of dishonesty or fraudulent concealment, thereby putting clients' money at risk.

2. The wilful or negligent operation of a system or failure to exercise control, such as might give rise to a breach of the Rules, but without any dishonest intent or bad faith.

3. The result of some inadvertence or error, not amounting to negligence . . .

the Tribunal said that it was hesitant to adopt the categories put forward by the Fiscal, but it was significant in this case that there was in operation a system which did not enable the Respondents to ensure that at all times they were complying with the Accounts Rules.

The Tribunal further said:

> The Tribunal is of the opinion that failure to maintain [an] adequate accounting system within a firm can have serious consequences to the extent of endangering clients' money and is therefore a matter of such gravity as to justify a finding of professional misconduct in the event of a breach of the Accounts Rules being established, even although the direct cause of the particular breach might be outwith the knowledge of the Solicitors concerned (Case 517/81).

19.03 ESTABLISHED PROCEDURES

In a case where the Tribunal found a solicitor guilty of Professional Misconduct in respect of a breach of the Accounts Rules in that he had a shortage on his client account resulting from the issuing of a cheque to settle a conveyancing transaction where he had not established that the cheques (one was from an Insurance Company and the other two cheques were from the client) he had received to effect the settlement were cleared, the Tribunal said:

> In the course of dealing with [the client's] affairs in June and July 1981, the Respondent encountered several exceptional circumstances. It was an unfortunate coincidence that the arrestment of funds in the hands of the [Insurance Company] coincided with the Respondent's interim settlement of [his client's] dispute with his Landlords and suppliers. It was also very unusual in itself for a company of the standing of the [Insurance Company] to stop payment on a cheque, particularly when there may have been some doubt about the justification for such an action, and further the Respondent was unfortunate in that his bank omitted to intimate to him that payment on two cheques had been stopped—particularly when these cheques had been lodged for special presentation.

> Nevertheless the foregoing circumstances are all of a nature which occasionally can arise and the difficulties encountered by the Respondent might have been avoided if he had followed certain well-established procedures. In particular the Respondent ought to have ensured the clearance of [the client's] cheques before drawing cheques on his own client account which were dependent on the same (Case 526/81).

19.04 RESPONSIBILITY OF PARTNERS *INTER SE*

In a case where two partners were charged with offences under the Accounts Rules and the senior partner was responsible for the cashroom procedures, the Tribunal in finding both partners guilty of Professional Misconduct said:

> It is accepted practice in a firm of two or more partners for one of the partners to be responsible for the cashroom of their office in the day-to-day compliance of the Accounts Rules, and a failure on the part of that solicitor will not necessarily result in a finding of Professional Misconduct against the other partner or partners in a firm. However, if there are circumstances which should cause another partner in the firm to be alerted, then it is that partner's duty to enquire further and in some circumstances he may reasonably be satisfied by assurances given by the partner who has responsibility for the cashroom. However where other partners see an ongoing matter which should be of concern Rule 13 [of the 1986 Accounts Rules] requires those partners to share the responsibility of resolving the difficulties (Case 790/90).

19.04 RESPONSIBILITY OF PARTNERS *INTER SE*

NB. The 1992 Accounts Rules now make provisions for the appointment of a 'designated Cashroom Partner or Partners' in addition to making each partner of a firm of solicitors responsible for compliance by the firm of the provisions of the Rules (rule 17).

19.05 INEXPERIENCE OF SOLICITOR

In a case where the solicitor for the Respondent pointed to the Respondent's lack of practical training and experience in keeping books of account and suggested that the profession should itself accept some responsibility for the Respondent commencing practice prior to having adequate training in the keeping and maintenance of accurate books of account, the Tribunal said:

> This submission is not accepted by the Tribunal. The Solicitors (Scotland) Accounts Rules are enacted for all solicitors in practice and it is the duty of a solicitor not to enter into business on his own account unless and until he can satisfy himself that he is in a position to keep properly written up records of his intromissions with clients' monies and to comply with all the provisions of the Accounts Rules. It was clear from the evidence before the Tribunal that the Respondent's book-keeping fell gravely short of the requirements of the Accounts Rules and not only did this contribute to the *de facto* shortage in the Respondent's client account, it also caused considerable inconvenience to the Complainers' accountant in that he had to prepare his own list of balances before proceeding to carry out an audit of the Respondent's books. It is an essential feature of the Accounts Rules that they require the solicitor to follow a course of action which enables the solicitor, and any third party requiring to examine the books, to be in a position readily to satisfy himself that the solicitor's client account is in order. The Tribunal is satisfied that in various respects the Respondent's standard of book-keeping fell gravely short of that which is expected in the Accounts Rules and accordingly there is a finding of professional misconduct in this matter.

The Tribunal later in the same case said:

> [I]t is not accepted that the profession must accept any part of the responsibility for the Respondent commencing practice whilst relatively inexperienced. A Diploma in Legal Practice is now a prerequisite for any new solicitor and whilst the instruction for the same will not necessarily cover the detailed application of the Accounts Rules such as might have precluded the possibility of the Respondent maintaining books which were less than adequate, nevertheless the whole training should have instilled in the Respondent such a degree of responsibility that he himself should not have commenced practice on his own until such time as he had satisfied himself that he was in a position to comply with the Accounts Rules at all times. The Tribunal accepts the Respondent's assurances that he will attend an early Practice Management course. Nevertheless the lack of judgment displayed by the Respondent in failing to establish a system which satisfies the requirements of the Accounts Rules and in seeking to continue in practice without Professional Indemnity insurance indicates that the Respondent should have the guidance and support which is available in an established business and it is for this reason that a limited restriction has been placed on his Practising Certificate; and it will be a matter for the Council of the Law Society to determine whether at the relevant time a particular firm is suitable for the Respondent (Case 857/93).

19.06 RULE 4(1)(*a*)

The Tribunal has observed in relation to this rule, which requires a solicitor to ensure that at all times the sum at credit of the client account, or where there are more such accounts than one, the total of the sums at the credit of these accounts shall not be less than the total of the clients' money held by the solicitor, that its purpose

> is to ensure that at all times a solicitor has sufficient funds in his client account to meet the aggregate of all the monies due by him to individual clients, and that this can be demonstrated from an examination of the solicitor's books. It is not simply a matter of maintaining solvency and it is not acceptable merely to demonstrate that funds are due and payable which will have the effect of producing a surplus. The terms of Rule 4 are strict, not only to protect the interests of clients but also so that the solicitor, and any other party requiring to examine his books, may be satisfied without reference to extraneous records that there are adequate funds in his client account. Accordingly it is not acceptable practice for a solicitor to draw a cheque on his client account in anticipation of funds which may be received later that day or shortly thereafter. It is the essence of the Rule that a solicitor is only entitled to draw money from his client account if he holds funds for that client or he has in his possession a cheque which he will deposit in his client account for behoof of his client later that same day. The Solicitor for the Respondent described the practice of anticipating a cheque as being 'slightly sloppy banking practice' but it is in fact a wholly unacceptable practice which strikes at the very root of the accounting principle upon which the Accounts Rules are based. It is an essential feature of the Accounts Rules that it can be demonstrated from the books themselves that a solicitor has sufficient funds in his client account and this cannot be so if the solicitor requires to rely on funds which he has still to receive in order to achieve a credit balance (Case 770/89).

A breach of rule 4 was found to constitute Professional Misconduct where it was established that a solicitor deliberately advanced the purchase prices of properties from his client account in each case three days before receiving the respective loan cheques covering the respective purchase prices, with the result that the sum at credit of his client bank account was less than the total of the clients' money held by him (Case 822/91).

The Tribunal took a particularly serious view where the Respondent's firm pursued a course of deliberate deception whereby substantial funds were transferred into the client account in order to achieve a temporary surplus at the end of each month and withdrawn immediately thereafter. Apart from the brief period each month, the client account was in effect funding the Respondent's firm to a significant extent and they said that this was wholly improper and a flagrant breach of the Accounts Rules (Case 759/89).

19.07 DEBITING FEES TO CLIENTS' ACCOUNT

The Tribunal has taken the view that it is a breach of the rule which permits 'money properly required for or to account of payment of a solicitor's professional account against a client which has been debited to the ledger account of the client in the solicitor's books' if the funds are taken from the account to meet the solicitor's fees without a fee note being prepared and without the permission of the client and in such a case found Professional Misconduct established (Case 826/92).

Rule 6(1) (*d*) of the Solicitors (Scotland) Accounts Rules 1992 provides:

> So long as money belonging to one client is not withdrawn without his written authority for the purpose of meeting a payment to or on behalf of another client, there may be drawn from a client account ...
>
> (*d*) money properly required for or to account of payment of the solicitor's professional account against a client which has been debited to the ledger account of the client in the solicitor's books *and where a copy of said account has been rendered.*

The words in italics have been added to the corresponding rule 6(1) (*d*) in the 1989 Accounts Rules.

In an Appeal to the Court by a Solicitor (*MacColl v The Council of the Law Society of Scotland* 1987 SLT 524), where the solicitor had been *inter alia* in breach of this rule in that he had charged grossly excessive fees against a client and debited them to the ledger account of his client, it was submitted on behalf of the Appellant at the Appeal that there had been no breach of rule 6(1) (*d*) of the Solicitors (Scotland) Accounts Rules 1981 and the Tribunal had erred in holding that such a breach had been established. The Court at page 528 said:

> Rule 6 defines the various circumstances in which money may legitimately be withdrawn by a solicitor from a client's account. Sub-paragraph (*d*) permits the withdrawal, without the client's knowledge, authority or consent, of 'money properly required for or to account of payment of the solicitor's professional account against (the client) which had been debited to the ledger account of the client in the solicitor's books'. The simple submission was that the eight professional accounts against the client in this case had been debited to the client's ledger account and the withdrawals accordingly represented money required to pay these accounts however grossly excessive they may have been. In our judgment this submission is not only simple but absurd. The rule is designed for the protection of clients' money. Rule 6(1) (*d*) is concerned with money 'properly' required. ... Money can never be properly required for payment of a bogus account however neatly it has been debited in the client's ledger account. The presupposition of the Rule, properly construed, is that the solicitor's account therein mentioned is a fair and reasonable one subject only perhaps to minor criticisms of detail.

19.08 FUNDS TRANSFERRED BETWEEN CLIENTS DIRECT

In a case decided in 1993, the Tribunal upheld the Respondent's plea to the relevancy to the effect that where a solicitor acts for both purchaser and seller in a conveyancing transaction and part of the consideration passes between the clients direct, the solicitor's failure to record that part of the consideration in his books of account does not contravene rule 10 of the Solicitors (Scotland) Accounts Rules 1989 (now rule 12 of the 1992 Accounts Rules); but the Tribunal found the Respondent guilty of Professional Misconduct *inter alia* in regard to her failure to comply with the provisions of rule 10 in respect of confusing and misleading entries on six ledger cards referring to a flatted property, W. In its Decision the Tribunal said:

> ... It was specifically averred, and admitted by the Respondent in her Answers, that in respect of certain specified conveyancing transactions, the Respondent had only recorded part of the consideration and that she had not set down in her books and accounts the balance of the price which in each case had passed direct between the purchaser and the seller. Where it was recorded, the stamp duty paid reflected the whole consideration but the total price was not specifically noted or referred to in the ledger sheet kept by the Respondent for each transaction.

It was averred in paragraph 6.3 of the Complaint that the Respondent's failure to disclose in her books the full price for each of the specified transactions constituted a breach of Rule 10 of the Accounts Rules 1989 (which were the operative Accounts Rules at the relevant time); and with the concurrence of the Fiscal, Counsel for the Respondent submitted a plea to the relevancy in respect of this charge. The charge in the preceding paragraph (6.2) also founded on Rule 10 and related to 'the confusing and misleading entries' on ledger cards relating to two properties at the same address; and Counsel incorporated a reference to this charge in his submissions.

Counsel pointed to section 35(1) of the Solicitors (Scotland) [Act] 1980 as the authority for the Complainers making the said Accounts Rules and referred to the provisions of Rule 10(1) of the Accounts Rules 1989 which provides that

> A solicitor shall at all times keep properly written up such books and accounts as are necessary:—
>
> (a) to show all his dealings with:–
>
> (i) clients' money held or received or paid or in any way intromitted with by him; . . .'

with the direction in Rule 10(2) that

> All dealings referred to in sub-paragraph (1) of this Rule shall be recorded as may be appropriate:—
>
> (a) (i) either in a clients' cash book, or a clients' column of a cash book, and
>
> (ii) in a record of sums transferred from the ledger account of one client to that of another; and in addition
>
> (b) in a clients' ledger or a clients' column of a ledger.

Counsel submitted that the foregoing did not require the solicitor to make a record of all the clients' financial intromissions in relation to any transaction which the solicitor might be handling and he refuted any suggestion that the omission of a reference to monies passing between the purchaser and the seller direct was confusing and misleading. Counsel referred to the similarity of the corresponding provisions applicable to English solicitors except that the English Rule excludes the words 'or in any way intromitted with'. *Halsbury's Laws of England*, volume 44, para 327, under the heading of 'Solicitors', observes that

> Every solicitor must at all times keep properly written up such accounts as may be necessary (1) to show all his dealings with client's money received, held or paid by him and with any other money dealt with by him through a client account; and (2) to show separately in respect of each client all such money which is received held or paid by him on account of that client and to distinguish

all such money received, held or paid by him from any other money received, held or paid by him. All these dealings, and no other dealings, must be recorded as may be appropriate either (*a*) in a clients' cash book, or a clients' column of a cash book or (*b*) in a record of sums transferred from the ledger account of one client to that of another, and, in addition (*c*) in a clients' ledger, or a clients' column of a ledger.

The direction that no other dealings are to be recorded is repeated in E. Lawson's *Accounting for Solicitors*, 1975, at page 110. Counsel also took an analogy from Halberstadt's *Basic Book-keeping for Solicitors* at page 39, where it is observed:

[I]f a cheque is received not payable to the solicitor but payable to a third person and the cheque is sent on to that third person there is no need to make any entries at all. However it is probably unwise to have no record of the receipt and despatch of the cheque. The recording can be done on the file of the papers and correspondence kept for the client, or it can be kept in the accounts themselves.

And in Janet Baker's *Solicitors Accounts: A Student Guide*, the author observed that the solicitor may make a memorandum entry. Counsel distinguished the reference in *Halberstadt* and *Baker* in that they referred to the situation where the solicitor physically receives and hands over a cheque made payable to another whereas in the present case the solicitor never handled any cheque for the balance of the consideration.

Counsel further submitted that accordingly the question of 'confusing and misleading entries' did not arise as the monies which the Respondent received were less than the full consideration.

[The Fiscal] sought to distinguish the English commentaries in that the corresponding English Rule did not include the words 'or in any way intromitted with' and he referred to the various transactions to illustrate the mischief which the said Rule 10 was intended to cover. In the sale of the first flat at [Property W] in November 1990 the consideration was £52,000 but only £48,704.90 was recorded in the Respondent's books as passing between [A—the seller] and [B—the purchaser]. The sum of £48,704.90 was the amount of the loan raised by [B]. Only the loan figure of [£. . .] was recorded in respect of the sale of [Property X] to [C] and similarly only the net advance of [£. . .] in the sale of the [Property Y] by [D] to [E], although [the Fiscal] acknowledged that in relation to the latter transaction, the Respondent's ledger had referred to 'the balance of price'. In [E's] sale of [Property Y] to [F], there was a record of the Respondent having received the 100% loan of £43,000 for the purchaser but only £38,590.17 was entered as the price paid to [E], that sum being the amount required by him to redeem his Building Society Loan. [The Fiscal] also pointed to a sale by [B] to [A] but the references were to the above-mentioned purchase by [B] in November 1990. [The Fiscal] stated that he did not make any imputation regarding the honesty of the Respondent but he explained that he would have expected to see some reference in the narrative to the whole price. He specifically referred to the words 'or in any way intromitted with' and he adopted the definition of 'intromit' in *Green's Glossary of Scottish Legal Terms* by A. G. M. Duncan, 1992, page 55, where the phrase 'intromit with' is described as meaning 'to handle or deal with, as funds or other property'. [The Fiscal] urged the Tribunal to take a broad view in that the monies passing did not correspond with the books which the solicitor was required to keep written up. Rule 10 in effect required the solicitor to tie up his book-keeping work with the real transaction and the Respondent's failure to do this constituted a breach of Rule 10.

At its widest, Rule 10 requires that there be recorded in the solicitor's books of account all intromissions [with] clients' money. In effect that represents all monies passing through the solicitor's hands. In this matter the Respondent had recorded the monies received and paid by her but her books did not contain any reference to the monies which may have passed between her clients direct or between one client and the other party to the particular transaction. Ordinarily, a solicitor will dissuade the client from making any payment direct in respect of the consideration passing in a conveyancing transaction, but it remains open to the client to make such payment; and indeed this may occur where the parties are related or there is some commercial connection or in certain special circumstances. The Respondent was in effect charged with failing to note the full sale price of each property in her ledger. The correspondence file kept by the Respondent would undoubtedly have contained this information but as the balance was passing directly between the purchaser and the seller, the Respondent would only have her client's word that this money had actually been paid. It is understandable that the English commentaries recommend that a record either in the file or in the accounts is made where a cheque is not cashed by the solicitor but is merely handed over to the other party, as the cheque which represents the particular funds is in that case being physically received and handed over by the solicitor. However, such was not the situation in the present case in that the Respondent did not handle any document representing the money which apparently constituted the balance of the consideration. Understandably it may be of interest to the inspecting staff of the Complainers to ascertain the whole price passing in a transaction but in the opinion of the Tribunal the purpose of Rule 10 is to enable the Complainers' accountants and any other party who may have an interest, to ensure that the *solicitor* has properly accounted for all clients' money which he or she may have held, received or paid. The Rule does not specifically state or otherwise require that the solicitor's books of account shall record all intromissions of the client and it would be inappropriate to infer such obligation from the precise words of Rule 10. There may be circumstances where the solicitor may have no evidence that the balance of the consideration has actually passed, and it would be expecting much more of the solicitor to enquire of such payment than is set out in that Rule. If the solicitor were obliged to record such extraneous matters, then it is to be expected that such requirement would be clearly set out in the Accounts Rules. The Tribunal was not directed to any such provision and accordingly it is not considered that the omission to record the balance of the price in any conveyancing transaction necessarily gives rise to a breach of the Accounts Rules.

Whether the particular entries were confusing and misleading, as averred in paragraph 6.2 of the Complaint, is another matter which will be considered separately.

In his submissions to the Tribunal in relation to the remainder of the Complaint, [the Fiscal] referred to the previous circumstances in 1988 and although he did not make any averment of professional misconduct in relation to this period, he founded upon these events in that they ought to have alerted the Respondent to the necessity of having her books properly written in conformity with Rule 10. Nevertheless at a subsequent inspection in March 1992 the Complainers' accountant was faced with confusing entries, particularly in regard to the references to [Property W]....

... In reply, Counsel for the Respondent explained to the Tribunal that the substance of the original complaint against the Respondent had been greatly diminished. He accepted that there had been some confusion relating to the entries for [Property W] and that someone reading the ledger cards might be misled but that there had been no intention on the part of the Respondent positively to mislead any party. He also acknowledged that there had been a mistake in that the ledger card relating to [Property X] had also been headed ['Property W'] but only the Law Society inspector had been confused and the matter had been instantly corrected when it had been drawn to the Respondent's attention. However, a reference to the correspondence file would have demonstrated that the particular transactions were in order. Counsel added that in relation to the sale of the top flat at [Property W], the Respondent had only acted for the seller [G] and that the purchaser [H] was separately represented. The transaction had been delayed and it was for this reason that the balance of the price was paid direct. Counsel submitted that what might constitute a breach of the Accounts Rules was ultimately a matter of degree and he referred to the Affidavit of [I], CA, the nominated accountant for the Respondent's practice. That Affidavit contained the following quotation taken from the *Bulletin of the Auditing Practices Committee of the Consultative Committee of Accounting Bodies*:

> Accounting records compromise the orderly collection and identification of the information in question, rather than a mere accumulation of documents. The accounting records need not be in book form; and may take the form of, for example, loose-leaf binder, or computer tape; it may even be sufficient if the books of prime entry are in the form of a secure clip of invoices with an add list attached. The essence of the matter is that the information recorded is organised and labelled so as to be capable of retrieval.

And Mr [I] concluded:

> I have little difficulty in confirming that based upon my examination of the accounting records of [the Respondent] so far as affected by the Statement of Facts as contained within the complaint at the instance of the Law Society, they conform with the above definition.

Counsel acknowledged that certain entries were laconic and that there was inaccurate noting but he submitted that the matters of confusion were capable of being resolved and that if there was indeed a breach of Rule 10 then this was on the borderline and did not exten[d] to professional misconduct . . . .

. . . Referring to the Affidavit of Mr [I], Counsel pointed out that the Respondent had some 800 live accounts and that between May and August 1992, the Respondent had transferred from a manual accounting to a computerised system. He submitted that although it was the Respondent's personal responsibility to comply with the Accounts Rules, she acted on the advice of her accountant and he questioned whether the Respondent's conduct might be regarded as deplorable to the extent that the book-keeping satisfied her accountant.

The Tribunal has carefully considered the very full submissions for each of the parties. Rule 10 of the Accountant's Rules sets down required standards of book-keeping and it is in the public interest, and in the interest of individual clients and the profession, that a solicitor keeps properly written up books and accounts. The Law Society had reason to express concern in 1988 regarding the standard of the Respondent's book-keeping and it is regrettable that the inspection by the Complainers' accountant in March 1992 disclosed shortcomings which undoubtedly confused and indeed misled the inspector to such an extent that the true position in relation to certain of the transactions only became apparent at the commencement of the Hearing. It was suggested that the precise circumstances of each transaction could have been easily ascertained from the client files; but it has always been understood that a solicitor's books of account should *in gremio* contain sufficient in themselves to explain the solicitor's financial intromissions. Having regard to the previous concern expressed by the Complainers in 1988, the further confusion in the Respondent's books as ascertained at the inspection in March 1992 was inexcusable and reprehensible and a Finding of professional misconduct is accordingly appropriate (Case 861/93).

19.09 BANK RECONCILIATIONS (Rule 13 of the 1992 Accounts Rules)
In a case in 1993 the Tribunal said:

> The essential feature of the Accounts Rules is to enable the solicitor to demonstrate not only to himself but also to the Law Society and any other party requiring to examine his books that the solicitor's client account is maintained at a figure which is not less than the aggregate of the monies due by the solicitor to all his clients. Such provision ensures that clients' funds are wholly safeguarded and free from attachment, even in the event of the solicitor's own estates becoming insolvent. . . . In order to ensure that the interests of clients are fully protected, it is also essential that the solicitor maintains accurate records of all his intromissions for clients. Mistakes can inadvertently occur, frequently through no personal fault of the solicitor himself, and the Accounts Rules further provide that checks in the form of reconciliations are carried out at regular intervals which should enable the solicitor to identify and immediately correct any such error. The Accounts Rules also provide that the solicitor retains his primary records together with these reconciliations so that the Law Society can exercise its supervisory role. It is accepted that in the majority of cases, the solicitor will delegate the day-to-day administration of his book-keeping activities to an appropriate member of staff and, ordinarily, such procedure will not give rise to any significant risk in that it is the invariable practice that only partners will sign any cheque or transfer and the solicitor either personally or through one of his partners will satisfy himself by personal examination that the monthly reconciliation procedure has been diligently followed through. Such procedures should, in ordinary course, protect the interests of the solicitor and his clients from any improper actions on the part of the solicitor's own staff and this Tribunal takes a serious view of a failure to institute and regularly monitor a system of making monthly reconciliations of the clients' Bank Accounts accompanied with a comparison with the total of the sums due by the firm to clients (Case 858/93).

19.10 INVESTMENT OF CLIENTS' FUNDS
The Tribunal has taken the view that notwithstanding that a solicitor is due fees by a client there is nevertheless a duty on the solicitor in terms of the Accounts Rules (rule 15 of the 1992 Rules—which requires interest to be earned for a client) to place clients' money, over a certain amount (which may be held to meet these fees), in an interest-bearing account specifically nominated for the client. In relation to a charge of Professional Misconduct on this ground the Tribunal said:

> [T]he provisions of the Accounts Rules have two distinct and separate objects, namely to protect clients' funds, and also to ensure that they can be distinguished at all times. It is for the latter reason that monies in a client account continue to be clients' monies even although there may be fees due by that client in excess of the funds held, as it is only on this basis that a proper check can be made on a solicitor's client account. If there are fees due to the solicitor, it is always open to

19.10 INVESTMENT OF CLIENTS' FUNDS

him to put through a proper fee note and withdraw these funds from the client account, but until this is done, the Rules require these funds to be treated as clients' monies and the solicitor must comply with the Accounts Rules to the extent of depositing these funds when it is appropriate to do so (Case 759/89).

20

INVESTMENT BUSINESS

20.01 INVESTMENT BUSINESS

In finding a solicitor guilty of Professional Misconduct in respect of his failure to comply with rule 9.1 of the City Code of Takeovers and Mergers and his failure to co-operate with the Executive of the Panel on Takeovers and Mergers in its investigation, and his knowingly making false and misleading statements to the Panel and the Appeal Committee, the Tribunal said:

> ... In the Introduction to the Code it is set down (paragraph 1(*a*)) that 'This Code and the Panel operate principally to ensure fair and equal treatment of all share-holders in relation to takeovers. The Code also provides an orderly framework within which takeovers are conducted'. At paragraph 3(*a*) of the Introduction it is stated that 'The Code is based upon a number of General Principles, which are essentially statements of good standards of commercial behaviour' and at para-graph 3(*b*) (where a matter may be referred to the Panel) 'The Panel expects prompt co-operation from those to whom enquiries are directed so that decisions may be both properly informed and given as speedily as possible'. It is observed (in paragraph 1(*c*) of the Introduction) that the Code has not and does not seek to have the force of law but that it has been acknowledged by both government and other regulating authorities, that those who seek to take advantage of the facilities of the securities markets in the United Kingdom should conduct themselves 'in accord-ance with best business standards and so according to the Code'. A solicitor has a professional obligation to maintain such standards not only within his practice but also in relation to any transaction for which he may be personally responsible. Additionally, Rule 9.6 of the Solicitors (Scotland) (Conduct of Investment Busi-ness) Practice Rules 1989 provides that
>
> > A certified person shall comply with generally accepted standards as to what constitutes good market practice in respect of the provision of financial services and the conduct of investment business and shall advise his clients as to what constitutes, and the consequences of failing to comply with, good market prac-tice.
>
> The said Rule 9.6 does not specifically refer to this Code, but it is significant that in a practice note attached to Rule 9.6 it is stated: 'As examples of good market practice, account may be taken of ... the Takeover Code. ...' Rule 9.9 of the said Practice Rules declares that 'Breach of any of these rules may be treated as professional misconduct for the purpose of Part IV' of the Solicitors (Scotland) Act 1980, which is the operative part of the Act applicable to this Tribunal.
>
> In his closing submission, Counsel for the Respondent conceded that this head of the Complaint had been established; and having regard to the finding of the Panel that the Respondent's actings constituted 'serious and deliberate' breaches of the Code and that there was a 'deliberate attempt' to avoid the obligation of Rule 9 of the Code, this Tribunal has no hesitation in making a finding of professional misconduct in respect of this charge ... (Case 851/93).

INDEX

All references are to page numbers

INDEX

Bank reconciliation, 181
Beneficiaries, duty towards, 138, 139
Bequests in favour of solicitor, 76 *et seq*
Blanks
  affidavit with, 162
  execution of deed with, 122
  withdrawal forms with, 170
Blank sheets of headed notepaper, 151
Breach of the peace, conviction, 115
Breach of trust, 124
Bridging loans, 116 *et seq*
  authority to arrange, 118
  duty of disclosure, 118
  failure to advise on, 151
  Solicitors (Scotland) Accounts Rules 1992,
    89

Cash flow, 73, 153, 159
Censure (by Discipline Tribunal), 3, 4, 43,
  46
Certificate of Interest issued without
  authority, 116
Certificate—legal aid fees, 166
Certifying a title, 128, 131
Cessation of practice, duty on, 153, 158
Chairman of Discipline Tribunal, 10
Chambers, proceedings in judge's, 135
Charge to Discipline Tribunal, specification
  of, 11, 15, 24
Cheque
  breach of condition, 123, 124
  drawn in anticipation of funds, 175
  drawn in favour of third party, 178
  failure to honour, 115, 158
  loan cheque, encashment of, 124, 128–129,
    131–132
  stoppage of, after settlement, 124–126
  uncleared, 173
Citation of witnesses before Discipline
  Tribunal
  Application to Court, 22
Clerk to Discipline Tribunal, 10
Client
  definition of, 71
Client account
  shortage on, 146, 155, 171, 173, 174, 175
  debiting fees to, 57, 175
  debiting funds, 176
Client of another solicitor, communication
  with, 106
Client, duties to, 57, 58, 60 *et seq*
Client, duties to former, 61, 96, 100

Client's funds
  embezzlement of, 56
  improper use of, 149
  investment of, 181
  standards required re, 169 *et seq*
Commission, evidence at, 57, 133
Communication with client of another
  solicitor, 106 *et seq*
Company shares
  minority holding, 141
Compensation, following Inadequate
  Professional Services, 7, 8
Competency
  examples of consideration of, 5, 6, 26, 30
Complaint to Discipline Tribunal
  adjustment/amendment, 22
  authority of Fiscal, 6
  criminal charge pending, 25
  dismissal of, 13, 14
  expenses, award of, 41
  form, 2
  further complaint, 22
  more than one solicitor, against, 6
  remit to Law Society, 2
  service of, 14, 15
  specification of charge, 11, 15, 24
  withdrawal, 30
Compliance certificate, 159
Confidentiality, 60
Conflict of interest (See also Solicitors
    (Scotland) Practice Rules 1986), 83 *et seq*
  accusation of criminal nature, 60
  civil proceedings, 89, 94, 95
  conveyancing, 83, 84, 88, 89, 95, 96, 99,
    100, 129
  criminal proceedings, 97, 98, 100
  executry, 139
  family member, 74
  matrimonial proceedings, 61, 83
  outwith professional relationship, 60
  partner, action by, 89, 90, 91, 94, 154
  partner, personal interest of, 74
  personal business, 72 *et seq*, 88
  prior to proceeding, 98
  termination of agency, subsequent to, 94
Consideration transferred direct between
  clients, 176
Constitution of Discipline Tribunal, 1 *et seq*
Consultation, failure to arrange, 26
Contempt of the Discipline Tribunal, 44
Correspondence
  solicitors, failure to reply to, 105, 106

All references are to page numbers

186

All references are to page numbers

INDEX

Expenses, award by Discipline Tribunal, 41 *et seq*, 59
   recovery, 43
Expert evidence before Discipline Tribunal, 36

Faculty of Advocates, report (complaint) by Dean, 3
False
   affidavit, 161
   date to deed, 120
Fees, 164 *et seq*
   client account, debiting to, 175
   counsel's fees, 153
   delay in submitting to taxation, 167
   duplicate claim, 29
   excessive, 57, 149, 164, 165, 169
   inaccurate claim, 165, 166
   inadequte advice re, 58
   Inadequate Professional Services, modification of, 7
   legal aid, 29, 165, 166
   payments to account, 164, 165
   quotation of, 58
   services not performed, 165
Fictitious
   entries, 169
   Industrial Tribunal Decision, 55
   testing clause, 57, 103, 119
Fictitious name/person
   bank account, 57
   deeds, in, 57, 120, 121
   letters involving, 57
   use of, by solicitor, 122, 160
Financial services, 183
Findings of Discipline Tribunal
   content of, 38
   intimation of, 4, 38
Fine (by Discipline Tribunal), 3, 4, 43, 46
Firearms
   unauthorised possession, 113
Firm of solicitors, complaint against, 5, 6
Fiscal appointed by Law Society, 2, 6, 33
Forged undertaking, 143
Forgery
   employee, 133
   client, 103
   notary signing, 161
   solicitor, 57, 119
Formality of Discipline Tribunal proceedings, 15, 32
Fraud (See also under Dishonesty), 30

Havers, citation of, 22
Hearing before Law Society re Inadequate Professional Services, 17, 21
Hearing by Discipline Tribunal (See also Decision and Evidence), 32 *et seq*
   absence of party, 32, 33
   application for restoration, 32
   notice of, 33
   preliminary, 32
   private/public, 32
   procedure, 32
   shorthand writer, 32

Identification of party, 34
Ignorance
   staff actings, 150
   Practice Rules, 54
Ill health of solicitor, 147
Impartial/independent advice (See also Conflict of Interest), 47, 72, 73
   testamentary writings, 76 *et seq*
Imprisonment of solicitor, 3, 4
Improper acting, 125
In cumulo findings of Professional Misconduct, 38
Inadequate Professional Services, 57 *et seq*, 151
   appeals from Council of the Law Society (See under Appeals)
   compensation award, 4, 7
   death of a partner, 71
   enforcement of directions, 2
   jurisdiction of Discipline Tribunal, 2
   powers of Discipline Tribunal in relation to, 7, 8
   relation to Professional Misconduct, 39
Income tax
   actings affecting firm's liability to, 56
Incompetence, 64, 122
Incomplete deed, execution of, 122
Incorporated practice
   appeal in relation to, 46
   duties of Council of Law Society as Registrar, 43
   Inadequate Professional Practice, 8
   powers of Discipline Tribunal, 3, 4
Inexperience, 55, 174
Inhibition, 89, 126, 129
Inquiry
   by Council of the Law Society re Inadequate Professional Services, 17, 20, 21

All references are to page numbers

All references are to page numbers

All references are to page numbers

All references are to page numbers

INDEX

Undertaking—*cont.*
  reckless issue, 142
  reliance on, 145
  staff, given by member of, 143, 145
Unprofessional conduct, 59
Unqualified person, 157

Value of property for loan purposes, 130
VAT
  actings affecting firm's liability, 56

Warning by Law Society, 25, 155
Warrant of registration, 121, 122
Will—bequest in favour of solicitor, 76 *et seq*

Withdrawal of complaint/appeal, 30, 31, 42
Withdrawal of instructions, 69
Witness in court proceedings
  citation of, 64, 133
  fee of, 152
  precognition of, 26, 133
  questioning of, 64
Witness in Discipline Tribunal Proceedings
  citation of, 22
  death/disappearance of, 35
  examination of, 32
  expert, 36
Witness to execution of deeds, 103, 120
Workload, control of, 146, 147